# GENEVA LAKE REFLECTIONS

## MORE STORIES FROM THE SHORE

FROM THE PUBLISHERS OF
At The Lake

**Publisher:** Barb Krause
**Editor:** Anne Celano Frohna
**Writers:** Anne Celano Frohna, Jamie Rhodes, Manya Kaczkowski, Catherine Driscoll
**Design:** Nathan Chow
**Production and Photography:** Kayla Collins, Ashley Duchemin
**Sales and Distribution:** Renee Zembal
**Cover Photo:** Clint Farlinger
**Advisor:** John K. Notz, Jr.

© 2010 by Nei-Turner Media Group, Inc.

All rights reserved. No part of this book may be reproduced in any form without written permission of the copyright owners. All images in this book have been reproduced with the knowledge and prior consent of the artists concerned and no responsibility is accepted by producer, publisher, or printer for any infringement of copyright or otherwise, arising from the contents of this publication. Every effort has been made to ensure that credits accurately comply with information supplied.

First published and distributed in the United States of America by:
Nei-Turner Media Group, Inc.
93 West Geneva Street
PO Box 1080
Williams Bay, Wisconsin 53191
Telephone: 800-386-3228
Fax: 262-245-2000
Web site: www.ntmediagroup.com

ISBN: 978-0-578-06295-2

Printed in China by C & C Offset Printing Co., LTD.

COURTESY OF PEG WILLIAMS

*"If one could make alive again for other people some cobwebbed skein of old dead intrigues and breathe breath and character into dead names and stiff portraits. That is history to me!"*

George Macaulay Trevelyan

*In* the aftermath of publishing *Geneva Lake: Stories from the Shore*—even before the archival dust began to settle—we realized that our mission was not over. Not only were there a few more stories to tell about some of the legendary estates surrounding the lake, but even more imperative was the telling of the many unassuming, long-forgotten stories about ordinary people in the midst of extraordinary events and epic eras.

So we hunkered down, got back to work and were soon rewarded with a wealth of precious tales about generations past—many of which have not been told since the history was literally being made.

We were able to bring all of these poignant, touching, enchanting and sometimes tragic stories back to life thanks, once again, to a dedicated staff and the many members of our very special lakeside communities who feel the same commitment to the great task of recovering the past and introducing it to the present.

We are pleased to present, *Geneva Lake Reflections: More Stories from the Shore*, and hope it helps us further along the road to understanding the common thread which links us all—whether past or present—our humanity.

# CONTENTS

## 6
### The Early Years
Life for the newcomers in the mid-19th century.

- Profile: Israel Williams, Sr., and Family
- Profile: A.H. Button Family

## 12
### Signs of the Times
An extensive 19th and 20th century timeline covering significant events—both near and far—affecting life along the shores.

## 34
### Encyclopedia Shore Path
A guide to understanding historical details.

- Who's Who...
- Estate Architects
- Landscape Architects
- Boat Builders
- Who's Buried Where?

## 50
### The Golden Age of Victorian Living
A look at the era of enchanted celebrations and colorful characters.

- The Private Yachts
- The Public's Transport
- Profile: John Burton
- Nero and the Trib
- Cisco Fishing
- The Fabulous Fourth of July
- The Midsummer Fair
- Profile: John Bullock

## 66
### Lake Life in the 20th Century
The dawn of the 20th century brought with it many changes—and struggles—for people living beside the lake, including: the arrival of the auto and the airplane, the onset of two World Wars, Depression, Prohibition, and civil unrest.

- Profile: William Trinke

## 74
### Lakeside Lodgings
For as many different types of tourists visiting Geneva Lake each summer, there were just as many types of accommodations.

- The Hotels
- Profile: Augustus F. Nightingale
- The Camps
- The Sanitariums
- Public Domain

## 102
### The Places and The People
The graceful houses lining the shores and the families who made them their "homes."

- Profile: Ethel Sturges Dummer
- Profile: Samuel Allerton
- Profile: Albert W. Harris and Kemah Farms
- Profile: Elizabeth Boynton Harbert
- A Letter to Emily Baker
- Not to Be Forgotten
- Geneva Lake's Little Sister

## 155
### Index

## 159
### References and Resources

COURTESY OF SUE MORTON

# THE EARLY YEARS

*Something* drastic must have urged Cyrus Church to leave his homeland of Ohio in the middle of winter in 1837, but amid the frozen gloom of February, he did just that, heading west on foot to a land he must have believed offered promise and a future of plenty. It took the young man fifteen and a half days to travel nearly 600 miles to the Wisconsin Territory, but he made it, as did many others.

Toward the end of his arduous journey, Church met fellow pioneer James Van Slyke on his way home from Chicago. With his pockets full of cash from the sale of part of his claim on land further north, Van Slyke seemed indisputable proof of the bounty this region offered.

"He received, I think, two thousand in cash," Church recalled some sixty years later in a newspaper interview, "He had a wife and three children and had been very poor. When he left home he was poorly clad, but on receiving the money he felt wonderfully elevated and bought himself new clothes from head to foot."

"He carried the money loose in his side overcoat pocket," the old settler recalled, "and would occasionally take out a large handful and say, 'See here!'…"

Van Slyke eagerly told Church all about his land and the fertile region surrounding it. This and the cash being waved before his tired eyes was all Church needed to continue his journey further north. And so, without delay, the young hopeful trudged north through twelve inches of snow, crossing half-frozen rivers, charting nearly indiscernible trails, with nothing to eat, his clothing frozen to him and his skin rubbed raw. Church was just about at his wits end when he saw signs of life at the head of a lake.

"I was never more pleased to see smoke than that night," he remembered, "when wet, cold, tired and hungry, I crawled, half dead, to the door of the hut, having reached at last the end of my journey."

There he found the Van Slyke family, as well as another family—ten in all—living in a sixteen by eighteen-foot log house. With little more than a cook stove,
© CLINT FARLINGER

lantern, a few candles, a pack of cards and a few books, these families had, like Church, come here to start anew beside the ancient lake.

As the days—and months—passed, these families, and others settling in beside the lake, would stake and protect their claims and gradually build modest homesteads, businesses, and communities amid the often merciless wilds of this post-glacial region. Luxuries were simple and unremarkable, such as letters from home. Arriving only a handful of times each year, these long-awaited words from home came at a steep cost: 25 cents paid upon delivery. This meant about half a day's pay for an already harried settler to find. Anxious to learn news from home, however, they managed to either find work, or… ways around the pricey postage. "…certain marks were made by the sender on the outside of a letter…," recalled Church, "the meaning of these marks would be agreed upon beforehand, and if the one to whom the letter was sent had not the money to pay the postage, he could by a glance at the letter tell whether or not all was well at the home he had left."

News from the Wisconsin Territory proved fairly good, so more and more settlers arrived to the shores of Geneva Lake. A mill was built, businesses began to crop up and homes were erected.

Charles Goodsell was among those induced to come to the region in 1838 to build the area's first flour mill and was grinding the first wheat for the community by autumn of that year. Although business was immediately a boom, Goodsell was determined to make this new settlement's impoverished spiritual community prosper as well.

Geneva Flouring Mills on Mill and Main Streets in Lake Geneva.

COURTESY OF THE LAKE GENEVA PUBLIC LIBRARY

"Mr. Goodsell found the little settlement of Geneva Lake without religious worship," recounted the *History of Walworth County*, published in 1882. "They had no Sabbath, but he carried one to them. One Sunday, the boys of Christopher Payne (the first settler of Walworth County) called upon him with fish to sell. He told them that he never traded on Sunday, but to come on any other day and he would buy of them. The boys seemed surprised. They had always lived on the far frontiers, in advance of Christian civilization and Sabbath observance. They ever after called him 'the Sunday man.'"

But Goodsell would not be deterred by the wild frontier ways, he opened his house for community worship without delay, inviting a young preacher who travelled the territory—some 600 miles on foot—to deliver the Word to newly settled communities like Geneva. But for Goodsell, this was only the beginning. In fact, he had a church built and established a Sunday school by the following spring. Along with his interest in bringing Christianity west, Goodsell was also an ardent abolitionist and a leader in the temperance movement. So committed to his beliefs was this early Geneva settler that he refused to grind the corn brought by two men who planned to use it in their distillery (see timeline, page 15).

As the trials of early settlement continued and the community began to grow, so too did interest in the lake and its surrounding lands. In an 1855 newspaper account, the paper reported that G. Montague sold thirty acres of land for $3,000, a far cry from the $1.25 per acre price tag of 1839. "If Geneva was not surprisingly attractive," wrote the weekly paper, "would men be apt to buy land at such prices?"

# PROFILE: ISRAEL WILLIAMS, SR.

Captain Israel Williams was a claim jumper. That's what newcomer Cole would have said when he saw Williams, five of his sons and family friend Robert Russell building a cabin where he had staked out a plot earlier in the year on the northwestern shore of Geneva Lake. But with seven muzzles leveled against his four—and realizing the land laws would be against him because he improperly staked his claim—Cole decided to live to fight another day. Captain Williams later made a peace offering by giving him a cow.

Prior to becoming the namesake of Williams Bay, Captain Israel Williams lived in Ashfield, Massachusetts. He and his wife, Lavina, had nine children. The eldest sons, Israel and Moses, were married and had families of their own. The other children were Royal, Austin, Francis, Fordyce, Festus, Hannah, and Lavinia.

In 1836 the father, along with his two married sons, decided they wanted to move their families to the Middle West, which was just opening for white settlement at the end of the Black Hawk War. So he, along with Moses and Israel and their wives, headed west until they reached Michigan. Hearing about this "Big Foot Lake" in Wisconsin, the boys went on ahead while Israel, Sr. stayed in Michigan. Upon arriving on the south shore of the lake, the boys built a rudimentary log cabin on the future site of Kaye's Park. They then built another log cabin farther west for Moses on what would be the Ayer estate. During this time, the Potawatomi were still living on the lake and the brothers were witness to Chief Big Foot burying his wife at what is now Williams Bay.

After they completed their cabins, the boys went back to Michigan for their families, sending word to their father about the fine lands at Big Foot Lake and the cabins they built. Israel Sr. went back to Massachusetts for the remainder of the family and Israel Jr. and Moses took their wives and sons back to spend the winter of 1836–37 in the cabins they had built. The next oldest Williams boys, Royal, aged 18, and Austin, aged 16, followed soon after, landing at Milwaukee before walking all the way to Big Foot Lake to join their brothers. Israel Sr. and the rest of the family arrived on July 4, 1837, only son, Francis, remained in Massachusetts to finish his studies, joining them once he finished. Francis, however, would eventually return east to become a minister in Chaplain, Connecticut.

While the Williams' built a cabin on an additional claim on the future Ayer site, the family stayed with Israel Jr., making friends with nearby settlers Mark and Robert Russell, the latter of whom would eventually marry Hannah Williams.

Another would-be settler named Cole attempted to stake his claim on some "low, fertile land on the north and northwest shores of the principal bay," where the Potawatomi had recently left. He staked out lots, but did so improperly, rendering them non-binding should someone want that land before Cole could return to complete the claim process the correct way. And someone did want it. Israel Sr. found the land to be quite desirable and he and his five sons, and future son-in-law began to build a log cabin on the claim. When Cole learned of the "jumping" of his deserted site, he brought three friends with guns and ordered Williams and company off the site. The men, gladly accepting the challenge, put down their axes and picked up their guns, and Cole's party suddenly found themselves out-muzzled with men who were not easily intimidated.

Captain Williams brought his family to the newly completed cabin in the spring of 1838, at which time much of the area was marsh, swamp and water. Son Festus would drain much of the land years later. Hannah also married Robert Russell that year, with her father (recently appointed Justice of the Peace of the neighborhood) presiding over the ceremony.

Israel Sr. also bought some cows and with their milk, Mrs. Williams made 800 pounds of cheese, the first cheese made in Walworth County. The cheese was rowed to the Geneva settlement, where they sold it. Mrs. Williams's mother, Mrs. Hannah Joy, whom they had brought with them from Massachusetts, died that year as well. The family made a basswood coffin for her and interred her near Chief Big Foot's wife. She was later re-interred at the East Delavan Cemetery.

The following year, Israel Sr., with the help of his sons, and Mark and Robert Russell, began cutting mostly black walnut timber for what would be a large frame house. When they finished its construction in 1840, the building was large enough to accommodate a tavern, as well as living quarters for the family. The Captain nailed a large set of deer antlers over the doorway and it soon became known as Williams' Buck-Horn Hotel, where many of the new settlement seekers likely took shelter. In 1844 Captain Williams was made the first postmaster of Geneva Bay now called "Williams Bay" in his honor. He was also appointed one of the first Commissioners of Walworth County and served as Supervisor for several terms. Honored pioneers, Captain Israel Williams, Sr., died October 14, 1846 at 57 years old; his wife, Lavina died in 1852 at the age of 65.

# PROFILE: ALEXANDER HENRY BUTTON

Alexander Henry Button was born in 1828 in Floyd, Oneida County, New York, to Riley Button (originally Buttongue, Alexander's father was a titled man with the House of Delemonte in France) who immigrated to Canada after marrying Patience Weter, a German woman. When the Buttons' offspring: Alexander, Ezra, Mayhew and their half-brother, Hiram Powell, were old enough, they began working for the Erie Railroad, in part, building bridges for the tracks being constructed from New York to Buffalo. When that work was done, they headed to Detroit and picked up a boat destined for Milwaukee.

A twist of fate and the hand of Nature brought the Buttons to the shores of Geneva Lake. For if the weather had not turned dark and violent when Alexander and three of his younger brothers set out across Lake Michigan, they might very well have made their original destination of Milwaukee, instead of finding safe harbor where they did, at Fort Dearborn (Chicago). For it was here—and not Milwaukee—where they learned of the Portage route (that included Chief Big Foot's lake in the southeastern portion of the territory) first taken by the John Kinzie party 20 years earlier.

Alexander and his brothers disliked Chicago and thoughts of the Wisconsin frontier excited them so much so that they began the grueling 75-mile trek to Lake Geneva in the early winter of 1850. Alexander would soon settle on the east end of the lake—what is now known as Button's Bay—purchasing 16 acres from Deacon L.W. Fuller on November 11, 1850 for $12.05. None of Alexander's brothers, however, would plant roots in Lake Geneva. Ezra settled in Hebron, Illinois; Mayhew in Genoa City; and Hiram in Iowa. Alexander also had a younger sister, Joanna, who settled in the Lake Geneva area; and a younger brother, Riley, about whom little is known.

Deemed "no good for farming" the wooded lakeside acreage purchased in 1858 was where Button, a skilled carpenter, built Shady Side, for his wife, Terissa Ann Barker of Niagara Falls, New York, and his five sons and two daughters: Elmer, Ezra, George, Frank, Silas, Clara and Mabel. Shady Side would stand along the shores of Geneva Lake for well over a century, until 1975. Eventually, Button would increase his lakeside holdings by acquiring the land extending south, to the corner of Highways BB and 120; and later, adding on further by purchasing what is now the Holly Bush subdivision and the Geneva Inn.

Button's skills kept him busy elsewhere along the shores, where he helped build other homes and structures, including the original dining hall at George Williams College Camp. In addition to carpentry, Button was also an educator, teaching in Linn and Bloomfield, even though he, himself, had only gone to school up to age 12. However, one only needed to be able to read and write, during this period, to be considered a qualified teacher. As the story goes, Button was also an expert in penmanship and taught large classes. He also served as the Town Clerk for Linn.

Button's greatest earnings came, however, when, in 1892, the early pioneer sold eight of his acres at $300 per acre; a tidy profit from his initial investment of 75 cents per acre paid 42 years earlier.

Alexander Button died peacefully after a short illness in 1918 at the age of 91 and was interred at Oak Hill Cemetery. His wife, Terissa, died a few years later in 1922.

Alexander Button and his wife, Terissa, in front of the house he built with his own hands at the east end of the lake, named Shady Side.

PHOTO COURTESY OF THE BUTTON FAMILY

1870

# Signs OF THE Times

History is something often shared by a common collective: a group of neighbors, a close-knit community, a struggling nation. Be it inconsequential or monumental, the wave created by each incident and experience, casts forth a ripple; each ripple soon encountering another, eventually melding into one great mass of unceasing, ever-changing swells directed forward only by the passage of time.

COURTESY OF THE UW DIGITAL COLLECTIONS CENTER

## 1836
■ **THE FIRST CABIN IS BUILT** along the western lakeshore by James and Catherine Van Slyke in the summer of 1836.

## 1837
■ **FIRST MILLS BUILT.** While Christopher Payne and Robert Wells Warren fight for their right to build a mill on the eastern shores of Geneva, at the west end of the lake, Matthias Mohr begins building a mill to process oak and maple trees into planks that will build the first homes in Fontana, including Mohr's own home on the south end of what is today Fontana beach. Mohr, a farmer and miller, is able to harness the power of nearby springs to run his operation by building a dam at the headwaters of the stream known today as Van Slyke Creek. Mohr's mill is quite a sight in the otherwise rural landscape—with a water wheel 30 feet in diameter.

■ **JOHN BRINK VS. CHRISTOPHER PAYNE.** In Geneva, ownership of the land at the White River outlet of the lake—especially the waterpower—is hotly contested by government surveyor John Brink, who, by his accounts, lays claim to the land in 1835, and by Christopher Payne, a frontiersman who arrives at the lake the following year.

When Brink first surveys the land here in 1835, in addition to marking the town lines surrounding the lake, he also maintains marking the outlet of the lake, carving the word "claim" on trees in the area, as is the custom of the day. Christopher Payne arrives at the site during the winter of 1836, walking the entire lake without, according to Payne, finding any marks. Payne cuts down several trees and marks off his own claim and returns a month later, building a small log cabin and beginning construction of a dam across the outlet of the lake.

When Brink's hired men return, they find Payne on Brink's claim and ask him to leave. Payne refuses. Brink's men depart, but Payne knows the fight is far from over. Three weeks later, a suspicious fire burns the framework for his new dam; and while visiting a neighbor, an unarmed Payne is accosted. Payne eventually manages to pay off Brink's men with $2,000; and although Brink is given the opportunity to formally bid on the land at the government land sale, for reasons unknown, he chooses not to.

## 1838
■ **THE GENEVA HOUSE** (later known as St. Denis Hotel) is opened by Robert W. Warren and just across the street, the Owl House is established by his brother, Greenleaf S. Warren.

## 1839
■ **GENEVA TOWNSHIP IS ESTABLISHED.** Land around the lake sells for $1.25/acre.

■ **THE FIRST TEMPERANCE SOCIETY** in the county is established by C.M. Goodsell.

■ As suggested by Matthias Mohr, the name **Fontana** (an Italian—not French—word signifying a place of springs) is made official during a meeting called to organize a township government at the west end of the lake.

The Lake Geneva Express.
COURTESY OF THE LAKE GENEVA PUBLIC LIBRARY

## 1840

■ **THE FIRST DISTILLERY IS ESTABLISHED** by Capron, Wheeler and Whipple. When Charles M. Goodsell refuses to grind corn brought to his mill by two distillers, his actions not only rile the men being denied service, but also does not sit well with local farmers who are looking to the distillery to buy their corn and surplus grain. However, as an ardent leader in the temperance movement, Goodsell will not be moved and will take his fight to the district court—even appearing before Madison's Territorial Legislature—where he successfully argues to alter a statute which requires millers "to grind customers in due turn."

His legislative maneuverings in Madison, however, will not end the conflict in Walworth County, where Goodsell continues his temperance battle for well over a year. "… I had resolved in early manhood," Goodsell explains, "neither to use my capital myself, nor permit it to be used by others, in the manufacture and sale of intoxicating drinks…"

Goodsell will live in Geneva only until 1850, yet he still outlasts the distillery, which will fail only a few years after opening. The Walworth County Temperance Movement continues on without its founder for many years to come, but that demon "intoxicant" will never be fully relinquished (not even during the Prohibition Era) from the shores of Geneva Lake.

## 1844

■ **THE VILLAGE OF GENEVA IS INCORPORATED.** One of four parts of the recently divided Town of Geneva, organized in 1839, the Village of Geneva is granted a charter of incorporation in the winter of 1844. Their first president is Charles M. Goodsell. James Simmons serves as Village Clerk and is well paid with a Boston rocking chair, which he uses long after serving as Village Clerk. Several of the first elected officials are men of the temperance movement who promptly prohibit the sale or giving away of liquor within village limits, taking effect a day or two before the Fourth of July, 1845. There is only one known case prosecuted under this prohibition, however: Greenleaf Warren, keeper of the Lake House.

## 1856

■ The first newspaper, *The Geneva Express / The Anti-Slavery Churchman*, is published by David M. Keeler and edited by Reverend John McNamara. Just one year later, the paper would move to Elkhorn and merge with *The Independent*.

■ The first railroad from Elgin, Illinois arrives in Lake Geneva, only to be discontinued four years later, in 1860.

## 1861

■ The Civil War begins and will last until 1865.

## 1863

■ On January 1, President Abraham Lincoln issues the Emancipation Proclamation declaring "that all persons held as slaves [within the Confederate states] are, and henceforward shall be free."

## 1864

COURTESY OF WISCONSIN HISTORICAL SOCIETY WHi-36459

■ **THE LAKE GENEVA SEMINARY IS ESTABLISHED.** The first of its kind in the region, the Lake Geneva Seminary is established as an institution for the education of young ladies. Built along the east side of the White River in downtown Lake Geneva, the campus eventually encompasses six lakeside acres and several buildings, including Seminary Hall, which has classrooms, exercise rooms, laboratories, music rooms, art studios, and a museum. The seminary is both a boarding and day school where the young Victorian lady can "receive a thorough education." Eventually, the day school will also welcome young male students. The Lake Geneva Seminary will close its doors some time after 1885. Shortly after the school's closing, the seminary buildings become home to a sanitarium for a few short years (see page 97). The land is eventually sold to the city in 1895 and the outbuildings razed in 1901. Today, Seminary Park is all that remains.

# 1870

**■ THE FIRST GRAND-SCALE HOME IS BUILT ON GENEVA LAKE.** Originally from Putnam, Ohio, Solomon Sturges's business interests had taken him all over the Midwest in the early 1800s, until a ten-year contract to store grain in Chicago for the Illinois Central Railroad enticed him to set his sights on the burgeoning city by the lake. There, in 1855, along with his brothers-in-law C. P. Buckingham and Alvah Buckingham, Solomon founded Sturges, Buckingham & Company, which would go on to be the city's largest and most successful grain warehousing firm. Solomon would also eventually own a number of grain-carrying vessels, a fleet of tug boats in the Chicago Harbor, as well as found the bank Solomon Sturges & Sons, in which his sons Buckingham, Albert, and William became involved.

After following their father to Chicago, three of Solomon's nine children discovered the jewel of Geneva Lake as an ideal spot for fishing and camping excursions, and within a few years decide to make this inland lake their summer (and for two, their permanent) residences. Shelton built Maple Lawn; Buckingham built Fairfields and George built Snug Harbor.

Born in 1838, George Sturges would not only do well with his father's grain and elevator fortune, but would also make a name for himself in the banking industry as president of the Northwestern National Bank and founder of the Illinois Trust and Savings.

"His shrewdness foresaw the growth of Chicago," read his obituary in the *Chicago Daily News*, August 13, 1890, "and it was he who suggested to a committee of bankers the expediency of establishing a clearing-house to avoid the loss of time incidental to the settlement of exchanges by the old means of personally delivering and receipting for funds between banks."

Yet even as a financial giant, George Sturges had a reputation for being a kind, generous man. "Mr. Sturges was in heart sympathy with those around him," his *Daily News* obit concluded, "and for even casual acquaintances, such as letter-carriers, watchmen, janitors, and junior clerks, he had ever a warm word and cheery smile."

George Sturges died at Snug Harbor at the age of 52.

The third of the Sturges' nine children, Shelton was born in 1828 and spent much of his years as a young man on his farm in Ohio. But when the Civil War broke out in 1861, Shelton enlisted in the 24th Ohio Volunteers and was chosen to be Captain of Company B. He would be discharged a year later having earned the rank of Major. Shelton returned to the Ohio farm following his service, but in 1863 packed his things and joined his family in Chicago, where he became a partner in his family's bank until leaving in 1865 (George would also leave the bank at the same time). It was then that Shelton turned his sights on the firm Lewis, Ham & Company, distributors of paints, oils, and glass. This endeavor would last less than a year before Shelton formed the firm Sturges, McAllister & Company, wool commission merchants.

Although Shelton was drawn to the west for a short time to try his hand at ranching in California, he spent the last twenty years of his life primarily residing at his beloved Maple Lawn. It is believed that it was Shelton who brought his brothers and the likes of Levi Leiter to the shores of Geneva Lake and it was he who did much to improve and attract people to the young lakeside settlement.

"Mr. Shelton Sturges," wrote the *Lake Geneva Herald* in September of 1872, "proposes to erect a large reservoir upon the hill near his residence, the water to be pumped from the lake by an immense wind-mill. All the business men and private families in the village who wish are at liberty to lay pipes and have water brought to any room in their stores or houses in city style. We think it a most liberal offer, and the intention appears to be to accept of its advantages."

As the Sturges brothers began to erect their estates and improve the lands, they also raved about the glorious nature of the lake and word began to spread among other affluent Chicagoans. As a result, over the next several years, more and more lakeshore real estate was snatched up by affluent men and women from Illinois.

Born in 1833, Buckingham was the Sturges' fifth child. He began his career with his father's firm of Solomon Sturges & Sons as a cashier, tried his hand as a clerk for Sturges, Buckingham & Company, then became one of the partners in his family's bank, and would eventually act as president of the Northwestern National Bank. Buckingham held this prestigious post only a few short months before opening the banking house, Sturges & Company (which became commonly known as the Union Stock Yards Bank) with his brother Albert. Selling the bank in 1867, Buckingham and his brother Albert would undertake a variety of different business ventures together, including warehousing and the building of a railroad.

Like his brother Shelton, Buckingham would eventually make his Lake Geneva estate, Fairfields, his permanent residence.

So strong was the Sturges family's love for Geneva Lake that fourteen family members were re-interred from Chicago and elsewhere in 1887 and laid to rest in Oak Hill Cemetery in Lake Geneva. Today, many members of the Sturges family are buried there. (See page 48.)

The children of Solomon Sturges circa 1868.
FROM *SOLOMON STURGES AND HIS DESCENDANTS*, COMPILED BY EBENEZER BUCKINGHAM, 1907

# 1871.
■ The Chicago and Northwestern Railroad reaches Lake Geneva in July.

■ **THE GREAT CHICAGO FIRE.** It is difficult to describe what began at 9 p.m. on October 8, 1871, in or near the O'Leary barn on Chicago's near south side. But by the end of the Great Chicago Fire, some 300 people had lost their lives and more than 100,000 were homeless.

It had been extremely dry in the months preceding the fire—only 1.5 inches of rain were recorded to have fallen since July 4. After extinguishing a large blaze the previous day, firefighters were exhausted even before they got word of the quickly spreading O'Leary fire; and it didn't help matters that they were mistakenly sent to the wrong address.

When residents first learned of the fire, they were concerned, but saw it as just another in the string of blazes over the last week—numbering twenty. As time went on, their concern changed to worry, to fear, and eventually, to panic. "The sky kept getting red and redder," wrote Ada Rumsey, remembering how she watched the scene from her living room with her mother and the other children of the Julian Rumsey (Shadow Hill) family; "the wind, already high, was increasing with the heat, and huge burning cinders were settling in every direction."

Although business in Chicago was booming, most structures had been rather hastily built to keep up with demand—and all of them contained wood, a lot of it. In addition, the roads were paved with wood and so were the sidewalks. With the dry conditions and a strong wind coming out of the southwest, the city—and the residents—didn't have much hope of escaping the inferno.

One by one, significant structures succumbed to the flames: the post office, the Chicago Historical Society, the Chicago Tribune, the Palmer House, the Field & Leiter department store and the courthouse—where prisoners confined in the basement had to be released, and just in time, before the huge bell on top of the courthouse came crashing through the tower as it collapsed.

By this time, the Rumsey family was distraught. Their father had left several hours before, presumably to check on his office, which was even closer to the approaching fire. "We had heard the Court House bell ringing and ringing the alarm, never stopping until the whole structure had fallen," wrote Ada, "and as that building was directly across the street from Father's office we were more alarmed than ever at his non-appearance."

He did return, finally, but soon the family was forced to evacuate their home. They took off on foot, joining the throngs of people in the streets, all displaced and hurrying to safety as the flames spread around them. On the streets, safety was compromised as the crowd grew and the sidewalks began to burn. People began to crowd the bridges to escape the flames. Everyone was hoping that the river would be able to hold the fire from spreading to the north side, but even boats that were moored were ignited, and the river itself seemed to burn, as oil on the surface caught fire. Some people were trampled on the crowded bridges or in the new Washington and LaSalle tunnels. More were trapped in their burning homes. The Rumseys made their way to the Northwestern Railroad station, and mother and children boarded a train bound for Lake Geneva. "The train was crowded with refugees, homeless, tired and hungry..." wrote Ada. Leaving his family safely heading north, Julian Rumsey returned to the scene of destruction to help.

The fire raged until the rains came two days later, extinguishing the remaining flames. The burned area was four miles long and an average of ¾ mile wide—more than 2,000 acres in total. That's more than twenty-eight miles of streets, approximately 18,000 buildings, and more than $200,000,000 in property destroyed. Only about half of all the burned buildings had been insured, and because of the huge losses, only about half of the payments owed were ever paid.

Still, within days after the fire, businesses—including Schock, Bigford and Company, selling cigars, grapes and apple cider—began to spring up again in sheds and little shacks that were quickly constructed. The post office was set up in a Methodist Church, and much of the rubble was pushed out of sight and into Lake Michigan on the south side of the river.

General Philip Sheridan was in charge of martial law in the city for the next couple of weeks, composed of troops, police and volunteers. Relief efforts were also begun, starting with the Chicago Relief and Aid Society, which offered food, clothing and funds to displaced Chicagoans. Within six weeks, construction was already underway on 212 new buildings in the South Division alone, not to mention in other parts of the city. The period of Great Rebuilding was on.

COURTESY OF THE LIBRARY OF CONGRESS, PRINTS AND PHOTOGRAPHS DIVISION, LC-USZC2-3788

## 1872

■ **THE *GENEVA LAKE HERALD*** is founded by George S. Utter, with John E. Burton (see profile page 58) as its chief editor.

## 1873

■ **CAPTAIN EDWIN QUIGLEY** launches the excursion boat, *Lady of the Lake*. At the time, this double-decker, side-wheeling steamer is unmatched by any steamer running on Wisconsin's inland lakes.

■ **GENERAL ULYSSES S. GRANT VISITS.** Charles L. Wilson, President Lincoln's wartime minister of Great Britain and publisher of the *Chicago Journal*, invites the famed General Ulysses S. Grant to visit his home on Geneva Lake during the summer.

## 1874

■ **THE FIRST PRIVATE STEAM YACHT**, *Gertie*, is brought to the lake on the new railroad for owners G.L. Dunlap and Julian Rumsey.

## 1874

■ **THE FIRST MAJOR ICE HOUSE, GROSS & BROOKS, IS ESTABLISHED ON GENEVA LAKE.** Because the lake is spring-fed, deep, and crystal-clear, it is ideal for ice production. Add to that the proximity of the railroad lines, and it proves the best possible scenario for harvesting and shipping ice to fill local ice houses; to pack into cork-insulated rail-cars in order to keep meats and vegetables fresh on long train rides; to ship in large blocks to Chicago for use in drinks, or to Milwaukee for use in brewery cooling systems; and for delivery all summer long, so that locals can have unspoiled food—not to mention ice chips to cool a tall glass of lemonade.

Ice harvesting is a labor-intensive, dangerous business, with power supplied through steam, horses and men. Grooves are cut into the snow-cleared ice in a grid pattern, using a double-bladed horse-drawn plow. Then the workers cut the ice blocks using handsaws. The blocks are floated through an open channel to a steam-powered conveyor that carries them up the shore to the ice house. The blocks are then hand-stacked in layers at heights of thirty feet or more.

Horses wear special wooden shoes on the ice to keep their feet from freezing, but the real danger is crashing through the ice. When that happens, the men immediately tighten a rope around the horse's neck, then quickly cut a channel to the shore and assist the horse with swimming the distance. Drying the horse and putting it right back on the ice is critical—if the horse doesn't get right back to work, it develops a fear of the ice and becomes useless.

Once in a while, a man falls through the ice and has to be rescued with the same pike-poles that the workers use to guide the blocks through the water.

COURTESY OF WISCONSIN HISTORICAL SOCIETY. WHI-9525

Frostbite is always a danger, as is loading the blocks on and off the conveyor, or into the ice houses. This is slippery work where in one false move, a man can fatally crack his skull on a block, or lose a limb to a conveyor.

The first operation to build a large ice house for commercial storage and sale is Gross and Brooks, operated by Daniel Gross and Elymas Brooks. Their house, built in 1874, is able to store 400 tons of ice, and there is such a demand that they double it in size by the very next season.

The "Ice King" of the lake is John Seymour, who builds his first ice house near the railroad, in 1876. It is, however, some distance from the lake, so Seymour constructs a 2,200-foot wooden slide so horses can drag the ice up the ramp. At its peak, Seymour utilizes 300 men and twenty horses per winter to cut approximately 35,000 tons of ice.

Seymour builds additional ice houses, which newspaper accounts claim are "as large as the World's Fair!" By 1896, his business is in full swing—he is shipping 10,000 tons (450 carloads) of ice to Illinois. In her memoirs, Seymour's daughter, Eva Seymour Lundahl, recalls her father coming in the house on the coldest winter days with icicles on his mustache, saying, "Grand weather for icing!"

By 1888 the Chicago Northwestern Railway is extended from Lake Geneva to Williams Bay, which enables ice to be shipped by rail from that side of the lake. Two early ice houses in Williams Bay are owned by the Lake Geneva Ice Company and J.P. Smith Ice Company, and by 1893, a two-story boarding house is built to house transient ice workers.

The Otto Jacobs Company, which begins harvesting ice from Button's Bay during the Depression for local use, employs some forty men each winter.

COURTESY OF THE GENEVA LAKE MUSEUM

Katherine, Otto's wife, feeds the men in shifts so that they can harvest and haul ice from daylight to dusk. Overnight, it is required to have a man rowing in the open water in the middle of the ice field to keep the ice from freezing.

Not all the ice is shipped out on trains; some is kept and delivered year-round to residents around the lake. It is customary to put a cardboard sign in your window stating how many pounds of ice you want that day. Children follow the ice delivery truck, hoping to find chips of ice to nibble on during the hot summer days.

Over time, the ice houses begin to disappear from the lake's shores. As early as 1899 there is an account that H. A. Beidler (Alpine Villa) installed a "modern patent refrigerator" in his ice house on the lake. Scientists are experimenting with various liquids that expand and evaporate, absorbing heat. The earliest refrigerators use toxic chemicals and, in fact, several fatal accidents occur in the 1920s when they leak noxious chloride into homes. But, in 1928, Thomas Midgley, Jr., aided by Charles Franklin Kettering, invents a safer compound called Freon. It is a major blow to the ice industry. One of the last ice harvesting companies on the lake, The Otto Jacobs Company, cuts its final blocks in the winter of 1946.

## 1875

■ **SHERIDAN SPRINGS** offers its healthy lake elixir. Said to provide "almost magic relief" for a list of ailments ranging from diabetes to inflammation of the kidneys to eruptions of the skin, the water from Sheridan Springs is marketed heavily by the *Lake Geneva Herald*, which, incidentally, is edited by John E. Burton, who establishes Sheridan Springs with A. C. Hogaboom.

Burton and Hogaboom begin bottling spring water from property they are leasing from John Beamsley, who is actually the first proponent of the water's curative properties, even though he never profits (financially) from the sales. He writes, in a signed and witnessed statement, an account of his battles with illness. After Beamsley suffers in his bed for several days, praying and saying farewell to family and friends, his son brings in some of the spring water for him to drink and watercress for him to nibble. Miraculously, after several days of drinking the water, Beamsley is out of bed, and even returns to work—after convalescing with a daily supply of fresh spring water—after a couple of months.

The springs are named "Sheridan" after a famed visitor, General Philip Sheridan, who drank—and praised—the water in 1873. After some sales success, the lease reverts back to the Beamsley family, and the springs are later sold off to be used in manufacturing Coca Cola.

## 1879

■ **THE FIRST TELEPHONE** line is completed around Geneva Lake.

## 1880

■ **THE BUILDING BOOM** around the lake begins.

## 1886

■ **VILLAGE OF GENEVA BECOMES THE CITY OF LAKE GENEVA.**

## 1888

■ **THE WILLIAMS BAY RAILROAD** spur is completed.

## 1890

■ On the evening of August 7, while summer estates are in full swing and campgrounds are full to capacity, the residents and visitors of Lake Geneva are shown their first demonstration of electric lights.

## 1892

■ Public resorts begin to close in favor of private residences.

## 1893

■ **THE WORLD'S FAIR**, the Columbian Exposition, begins in Chicago.

# 1895

■ **THE SINKING OF *DISPATCH*.** It's a Sunday afternoon during the height of summer, when Reverend Hogan of Harvard, Illinois, and his sister, Mary, along with Dr. John E. Hogan of Elgin, Illinois, and his wife and child, decide to charter the steamer, *Dispatch*, for a tour of the illustrious Wisconsin lake. The happy vacationers hop aboard the steamer from the pier of the renowned and reputable Kaye's Park Resort and chug their way east along the south shore, toward Lake Geneva. There they dock the boat until later that afternoon, when the party boards the steamer once more and begins their tour of Geneva Lake's northern shores.

'Before they started," reports the *Lake Geneva Herald* the following Friday, "the clouds had began [sic] to gather in the west and there was every appearance that a severe wind storm would break upon us before very long."

Just as the small vessel, with its five passengers, reaches Elgin Park, the storm begins in earnest. Witnesses, undoubtedly abandoning their own lake tours for land, are standing on the pier of Elgin Park when *Dispatch* comes within fifteen feet of the dock they are standing on.

Surprisingly, however, instead of tying up to the pier with the rest of the shelter seekers, *Dispatch* continues on its way. Perplexed as to why the small vessel doesn't seek safety, those on the pier continue to watch *Dispatch* as it moves westward—first, toward the pier of the Crane estate, then changing direction toward the south shore. Almost as soon as *Dispatch* is redirected, the vessel changes course yet again, this time back towards Cooke's pier. Under what appears to be great confusion or severe indecision, the helmsman of the steam launch redirects the bow of the vessel one final time, setting its sights across the lake to Kaye's Park, where the excursion began.

Before it's halfway across the lake, however, the storm peaks and the rain begins to fall in blinding torrents. Witnesses on the pier say that that is the last they see of *Dispatch*.

George Manson, Captain of the steamer *Admiral*, later reports having passed *Dispatch* during the storm. With the curtains of the steam launch closed to protect the passengers from the downpour, Manson isn't able to see any of what was happening on board, but states that "when he last saw the boat it had luffed up to the wind—a wise thing to do—but, in his judgment, too late, for the storm is the worst he ever saw on the lake in his nineteen years' experience."

The storm, with its reported fifty-mile-per-hour winds, is, in fact, so severe that parts of southern Wisconsin and northern Illinois are ravaged and five additional lives are lost that day to the wildly churning waters of Lake Michigan.

After the storm passes, news spreads of the disappearance of *Dispatch* and every available steamer on the lake joins the search party. The *Arthur Kaye*, which had been docked at Williams Bay during the storm, reports having seen life preservers and cushions floating off the shores of Black Point on its return home. Several boats head in this direction, while others steer a course for Cedar Point where, sadly, they discover the body of the first victim, Mary Hogan, held afloat by the "large puff sleeves of her dress." Over the following three days, the search for more bodies continues and using the *Arthur Kaye* and the *Majestic*, the lake is dragged, but all in vain.

On July 11, the steamer is finally located about one-quarter mile off of Cedar Point in more than 100 feet of water. The following Sunday, Mr. Nelson, a diver, and his team are called to the scene of the tragedy. Slowly lowering the diver to the lake bottom 108 feet below, it's only a matter of moments until the second body is recovered, that of the Reverend's, who is found lying beneath the bow of the boat. The next body to be discovered is John Hogan, the reverend's brother, found on the opposite side of the hull. As the diver prepares to descend again, the winds pick up speed and the mission to recover the remaining bodies is delayed.

The following day, the search continues and brings to the surface the child of Dr. and Mrs. J. E. Hogan and that of John Preston, the *Dispatch's* 21-year-old engineer. But having no further luck locating the final fatality, the diver returns to Chicago on Wednesday. Determined to lay their sister to rest, the brothers of Mrs. Hogan, the last missing victim, return to the site of the wreckage to, once more, drag the lake. Their labor is sadly rewarded.

"We hope we may never have to write up another item of this same character," concludes the front page story in the *Herald*. Since then, the lake has certainly been marred with misfortune, but none (as the *Herald* hoped) as wretched as the sinking of *Dispatch*.

## 1896

■ **BIG CITY LIGHTS COME TO LAKE GENEVA.** The Haskins Electric Company switches on in March for the very first time and offers local residents their choice between arc or incandescent electric lighting systems. By the following month, they hope to have two hundred "little balls of fire that give forth a steady and brilliant light" burning and plan to offer more and more Lake Geneva residents electric services as soon as buildings can be wired.

## 1906

■ **THE CONSTRUCTION OF LAKE SHORE DRIVE IS COMPLETED.** With the rising popularity of the automobile and an increase in population, as well as local tourism, the public is anxious to see a road constructed around the lake. So, in 1903, with an estimated length of 20.75 miles, at an average cost of $5,000 per mile, the creation of Lake Shore Drive is the hot topic of the day. The attitude of local residents is that the development of the road will "add a new source of diversion to those who already make the lake so popular." By late 1905, the road is nearly complete and is the pride of all, especially the estate owners who ultimately pay for most of its construction. "Those men put their money into it," writes the *Herald*, "in order that they might have a fine drive around the lake...And yet, it is no more their road than it is yours. It is a public road...."

## 1905

■ **LEVI LEITER OF LINDEN LODGE** passes away. The Leiter family, who had been spending the past several summers in Maine (where Levi died), sells parcels of the estate to: A.C. Bartlett, who will build House in the Woods, N.W. Harris, who will build Wadsworth Hall and E.F. Swift who will build Villa Hortensia. The remaining property will remain in the family until 1923 at which point the land is sold and further subdivided. The main house will be razed in 1939, but the estate will forever be remembered as a place where generations of Lake Geneva residents gathered to rejoice in their bounty, revel in their history and relax by the shores.

COURTESY OF THE LAKE GENEVA PUBLIC LIBRARY

## 1908

■ **DESIGNED BY IRVING K. POND**, the Y.M.C.A. is built along the shores of the lake.

## 1910

■ **ALL EYES ON HALLEY'S COMET** and Yerkes Observatory. The world watches the skies expectantly during the spring of 1910—many fearing the worst—as Halley's Comet hurls toward the planet. News from Professor E.E. Barnard at Yerkes Observatory in Williams Bay is both welcome and feared around the globe. As astronomers at Yerkes point their telescopes towards the stars to snap some photos, the people of Chicago and Lake Geneva also catch their first glimpse of the famed comet in the early morning hours of April 20. Yet it will not be for another month that the dreaded comet is supposed to come close enough—as some predicted—to penetrate the earth's atmosphere. The month passes and, "Without so much as denting the air envelope," writes the *Chicago Tribune*, on May 19, 1910, "mother earth last night plunged into the tail of the long-awaited terrestrial visitor, whizzed madly forty-five miles a second through a million miles of it, and came out of the other side unscathed."

COURTESY OF SUE MORTON

## 1911

■ The Gardeners and Foremans Association is founded.

## 1912

■ **HORTICULTURAL HALL** is officially opened in June with a Peony Show given by the Gardeners and Foremens Association.

# 1916

■ **IN 1916 RED CROSS TRAINING CAMPS** are just beginning to sprout up around the country, but will eventually train many women (and young ladies) to help serve their nation in times of need. Sponsored by the Navy League, the third camp to be established in the nation opens on the shores of Geneva Lake in July on the grounds of the Northwestern Military and Naval Academy. "Here," reports the *Lake Geneva News*, "the women of Chicago and of the middle west will have the opportunity to go into camp and experience the sort of life led by Red Cross nurses in actual service in the field."

The camp consists of two two-week training courses during which time about 100 women reside in regulation tents, practice military calisthenics and take coursework in first aid, diet, home care of the sick, surgical dressings, sewing (Red Cross Relief garments), and are instructed in ambulance driving. The training camp also holds classes in telegraphy, wireless and other signal work. "…it is the belief of the Navy League," explains the article, "that women could be of real service as telegraph operators in the event of war, because there are 40,000 telegraph operators in the United States, mostly able bodied men, who could do service at the front if their places at home were taken by women."

The Red Cross Training Camp in Lake Geneva proves very successful and another like it will follow, but only after the end of World War I and the 1918 influenza epidemic. Established in 1919, the second training camp to be located on the shores of Geneva Lake will include much of the coursework offered by the Red Cross Training Camps, but will be financed mainly by Chicago businessmen; conducted by Washington departments, such as the Bureau of Education and the Public Health Service, and supported by the U.S. government.

Opening in August, the United States Training Corps for Women is the prototype camp that will act as the testing ground for a nationwide program. It welcomes women (over the age of 20) to Northwestern Military and Naval Academy for yet another opportunity to train and drill. Nearly 200 women (many of whom are employee sponsored) come from all around the nation to join in the training that includes swimming, hiking, household management, military exercises, physical and mental fitness, community sanitation, social hygiene, and home care for the sick.

And although the newspaper reports, by today's standards, don't seem to take these women very seriously (nor do some of the women themselves), the "soldierettes" are expected to rise for reveille at 7 a.m., drill and train all day until taps at 10 p.m. and receive training that will allow each of them to take some very important lessons and skills back to their communities.

COURTESY OF THE DORIS M. REINKE RESOURCE CENTER

# 1917 ■ THE U.S. ENTERS WORLD WAR I.

■ **THE SILENT FILM INDUSTRY DAZZLES LAKE GENEVA.** "'Help!' screamed a young lady bather in front of the William Wrigley, Jr. summer mansion Monday afternoon—and she threw up her hands and went under," begins the front page article in the *Lake Geneva Herald* in June of 1917.

The *Herald* is not reporting a tragic accident, but the scene from a silent picture being filmed on Geneva Lake. Movie producer Andrew J. Callaghan and film director Arthur Berthelet chose Lake Geneva as the setting for their Essanay film production of *The Golden Idiot*.

Chicago's Essanay Film Manufacturing Company would play a leading role in the young filmmaking industry, producing thousands of early motion pictures (of which only 215 survive today) featuring soon-to-be legendary film stars, such as Ben Turpin (who began as the studio's janitor), Charlie Chaplin (who would make a series of comedies for Essanay in 1915, including the celebrated film, *The Tramp*), Wallace Beery, Gloria Swanson, and Gilbert M. Anderson—not only one of the company's founders, but one of its biggest box office draws for his character, Broncho Billy. The success of this Chicago film company would also be attributed to their genius for distribution and promotion, which would turn the fledgling industry into big business.

Even though Essanay's producer assures reporters that Lake Geneva has potential for attracting more movie-making magic, the production of *The Golden Idiot* will prove to be one of the last films to be made by the company which closes just months later due to a number of factors, including: industry changes (the California foothills winning favor over the Windy City), conflicts between co-founders, the loss of Chaplin (who was looking for more money and more creative control), and the arrival on the scene of other studios, such as Universal and Paramount, which prove stronger competitors. One of its founders, George Spoor, however, would retire from Essanay a millionaire.

Unaware of the company's doomed future, Lake Geneva welcomes the film crew with much excitement. Starring in this film are silent film stars Bryant Washburn, William Long, and Virginia Valli. Although known by only a few today, these actors are some of the movie-goers' favorite silent film stars of the time. The cast and crew are put up at Frank Lloyd Wright's illustrious Hotel Geneva and treated to the best of everything.

G. M. ANDERSON—BRONCHO BILLY.
ESSANAY PHOTO PLAYER.

COURTESY OF THE NILES ESSANAY SILENT FILM MUSEUM

The John J. Mitchell (Ceylon Court) and the Wrigley estates (Green Gables) will be two of the liveliest spots during the production of the movie—not only as backdrops for the film, but as lively social centers for the film company and invited local residents. Even Phillip Wrigley shows his enthusiasm for the event, purchasing his own camera and filming scenes of summer fun for the amusement of his family and friends sojourning at Green Gables that summer.

*The Golden Idiot* premiers to "rave" reviews in July of 1917. "Mae Tinee of the *Tribune*, Luella Parsons [a former screenwriter for Essanay] of the *Herald*, and Hollander of the *News*…proclaiming the Essanay picture… one of the greatest pictures taken for a number of years." Sadly, *The Golden Idiot* was not among the handful of Essanay films known to survive.

COURTESY OF THE LIBRARY OF CONGRESS, PRINTS AND PHOTOGRAPHS DIVISION, LC-US262-123257

**1918**
- World War I ends.
- The influenza epidemic kills 50 million people worldwide.

- **WILLIAMS BAY IS INCORPORATED.** Named after Captain Israel Williams, who settled the area with his family in 1836, Williams Bay is faced with whether or not they wanted to "govern themselves" in October 1919. After much discord, the people of Williams Bay (with a population of 450 and an assessed value of $1,180,000—the highest of any village in Walworth County) vote 66 to 41 to incorporate as an autonomous village.

- **THE AVIATION ERA.** It's "all the rage" in July of 1919, a new way to view Geneva Lake—from high above—in a bi-plane flown by medalled World War I pilot and world alltitude record holder, Lieutenant Paul R. Blair, who arrives at the shores of the lake to offer customers a $15 experience that they'll remember all their lives. Taking off and landing from a tract of ground on the Otto Young (Younglands) estate, Lieutenant Blair flies people of all ages into the wild blue yonder and across the glacial lake for a month that summer. Leo J. Host, a local garage mechanic, is the pilot's first passenger from Lake Geneva.

- **WILLIAM WRIGLEY JR.** purchases the three-year-old, pure bred Poland China hog for a record $15,000. The highest price ever paid for a boar, beating the last record by $2,500, "The Clansman" is shipped to the Green Gables farm in August where Wrigley, Jr. hopes to continue the award-winning line by breeding this prince of porkers to some of the Poland China sows already living on the farm.

- **LAKE GENEVA GOES DRY.** "Booze Buried in Foamy Funeral," is the headline of the July 3, 1919 edition of the *Lake Geneva News*, as the country's new era of prohibition (which would last from 1919–1933) begins as a result of the powerful Temperance Movement's success in pushing the "Volstead Act"—a nationwide ban on the sale, manufacture and transportation of alcohol—into being.

"Looks like a long, dry summer," states one of the patrons of the nine saloons and hotel bars in Lake Geneva that will be forced to switch gears or close their doors.

"Monday night, bartenders swished the last scuttles of suds along the polished counters, and lingering customers cast fond departing glances at the old scenes of brass rails, gleaming glassware, clinking bottle and foaming amber," states the paper forlornly.

Although the sale of soft drinks will be the new order of the day (at least above the counter), the new era brought on by the passing of the National Prohibition Act (the 18th Amendment) will soon prove to be highly explosive and extremely unsuccessful, especially with regard to the government's inability to enforce this coast to coast ban. It also gives rise to a powerful criminal element which will make great fortunes (illegal liquor sales will climb to $100 million annually) and cause great destruction.

Ultimately, the enraged American public —as it falls headfirst into the Great Depression—says enough is enough and in March of 1933 (after nearly a decade and a half of enduring this failed policy,) President Franklin Roosevelt signs an amendment to the Volstead Act known as the Cullen-Harrison Act, which allows the sale and manufacture of certain alcoholic beverages. By the year's end, the President takes it one step further by ratifying the 21st Amendment, which ultimately repeals the 18th Amendment.

## 1920

■ **WOMEN GET THE VOTE.**

■ **SIMEON B. CHAPIN FOUNDS GENEVA LAKE'S WATER SAFETY PATROL**, an organization dedicated to teaching people how to swim and keeping lake residents and visitors safe.

## 1924

■ **THE VILLAGE OF FONTANA IS INCORPORATED.** Since 1839, "Fontana" referred to an area (which now encompasses Sharon, Walworth, Fontana and western Williams Bay) within Walworth Township. The name, first suggested by early Chicago settler, Matthias Mohr, was agreed upon by settlers during an organized meeting, but soon ignored by a county representative in Madison who changed the name to Walworth in order to flatter a New York state judge. Samuel Phoenix, founder of nearby Delavan, knew Judge Reuben Hyde Walworth and proposed, instead, that it be the name of the county. It would, however, be nearly a century later before the name is made official through the incorporation of the Village of Fontana.

Surrounded by onlookers of the opposite sex, a lone women stands firm for her right to vote.

COURTESY OF THE LIBRARY OF CONGRESS, PRINTS & PHOTOGRAPHS DIVISION. LC-US262-135533

# 1927

■ **THE AREA'S FIRST HISTORICAL SOCIETY, THE GENEVA LAKE HISTORICAL SOCIETY, IS ESTABLISHED.** Efforts to trace the lake's history begin as far back as early settlement with men such as James Simmons, a lawyer and leading citizen who had a penchant for history; and organizations such as the Old Settlers Society (founded in 1869 and later evolving into the Walworth County Historical Society), dedicated to recording firsthand experiences of early pioneer life. However, in 1927, an effort is made to form an *official* historical organization that will not only delve into early settlement, but explore the area's pre-settlement and ancient history.

Prior to this happening, one of the first "unofficial" attempts to explain to the public the lake's post-glacial history occurs in 1922, when citizens organize the Lake Geneva Historical Pageant Association, whose first order of business is to plan a pageant to be held on May 29. The idea for the pageant originates in the schools, but soon becomes a bit too extravagant for a small group of teachers to pull together, thus the association is formed. The call for volunteers from every community organization to get involved goes out and Joseph Leiter offers his estate (Linden Lodge)—and its natural amphitheater-like setting—for the final staged performances. The ambitious goal of the pageant association is to tell the story of the lake from the time of the mound builders forward and includes a parade, the usual array of speeches, a regatta and a spectacular pageant finale.

The day proves to be very successful in almost every aspect. Nearly 4,000 visitors join in the festivities that Monday in spring, arriving from all around the region by boat, by train, by horse, and by auto. There are newspaper reporters and film crews, warm days and cloudless skies for the spectacular event that presents Greek goddesses, fairy queens and an elaborate and kaleidoscopic display of dancing girls who are a fantastic site—if not for their historical accuracy, than for their delicate, passionate, enthusiastic frolicking.

In truth, historical accuracy seems to be little on the minds of the pageant organizers, its director, Mary Short Baxter (a local resident and dramatist who appeared on the lyceum and chautauqua circuits); or for that matter, its author and producer, Mr. Tucker for the pageant's attempts at presenting the region's pre-history is both misinformed and misguided.

"The muffled sound of tom-toms heralded the coming of the procession of the Mound Builders marching to perform a human sacrifice..." reports a local paper. "The white robes of the Mound-Builders were stained and spotted as with the blood of former sacrifices..." And on this extraordinarily erroneous performance goes, until the victim lay sacrificed and "the waves and winds and flowers and fairies screamed, and Lake Geneva [another dancer] ran forward, horror in her face, and drove the bloody group away into the silence of oblivion."

A few years later, in 1925, the Lake Geneva Women's Club organizes another historical event, Pioneer Day, during which time old stories of early settlement are dusted off and retold by family members of early pioneers.

Despite the community's efforts to tell its history, it isn't until July of 1927 that steps are taken toward the formation of the Geneva Lake Historical Society. The first meeting is held at Yerkes Observatory in Williams Bay and is spearheaded by local notables, such as S. B. Chapin (Flowerside Inn), J. S. Hotton (Williams Bay's Village President,) Paul and Edward Jenkins, Edwin B. Frost (Director of Yerkes), M. A. Healy (Healy estate), Dr. Otto Schmidt (Black Point) and is led by Charles Brown, head of the Wisconsin State Historical Society.

A few days later, the Society dedicates four bronze tablets around the lake marking Big Foot's village, the Kinzie party's arrival, and John Brink's survey and renaming of the lake. Over the following months, the newly formed society (led by Dr. Paul Jenkins) attempts to educate the public as to the facts unearthed by local archeological investigations by exhibiting various Native American relics discovered by land owners around the lake. (Many of these items are to form the nucleus for the future Geneva Lake Area Museum that would be established by the Geneva Lake History Buffs in 1984.)

In 1930 the Geneva Lake Historical Society begins plans to mark the centennial anniversary of the "discovery" of Lake Geneva. Gathering local leaders, the society organizes a weekend-long celebration, inviting guests from near and far (including Potawatomi men, women, and children) to partake in the historical observance.

Their efforts to gather accurate historical information while old settlers still lived—relics were still being uncovered and Chief Simon Kahquados (a Potawatomi spokesperson, historian and interpreter whose grandmother was said to have been a member of Big Foot's village) was still alive to retell his tribe's vivid oral history of the lake—have been invaluable to every generation that has followed in their footsteps.

The Pioneer Pageant during the centennial anniversary celebration of the discovery of Geneva Lake by white setters, 1930.
COURTESY OF THE DORIS M. REINKE RESOURCE CENTER

## 1929
- Wall Street crashes.

## 1933
- **"BEER! SPARKLING, FOAMING, BREW,"** revels Lake Geneva's *News Tribune* on April 13. After fourteen years of a failed prohibition attempt, barrels of beer arrive in town; the first barrel being delivered to the J.W. O'Brien Tavern where it is rolled into the cellar, uprighted and tapped immediately. "The return of the brew seemed to carry with it a return of uplifted morale," reports the paper. "There was a grin on everyone's face and a general feeling of good fellowship." Reports from Chicago say that huge crowds (larger than those amassed in the aftermath of the market crash of 1929) gathered in the Loop to celebrate and, for the first time since prohibition began, no arrests for drunkness were made. "...thus proving the theory advanced" concludes the paper, "that the beer is not intoxicating."

## 1934
- **COLLECTIONS AT THE AYER ESTATE, THE OAKS, ARE AUCTIONED.** Edward E. Ayer and his wife, Emma Augusta Burbank Ayer, had lived on the southwest side of Geneva Lake since 1875 in a rambling estate named for its many trees on the grounds. A philanthropic, self-made man, Edward and his wife traveled the world collecting artwork, artifacts, books, weapons, furniture, and other rare antique and unique items. Not long after Edward's death in 1927, and Emma's death in 1932, the estate went bankrupt and by 1934, their lovingly built treasury is on the auction block. Items such as Chippendale furniture; rare Oriental rugs; an envied collection of arms, such as a 13th-century crossbow inlaid with ivory, an ancient Japanese cannon, two-handed swords and more; a collection of thousands of dollar's worth of ruby glass; historical development data on American Indians, birds in America and Americana go to the highest bidder. Among other items of pride decorating the interior of the Ayers' home up for bid are wrought iron fire dogs from Italy; two old German guns; a huge Mexican water jar; two finely carved cabinets, one Italian, one Dutch; and Della Robbia's "Madonna and Child." Auctioned objects once gracing the estate's grounds include: Egyptian statues and a Japanese death gong, gotten at great expense from a temple, which the Ayers sounded as a dinner bell for many years.

## 1936
- Dr. Paul B. Jenkins, two-time president of Williams Bay, historian and author of two invaluable historical publications: *The Book of Lake Geneva* and *History and Indian Remains of Lake Geneva* passes away at his home in Williams Bay.

## 1940
- To help with the Red Cross War Relief effort, women of the Lake Geneva Garden Club put many hours into fundraising, sewing, knitting and food conservation efforts—one household reporting 1,000 jars of jelly preserved and forty-five gallons of fruit juice made.

## 1941
- The U.S. enters World War II.

## 1945
- World War II ends.

- **UFOS ARE SIGHTED OVER GENEVA LAKE.** Flying saucers are first reported on the evening of Sunday, July 13, by two women staying at the lake. While dining on the porch of the home they are visiting at Sunset Hills, the two women witness a strange sight in the southern skies: "a circular disc, blueish-green in color, with a light extending through the center from front to back, indicating a row of windows." Both women claim the object moved slowly and silently for a few seconds and then vanished from the skies. No other sightings are reported that evening, but one week later the *Regional News* reports that five more persons claim to have sighted strange objects in the skies over Geneva Lake.

One witness claims seeing basketball-sized saucers hovering in three groups of six; while another group reports watching an object "larger and brighter than an ordinary star [that] moved slowly back and forth as if on a pendulum" for over an hour. Dr. Georges Van Blesbroeck of Yerkes Observatory is asked to comment on the events and suggests that the sightings might very well be the planet Jupiter, which would be highly visible each night in July. Ignoring the astronomer's professional opinion, more flying saucer sightings are reported for a third week, including a mother and son who maintain they watched a fast-moving craft (which was round and entirely illuminated by a bluish light) travel north to south over the lake and then disappear.

© GENE PESEK, CHICAGO SUN-TIMES

# 1967

■ **THE RIOTS.** It is a tumultuous year in American history. Hair is getting longer as America's patience regarding the Vietnam War is growing shorter and shorter; Flower Power is blossoming and thinking the way your parents thought is fast dying. Everywhere one turns this year, societal norms are being questioned and redefined—not only by the likes of Timothy Leary, Muhammad Ali and Martin Luther King, Jr., but by young men and women in both small towns and urban centers across the nation.

Great change such as this always comes at a cost and occasionally loses its way, as it did around Geneva Lake during the weekend leading up to the Fourth of July, when thousands of youth (ranging from sixteen to their early twenties) turn from a mass of vacationing youngsters to a throng of rioters bent on violence and destruction.

This is not the first time such an event had occurred along the shores of Geneva Lake. In fact, the summer before, during the very same holiday weekend, nearly 200 "pleasure-bent" teens had been arrested among a reported crowd of 5,000; one youth was shot in the foot and thousands of dollars in damages had been caused. So there is good reason that local authorities gear up for an encore performance by having 300 National Guards (later increased to 600) at the ready in the nearby Elkhorn Armory and barricades erected at Broad and Main Streets, Main and Center, as well as Highway 120.

Signs of trouble first begin on Friday evening, as a reported crowd of 5,000 gathered in the resort town begin to show signs of unconstraint. However, it isn't until the following night and into the early Sunday morning hours that events escalate and the crowd begins a tour—on foot and in automobiles—of plundering and mayhem.

"It was Saturday night that youths tore the decorating flags from south Broad Street light poles, destroyed the Andy Gump statue, smashed windows and tried to set fire to the lakefront ACI building," reports a Lake Geneva newspaper.

As the weather worsens and the temperatures drop, events begin to rapidly deteriorate as the frenzied crowd lobs firecrackers, bottles, rocks—even phone booths—not only at storefronts, cars, boats, and residences, but at local police, police dogs, and the police station.

Among the most senseless of acts is the beating of a Vietnam veteran, Leston Renth, a 19-year-old Marine and two-time Purple Heart recipient from Chicago who attempts to stop the burning of an American Flag torn from a flagpole outside the Riviera Ballroom.

At 11:05 p.m., Lake Geneva Mayor, Emil Johnejack, orders officials to "Close it up." and issues an immediate curfew, ordering taverns closed, streets cleared and main roads blocked; several citizens are also sworn in as auxiliary police.

Those who remain on the streets are "herded into a roped-off area in Flat Iron Park while police with bull horns warn the youth that guardmen were standing by," reports the *Chicago Daily News* the following day. It is then that the unruly crowd picks up wooden park benches and smashes Sidney Smith's Andy Gump statue to bits.

Hoping to avoid further damage and trouble, a 5 p.m. curfew is set for the following evening. But this does not stop a smaller crowd of about 200 teens (mobilized by automobiles) who, after being blocked from entering Lake Geneva, turn their attention toward Fontana. Here, they smash store windows and telephone booths, loot a Blatz Beer truck and thoroughly frighten residents of the sleepy town who sound the alarm and call in the National Guard. As the rioters see the Guard approach, the mob heads further around the lake toward Williams Bay where police, residents, storekeepers and firefighters stand their ground, armed with sticks, clubs, firearms and determination.

"After a 15-minute rampage," reports a local paper, "the motorcade headed for Delavan where authorities, forewarned of the rioters, erected a roadblock." The mobile mob soon find themselves caught between Delavan authorities and the National Guard and finally become calm and complacent as they are herded into a field and surrounded by rifle-wielding guardsmen.

"They're like children at recess now," one observer is heard to say of the young mob which, now trapped, looks frightened and repentant.

Confiscated from the unruly crowds are sticks, firecrackers, pieces of steel, homemade blackjacks formed with rags and sand, and potentially lethal weapons made by attaching boat tacks to shortened oars.

With a convoy of National Guard trucks, squad cars and local residents' cars, between 250 and 300 of the rioters are caught and carted off to the county jail and to the Walworth County Fairgrounds in Elkhorn where they are held in a temporary stockade set up in the cattle barns until they can be formally charged with drunk and disorderly conduct.

Judge Russell, who will hear many of the cases of those arrested during the riots, is unsympathetic to the pleas of the parents (who arrive to bail out their children) and tears of the defendants.

"You do not meet our moral standards," he says to the young people before him. "You have shaggy manes and dirty clothes and I wish you would not come here again. The civil rights act prevents us from keeping you from coming here. The only tool we have against you…is to sock you hard in court." Most of those facing the judge are fined $150 to $200, while others, unable to pay, are sentenced to jail for 30 to 60 days.

In the following years, the towns around the lake are ready for the worst and occasionally those fears came close to being realized, but never with the ferocity of the summer of '67. Hoping to avoid any further outbursts, Lake Geneva enforces a midnight curfew during the Fourth of July weekend in 1968, increasing the fifteen-man police force regularly on duty that weekend to 200 with the aid of Walworth County deputies, and police and deputies from a dozen other Wisconsin communities—all clad in riot gear.

"At times," reports the *Tribune*, "as many as 10 policemen were stationed on a street corner, sometimes outnumbering the young men and women…"

In the wake of the 1967 riots, the town moved quietly and slowly toward putting things right again, shocked and dismayed by what they deemed to have been a "rampaging, howling mob bent on violence." Yet as frightening and costly as the days of unrest might have been for the residents, other than minor injuries suffered by a few dozen individuals (and a concussion suffered by a police dog), in hindsight, with thousands of drunken, frenzied youngsters, 600 National Guards equipped with loaded side arms, rifles fixed with bayonets, nightsticks and a machine gun, and 125 armed policemen with orders to fire if absolutely necessary, the events could have erupted into something far more tragic…as it would at Kent State just three years later.

# 1974

**■ GIRL POWER: THE *WALWORTH II'S* FIRST FEMALE MAIL CARRIER.** When Elaine Kanelos was a child, she had a rather unusual dream: she wanted to be the mailboy who hopped on and off the *Walworth II*, Geneva Lake's unique system of mail delivery—the only one of its kind that remains active in the nation.

In 1974 18-year-old Kanelos achieves her dream and the distinction of becoming the *Walworth II's* first mailgirl, an honor that is not lost on the community. Subject of several newspaper stories, including the *Wall Street Journal*, Kanelos becomes an overnight celebrity, all because she broke the mold for mail carriers, proving that girls can do anything boys do—even if it means putting mail in her teeth, jumping onto piers and then back onto a moving boat—55 times per day.

Kanelos watched mail being delivered for many years to her own family's pier and thought it looked fun. She soon discovers for herself that it is—if not also slightly treacherous. During her first summer, Kanelos takes a couple of dunks into the lake—after all, those piers can be slippery—but each time manages to climb right back onto the pier and leap across the water, back aboard the *Walworth II*, all to the applause of cheering passengers. And, in between mail duties and deliveries, she functions as tour guide, finishing her day by swabbing the hull of the boat and getting it in shape for the next trip.

Today, the "mailboy" is still a coveted position on Geneva Lake—and girls now tend to be the main staffers—all thanks to one young girl following her dreams. This unique service is still the subject of press stories: in October 2009, the *Walworth II* was graced by the likes of Andrew Zimmerman, who took a stab at delivering mail by boat for his show, *Bizarre World with Andrew Zimmerman*.

COURTESY OF VIRGIL WUTTKE

COURTESY OF THE RON POLLITT COLLECTION

*"Community cannot for long feed on itself, it can only flourish with the coming of others from beyond, their unknown and undiscovered brothers."*

~ Howard Thurman, American Theologian, Clergyman and Activist (1900–1981)

# Encyclopedia
## SHORE PATH

When faced with a vast amount of stories to tell, it's sometimes difficult to focus enough attention on the details, especially on the people—some of whom regularly made the headlines in the history of Geneva Lake—but even more of whom could be found behind the scenes, playing quieter, yet nonetheless influential, roles in helping define the character of the community and in developing its unique identity, still recognizable in the lake's aesthetics today.

The following guide was created to introduce you to just a few of the key players in the fashioning of life on and around Geneva Lake during the late 19th and early 20th centuries.

# ENCYCLOPEDIA: WHO'S WHO

### THE ART INSTITUTE OF CHICAGO:

**Edward E. Ayer** (The Oaks)
Trustee

**Adolphus Clay Bartlett** (House in the Woods)
Trustee

**Charles L. Hutchinson** (Wychwood)
President, 1882–1924

**Martin A. Ryerson** (Bonnie Brae)
Trustee

### BANKERS:

**C. K. G. Billings** (Green Gables)
Director, Chicago National Bank

**William J. Chalmers** (Dronley)
Director, Commercial National Bank

**General A. C. Ducat** (Green Gables)
President, Board of Underwriters

**Nathaniel K. Fairbank** (Butternuts)
Director, Commercial National Bank

**Warren F. Furbeck** (Buena Vista)
President, W. F. Furbeck & Company

**Norman W. Harris** (Wadsworth Hall)
Founder, Harris Trust and Savings Bank

**Charles L. Hutchinson** (Wychwood)
President, Corn Exchange Bank

**Albert Keep** (Fair Oaks)
Director, Merchants Loan & Trust

**John J. Mitchell** (Ceylon Court)
President, Illinois Trust & Savings

**Henry H. Porter** (Maple Lawn)
Director, First National Bank of Chicago

**Julian Rumsey** (Shadow Hill)
President, Corn Exchange National Bank

**John M. Smyth** (Tyrawley)
Director, Chicago National Bank

**General Henry Strong** (Northwoodside)
President of Municipal Bond Association

**Buckingham Sturges** (Fairfields)
President, Northwestern National Bank

**George Sturges** (Snug Harbor)
President, Northwestern National Bank; founder, Illinois Trust & Savings

### CHICAGO BOARD OF TRADE EXECUTIVE OFFICERS:

**Wiley M. Egan** (The Anchorage)

**Nathaniel K. Fairbank** (Butternuts)

**Charles L. Hutchinson** (Wychwood)

**Juliam S. Rumsey** (Shadow Hill)

### CHICAGO CITY RAILWAY COMPANY BOARD OF DIRECTORS:

**Samuel Allerton** (Folly)

**Joseph Leiter** (Linden Lodge)

**Otto Young** (Younglands)

### FIELD MUSEUM OF NATURAL HISTORY BOARD OF TRUSTEES:

**Edward E. Ayer** (The Oaks) First President

**William Chalmers** (Dronley)

**Martin A. Ryerson** (Bonnie Brae)

### POLITICIANS AND CITY OFFICIALS:

**Samuel Allerton** (Folly)
Republican mayoral candidate, 1893

**George L. Dunlap** (Moorings)
Police Marshall of Chicago

**Julian Rumsey** (Shadow Hill)
Republican, Mayor of Chicago, 1861–1862

**Nathaniel C. Sears** (Glen Fern)
Republican mayoral candidate, 1897

### UNIVERSITY OF CHICAGO TRUSTEES:

**Adolphus C. Bartlett** (House in the Woods)

**Charles L. Hutchinson** (Wychwood)

**George C. Walker** (Point Comfort)

**Martin A. Ryerson** (Bonnie Brae)

### WORLD'S COLUMBIAN EXPOSITION, CHICAGO WORLD'S FAIR 1893 EXECUTIVE COMMITTEES:

**Samuel Allerton** (Folly)

**C.K.G Billings** (Green Gables)

**Charles L. Hutchinson** (Wychwood)

**Thies Lefens** (Lefens)

**William C. Seipp** (Black Point)

**John M. Smith** (Tyrawley)

**Charles Waker** (Fair Lawn)

**Otto Young** (Younglands/Stone Manor)

JULIAN RUMSEY COURTESY OF CHICAGO HISTORY MUSEUM ICHi-27270; ALL OTHERS COURTESY OF THE NEWBERRY LIBRARY.

# ENCYCLOPEDIA: ESTATE ARCHITECTS

In the late 1800s, the architecture of homes on the lake changed dramatically; architects with training from the best schools in the U.S. and Europe were retained for their expertise in elegant and sometimes whimsical styles, creating unique homes, many of which have stood the test of time.

**Henry Ives Cobb** (1859–1931) was born in Massachusetts and attended both MIT and Harvard, studying engineering and architecture. He practiced his profession in Boston, then came to Chicago, where, in 1881, he was commissioned to design a new clubhouse for the Union Club (of which his brother was an officer). His skill was apparent and he soon became an important Chicago architect, known for his Romanesque and Victorian Gothic styles. Cobb designed many residences, important public buildings, and churches. Partnering with Charles S. Frost from 1882–1898, the firm was commissioned for the Newberry Library (1887), Historical Society Building (1887), several University of Chicago buildings, the Fisheries Building at the Chicago World's Fair (1893), and the Potter Palmer mansion, among many others. His partner Frost, who had married the daughter of a railroad magnate, became known for his design expertise in railroad stations, and designed The Lake Geneva Depot, which is listed on the National Register of Historic Places.

On Geneva Lake, Cobb designed the University of Chicago's Yerkes Observatory.

**Jarvis Hunt** (1863–1941) was born in Vermont, into an artistic family. His father, Colonel Leavitt Hunt, was an attorney and photographer, his uncle was famed New York architect Richard Morris Hunt—architect for the Vanderbilts and Astors—and his brother was a painter in Boston. Jarvis Hunt graduated from both Harvard and MIT, and began his career in building design. In 1893 he supervised the construction of the Vermont State Building at the Chicago

Yerkes Observatory
© CLINT FARLINGER

World's Fair, then opened the firm of Hunt and Bohassek. A fine golfer himself, Hunt later designed clubhouses for several courses, including the Chicago Golf Club and the National Golf Links of America Golf Course, of which he was a founding member. His design career resulted in many types of buildings, including the 39 original buildings at the Great Lakes Naval Station, the Newark Museum and Bamberger's Department Store in Newark, New Jersey. He also designed Kansas City's Union Station, listed on the National Historic Register, which was the scene of the Kansas City Massacre in 1933, when Charles Arthur "Pretty Boy" Floyd, Vernon Miller, and Adam Richetti gunned down four police officers in an attempt to free their cohort, Frank Nash, who was on his way to the U.S. Penitentiary in Leavenworth, Kansas. Hunt's buildings are known for their varying architectural styles, from Beaux Arts to Colonial Revival to Renaissance Revival.

On Geneva Lake, Hunt designed the buildings of Loramoor.

COURTESY OF NEWBERRY LIBRARY

**William Le Baron Jenney** (1832–1907) is generally thought of as the first to build the modern skyscraper—the Home Insurance Building in Chicago, designed in 1883. Born in Massachusetts in 1832 to affluent parents, Jenney was able to travel as a teenager, sailing around South America to California, Hawaii, and the Philippines. On his journeys, he witnessed a method of construction in the Philippines that he never forgot: lightweight bamboo used as framing in buildings needing to withstand the rigors of tropical winds. Perhaps this influenced his use of steel girders in tall buildings—the weight was much less than the concrete typical of the times. Jenney studied engineering at Lawrence Scientific School at Harvard, then received a diploma in architecture from the École Centrale des Arts et Manufactures in Paris in 1856. He did a stint on the Engineer's staff for General Grant and General Sherman during the Civil War, and then, in 1868, went to Chicago, forming the firm Jenney, Schermerhorn and Bogart. Jenney first acted as a civil engineer, with his first commission as designer of the West Parks system in Chicago in 1869, including Humboldt, Garfield and Douglas parks and their connecting boulevard system, which he borrowed from Paris. He also supervised the implementation of Frederick Law Olmsted's landscape design of Riverside, Illinois, before turning his sights to true architecture. Jenney designed a number of important buildings in Chicago, including the First Leiter, the Luddington and the Manhattan buildings.

In Lake Geneva, Jenney designed the Metropolitan Block building, and on the lake, he was responsible for the design of Blacktoft and Villa Thekla.

**Eben E. Roberts** (1866–1943) was born in Boston, Massachusetts, in 1866. The son of a woodcarver, Roberts was taught the art of mechanical and freehand drawing at an early age. His formal education was completed at Tilton Academy in New Hampshire and, in 1889, he left his home for Chicago. Roberts's first job was with the architect Solomon Spencer Beman as a site superintendent for the Pullman Company town in Chicago. In 1893 he opened his own practice in Oak Park, Illinois, where he focused on residential projects. Some 200 homes have been attributed to Roberts—at least a dozen of which are now designated as historic landmarks and located in Oak Park and River Forest. Roberts used many different architectural styles to create his homes, including Queen Anne, Classic Revival, Medieval Revival, Shingle, as well as Early Modern and Prairie style. As Roberts's practice began to flourish and the architect began to mature, his designs began to lean toward the simpler, rectilinear lines characteristic of the Prairie School. Roberts would eventually move to Chicago in 1912 so that he could focus on commercial architecture and would become partners with his son, Elmer, in 1923. Three years later, he would go into semi-retirement due to health issues.

His projects on Geneva Lake are believed to include House on the Hill and Pinegate; perfect examples of the architect's versatility.

**Joseph Lyman Silsbee** (1848–1913) was born in Massachusetts in 1848, studying architecture at both Harvard and MIT. At twenty-six, Silsbee became a professor of architecture at Syracuse University. In 1882 he moved to Chicago, and is generally credited for bringing Shingle style to the Midwest, although he also designed in other styles such as High Gothic. He is recognized as an important teacher, with architects George W. Maher, George Grant Elmslie and Frank Lloyd Wright apprenticing in his office. In addition to residential work, Silsbee created many prominent commercial and public buildings, including the Lincoln Park Conservatory in Chicago. In Wisconsin he designed the Unity Chapel in Spring Green, the original burial site of Frank Lloyd Wright. Silsbee and another designer are also responsible for the Moving Sidewalk at the Chicago World's Fair of 1893, the prototype for moving platforms and escalators seen today.

On Geneva Lake, Silsbee designed Fair Oaks, including the caretaker's house and barn; and Hill View.

Clear Sky Lodge was designed by R. Harold Zook in the 1920s.
© KAYLA COLLINS

**R. Harold Zook's** (1889–1949) work is strikingly different from the work of other designers around Geneva Lake. His romantic residences typically feature signature touches: chevron-shaped windows, curving stairways, scalloped wood trim, spiderweb patterns, shingles that appear to undulate, and uniquely crafted custom shutters and window boxes. His homes have been described as "Hansel and Gretel" houses. Zook, born in Indiana in 1889, received a degree in architecture from Armour Institute of Technology, and then stayed in Chicago, specializing in residential architecture. He initially worked in the offices of Howard Van Doren Shaw, another important architect with designs at Geneva Lake, but eventually branched out on his own. Zook designed many homes in the Chicago suburb of Hinsdale, but also in other western suburbs, as well as in Wisconsin, Iowa, and Tennessee.

On Geneva Lake, he designed Clear Sky Lodge, with seven log structures, and a charming Cotswold-style cottage on Geneva Lake's south shore.

**Robert C. Spencer, Jr.** (1864–1953) was a man of many talents. He was born in Milwaukee, Wisconsin in 1864, graduated with a degree in mechanical engineering from the University of Wisconsin, then studied architecture at MIT. After working briefly with two Boston firms, he received the prestigious Rotch traveling scholarship in architecture, which allowed him to travel throughout Europe for two years. In 1893 Spencer came to Chicago, where he worked briefly for Shepley, Rutan & Coolidge, then established his own practice. He was also a partner in the firm Spencer & Powers from 1905–1923, then again worked independently, and taught at Oklahoma A & M and the University of Florida. Homes designed by Spencer had clean, modern lines, but were also influenced heavily by English half-timbered styles. In fact, he was thought to sometimes struggle between modern and historical influences. Spencer was also an accomplished painter, and produced watercolors such as one of the Italian palaces of Mantua, that were reflected in later works, including his flowing, colorful mosaic designs on the interior walls of the Chicago Public Library. He was also an accomplished writer, producing the first-ever review of Frank Lloyd Wright in *Architectural Review*, and writing more than 50 articles in *Ladies Home Journal* and other shelter magazines and professional journals. Finally, from 1934 to 1938, Spencer painted murals for the U.S. Government before retiring.

On Geneva Lake Spencer designed the second Lake Geneva Country Clubhouse, Horticultural Hall, Deepwood, the Storrs B. Barrett House (Williams Bay), and the interiors and outbuildings of Wychwood.

COURTESY OF NEWBERRY LIBRARY

**Benjamin Howard Marshall** (1874–1940) was born into a wealthy family in Chicago in 1874, but left prep school when he was 17 to join Chicago architects Marble and Wilson as an apprentice. In 1893, at the age of 21, he became a partner with Wilson when Marble passed away. By 1902 he was working independently, then formed the firm Marshall and Fox with Charles Eli Fox. The firm designed elegant mansions and commercial buildings, and soon gained a reputation for expertise in luxury hotels, apartments, and theaters. Marshall designed the Blackstone and Drake hotels in Chicago, the Edgewater Beach Apartments in Edgewater, Mississippi and the Blackstone and Iroquois theaters in Chicago. Sadly, the Iroquois was a tragic story; it burned to the ground in 1903, one month after completion, resulting in the deaths of 602 people. Ironically, Marshall also died in one of his own buildings, the Drake Hotel in Chicago, at age 66.

On Geneva Lake, Marshall's firm designed Northwestern Military and Naval Academy and the Flowerside Inn.

# ENCYCLOPEDIA: LANDSCAPE ARCHITECTS

**Franz Aust (1885–1963).** A protégé of Jens Jensen and a foreman for Jensen's projects in the Chicago area and in Wisconsin, Aust eventually went on to become a Professor of Landscape Architecture at the University of Wisconsin at Madison. During his tenure in Madison, Aust continued corresponding with Jensen, seeking his mentor's advice on projects, such as his design of Frost Park in Williams Bay (only a fraction of which remains today as a result of road widening). Today the little triangular park is still distinguished by the remnants of a dry stone wall which Aust designed at the park's northeast corner. One can find a similar wall—also designed by Aust and funded by Simeon Chapin (Flowerside Inn)—to the east and to the south, at the north portion of Yerkes Oberservatory's golf course on Williams Bay's Geneva Street. Another convert to the joys of summer living on Geneva Lake, Aust also spent many summers at George Williams College, where he designed the camp's "Council Rings"—a feature for which his garden guru, Jensen, is famed.

**Alfred Caldwell (1903–1998).** A foreman for and protégé of Jens Jensen, Caldwell designed significant parts of the Chicago Park System during The Great Depression of the 1930s; most notably Promontory Point near Chicago's Museum of Science and Industry and The Lily Pool, between Chicago's Lincoln Park Zoo and Chicago's Notebaert Museum. Caldwell's design contribution to Geneva Lake is the rock work at Harley Clarke's Clear Sky Lodge. There is also evidence that Caldwell participated in the landscape design of Charles Wacker's Fair Lawn, as well as L. E. Myers's Allegheny.

**Horace W. S. Cleveland (1814–1900).** Funded by Chicagoans Richard Teller Crane (Jerseyhurst), Simeon B. Chapin (Flowerside Inn), Frank Chandler (Ceylon Court), Harry Selfridge (Harrose Hall) and Judge Nathanial C. Sears (Glen Fern), Cleveland would design Lake Geneva's municipal Oak Hill Cemetery in the mid-1880s. A protégé of Frederick Law Olmsted (who was instrumental in the development of Chicago's South Parks and Boulevards), Cleveland also became involved in the development of Chicago's South Parks. Due to changes in politics, park management and a dispute with the South Park Commissioners, Cleveland closed his Chicago offices and moved his landscape design practice to the Minneapolis-St. Paul area in the mid-1880s. Before leaving Chicago, however, Cleveland had gained a reputation for being one of the finest landscape architects in the country, taking his cue from the natural world. The Chicagoans who secured the acreage for Oak Hill Cemetery had good reason to retain Cleveland for the design of the new cemetery where they and their families would rest for all eternity.

**Warren Manning (1860–1938).** Another protégé of Frederick Law Olmsted, Manning eventually left Olmsted's firm, taking with him many of the firm's clients (a plan arranged by Olmsted himself). Manning soon built a nationwide practice and gained a reputation for being one of the country's finest landscape architects. Today there remain two of Manning's designs on Geneva Lake—both readily visible from the shore path: one, being the property once belonging to Henry H. Porter (Maple Lawn), which had undergone a complete redesign and remodeling by William Le Baron Jenney when Manning was retained; the other being James H. Moore's Loramoor. (Manning came highly recommended by Moore's brother, Judge William H. Moore of Pride's Crossing, Massachusetts, who had hired Manning to design the landscape for his own East Coast estate.)

**Ossian Cole Simonds (1855–1931).** A student at the University of Michigan and a protégé of Chicago's William Le Baron Jenney, Simonds is best known for his landscaping designs for Chicago's famed Graceland Cemetery. During his career, Simonds would continue to design cemeteries, as well as educational institutions and private estates throughout the Midwest, which included: the Glenview Country Club (not including the golf courses) and the Indian Hill Club, both on Chicago's North Shore, as well as landscape at the then-new University of Chicago (before Simonds was, at the insistence of Martin A. Ryerson, (Bonnie Brae) and Charles Hutchinson, (Wychwood) supplanted by John Olmsted of Olmsted Bros.) Simonds had only one project on Geneva Lake, but it was a substantial one: Hubbard Carpenter's Rehoboth. Little of that design can be seen from the shore path today. However, Simonds's original designs remain relatively pristine (albeit much grown in) at the back acreage of that property. Simonds, while the only non-East Coast founding member of the American Society of Landscape Architects, refused to refer to himself as a "Landscape Architect." Instead, he saw himself a "Landscape Gardener."

© CLINT FARLINGER

COURTESY OF THE DORIS M. REINKE RESOURCE CENTER

# ENCYCLOPEDIA: BOAT BUILDERS & DESIGNERS

*There was water, there were sunny summer weekends and there was money. Ergo, by the 1870s, there was enough demand for luxurious boats on Geneva Lake to support a local boat-building industry.*

**William Matthew Napper**
The best known boat builder on the lake was known to everyone simply as "Mate." Born in Sussex County, England, in 1838, William Napper did an apprenticeship with a ship builder, then in the early 1860s became Chief Carpenter's Mate on a huge ship, the *Great Eastern*. The role of this ship was transformational, designed to transport and facilitate the laying of the first reliable transatlantic cable across the ocean, forever connecting Europe and North America. The ship sailed on July 11, 1865, with 36,000 tons on board. The cable was fed out into the deep water off the stern of the boat and allowed to let sink to the bed of the sea. But 12,000 miles from the coast, a crisis occurred: the cable snapped. When Napper was interviewed many years later for the book *The Story of Telecommunications*, by George P. Oslin, he remembered how it was "a bitter disappointment to everyone on board. Four full weeks we grappled for the end that slipped into the water, but without success…" They returned to port, and tried again one year later…this time successfully.

In 1874 Napper and his family came to Geneva. It's believed that he first worked with John French, perhaps on the *Lady of the Lake* or the *Lucius Newberry*, and then opened his own business on the lakeshore at the end of Maxwell Street, with a short section of the infamous cable always on display. His sons joined in the business and they operated the highly regarded Napper Boat Company until at least 1912. An 1889 newspaper story describes one of their newly completed yachts as ready to "ride the waves like a northern diver, the loon."

Some Napper boats to grace the lake were:
*Alert*, for Wesley Johnson
*Alice*, for Ted Napper
*Aurora*, for Wesley Johnson
*Bavaria*, for Wesley Johnson
*Blanche*, for William Napper & George Manson
*Daisy*, for Levi Leiter (Linden Lodge)
*Dora*, for George C. Walker (Point Comfort)
*Ethel Mary*, for George C. Walker (Point Comfort)
*Geneva*, for Wesley Johnson
*Harvard*, for Wesley Johnson
*Majestic*, for Wesley Johnson
*Passaic*, for Richard T. Crane (Jerseyhurst)
*Shadyside*, for Judge T. F. Withrow (Bonnie Brae)
*Topsy B.*, for G. B. Barnard (Oak Lodge)
*Tula*, for Edward E. Ayer (The Oaks)

### Tilford ("Til") Stuyvesant

Born in Port Washington, Long Island, in 1863, Stuyvesant first came to the lake at the request of Julian Rumsey, who asked him to build a sailboat for a race in 1891, and there he stayed for the remainder of his life. Finding a big demand for his craft, he moved to Lake Geneva and began building sailboats and other small vessels for the residents. He decided, in 1911, to try his hand at building and operating larger sightseeing vessels under the name Lake Geneva Motor Boat Line. In 1918 Stuyvesant merged his business with Ernest Liechty, who had just purchased the Lake Geneva Steam Line. They called their new business the Wisconsin Transportation Company, running it until 1957. Some of Stuyvesant's commercial boats, all built between 1911 and 1928 were: *Sterling, Jennie, Jackie, Billie, Walworth* (the mail boat) and *Tilford S*.

COURTESY OF SUE MORTON

### Thomas and Walter Jewell

This father and son team began a boat building business, the Jewell Boat Company, in 1892, near Camp Collie in Williams Bay. Thomas came to Lake Geneva in 1874 to supervise the building of the *Arrow* for George Sturges, and moved his family to the area ten years later. Jewell Boat Company constructed sailboats, motorboats and rowboats, and also repaired and stored them. Born in Chicago in 1871, Walter Jewell liked to race yachts and won many honors. Walter continued the boat building business after his father's passing in 1910, running it until 1936, when he retired and sold it to Walter Beauvais. Prior to the sale, Beauvais, who had built boats for many years in other locales, worked for Jewell Boat Company, which built the steam yachts *The Ripple* and *The Cygnet*.

### Charles Palmer

Charles Palmer, who ran Palmer Boat Company, was the designer of the original Inland Scow. He also created light, fast skeeter iceboats. His first factory opened in 1905, east of St. Benedict Church in Fontana. The factory burned in 1934, so Palmer moved to the "building behind Mau's" (which became the Steak House), and then, eventually, back to the lakeshore, where customers could also purchase gas, oil, and other supplies at his shop. Palmer held the distinction of convincing Colonel Davidson to move Northwestern Military and Naval Academy to the lake from Highland Park, Illinois.

### George Warrington

Warrington was a naval architect and later founded Warrington Iron Works. In addition to running the business and designing boats, he functioned as Commodore of the Chicago Yacht Club in 1900. His yacht designing days were cut short when, in 1903, he was asked by Theodore Roosevelt to serve as the engineer commissioner of the Bureau of Lighthouses and Lightships, Department of Commerce, a position he maintained through President William Howard Taft's administration and for half of Woodrow Wilson's. He was known to design some of the most luxurious yachts on Geneva Lake between the years of 1897 and 1899, including:

*Gertrude*, for E.A. Potter (Stoneybrook)
*Hathor*, for Martin A. Ryerson (Bonnie Brae)
*Kaiulani*, for Tracy Drake (Aloha Lodge)
*Lorelei*, for Mrs. Conrad (Catherine) Seipp (Black Point)
*Olivett*, for Otto Young (Younglands)
*Passaic*, for Richard T. Crane (Jerseyhurst)
*Tula*, for Edward E. Ayer (The Oaks)

### Alben F. (Peter) Bates

Beginning in the 1930s, as a child at his family's summer cottage in Fontana, Peter Bates had always been fascinated with boats, and had a particular fascination with steam-powered vessels. Yet it wouldn't be until 1991, when the boy had grown and become an attorney in Elmhurst, Illinois, that he designed his own sixty-three-foot-long tugboat-styled yacht. Naming it after his great-great-grandfather, *Benjamin F. Bates*, (who had served on a whaling ship that was requisitioned for use in the Revolutionary War and subsequently sunk), Peter Bates finally drew up the plans for the vessel of his dreams and had Palmer Johnson Company of Sturgeon Bay build the elegant *Benjamin F. Bates*, which still graces the waters of Geneva Lake.

*Benjamin F. Bates was designed by Alben (Peter) Bates of Elmhurst in 1991 and named for his great-great-grandfather, whose ship was requisitioned and sunk in the Revolutionary War.*

© KAYLA COLLINS

# ENCYCLOPEDIA: WHO'S BURIED WHERE?

A quiet stroll around some local cemeteries will afford one the opportunity to visit some familiar individuals in the history of Geneva Lake.

### BRICK CHURCH CEMETERY: Walworth, est. 1845
**Cyrus Church** (early settler) and Family, 1817–1899
**Catherine** (nee Cummings) **Van Slyke** (early settler),
died May 21, 1855 at age 47

### EAST DELAVAN UNION CEMETERY: Delavan, est. 1854
**Walter Jewell** (boat builder), 1871–1952
**Israel Williams, Sr.** (early settler) and Family,
died October 14, 1846, age 57 years and 20 days

### PIONEER CEMETERY: Lake Geneva, est. 1837
**Colton Family** (innkeeper)
**O. T. Lasalle** (estate builder)

### OAK HILL CEMETERY: Lake Geneva, est. 1883
**Button, A. H.** (early settler/founder), born May 15, 1828;
died October 12, 1918 and Family
**Chapin, S. B.** (Flowerside Inn), born May 31, 1865;
died January 6, 1945 and Family
**Crane, R. T.** (Jerseyhurst) and family,
born May 15, 1832; died January 8, 1912
**Sears, Nathaniel C.** (Glen Fern) and family,
August 23, 1854; died May 7, 1934
**Sturges, George** (Snug Harbor) and family, born 1808; died 1885
**Stuyvesant, Tilford E.** (boat builder) and family, born January 1, 1855;
died June 8, 1928
**Trinke, William F.** (State Senator/developer), born January 25, 1897;
died September 25, 1982
**Warren, Robert W.** (early settler/innkeeper), born October 5, 1798;
died December 30, 1875

### WALWORTH CENTER CEMETERY: Walworth, est. 1847
**Charles Andrae** (estate builder), 1867–1943
**J. D. Beebe** (builder), 1836–1922
**William Long** (innkeeper), 1894–1965

Oak Hill Cemetery
© CLINT FARLINGER

# THE *Golden Age* OF VICTORIAN LIVING

In the years following the Chicago fire of 1871, the population of Lake Geneva would grow by 100 percent and would attract nearly 100,000 visitors each summer, as well as more and more well-to-do Chicago families who began acquiring land and building estates encircling the entire Geneva Lake shoreline. These were not to be mere summer cottages, but exotic pleasure palaces with near-fantasy landscapes and outbuildings, reflecting not only the golden age of American industry, but the world power that neighboring Chicago was aiming to become.

COURTESY OF PEG WILLIAMS

I. M. Beidler's place, near Chicago Yacht Club.

"Each owner has developed his own idea, or that of his family in the arrangement of wide verandas, a succession of angles, windows set for fine lake views," wrote the *Chicago Daily Tribune* in July of 1894, "and rustic seats and winding paths through swards kept constantly green. Each cottage is approached from a pier built out in the lake, near which one finds anchored a sail boat, or, quietly lying to, a modern steam yacht."

The money pouring into the area was not only reflected in the lakeshore homes being built, but in just about every manner of daily accoutrements.

"The number and kind of equipages at the depot on arrival of the fast express train in the evening, generally, is a sight to behold," wrote the *Herald* in 1883. "All of the latest styles, from jaunty dog carts to stately barouche with liveried footmen and coachmen, line the walk for a block on either side."

"There were tally-hos with four or six horses for special occasions," recalled Henry Hill Fuller in his unpublished memoirs. "There were traps with horses in tandem and dog carts for informal use…When the master wished to drive himself, a footman in full regalia perched up behind, ready to jump down and hold the horses' heads while his lordship went in after the mail."

From spring until autumn, the streets of Lake Geneva came alive with visitors —both young and old, dressed in the latest Paris fashions and out to find any and all amusements money could buy—both on land and atop the waters. In fact, Lake Geneva soon became the toast of the tourist season and its lake the "Queen" of all those found in Wisconsin.

"Mr. Wallace Delafield of St. Louis, brother of Mrs. George Sturges," reported the *Herald* in May of 1891, "has been in town this week, trying to find a satisfactory house for the summer. He has been here nearly every year since Columbus discovered this lake and both he and his estimable family dislike to think of going elsewhere, but the fact is that houses on the lake shore are about as hard to find as strawberries on a cactus."

*The Harvard* docking after a moonlight cruise.

COURTESY OF THE LAKE GENEVA PUBLIC LIBRARY

During the height of the Victorian summer season, it must surely have been a sight to behold, with grand manors, cozy cottages and crisp white tents lining the shore; while sleek yachts and steamboats chugged along the waters and rowboats quietly glided from one cove to the next—all filled with twirling parasols and straw hats, jaunty sailor suits and delicate lace dresses.

Each summer day, as the cool lake breezes comforted the crowds, there were ice cream socials, fishing excursions, wilderness hikes, "base ball" games, buggy rides and dips in the lake—even the occasional parade. And the setting of the sun did little to persuade the people to call it a day, for there were always concerts and hotel socials, dances, receptions and, among the favorite of all evening activities, moonlight rides.

"A moonlight-row upon the lake will not soon be forgotten," recalled one tourist. "The lights twinkled along the shore. The music of the band at the village grew fainter and fainter. There was no sound but the steady splash of the oars. Then we waited in utter silence in a lonely cove, and were startled:

> *When sometime a leaping fish*
> *Sent through the tarn its lonely cheer; while all the time*
> *The moving moon went up the sky, And nowhere did abide;*
> *Softly she was going up, And a star or two beside."*

Yet the love affair with this lovely spring-fed lake came at a price. As Lake Geneva's popularity grew, so too did its vices and noises, from beer drinking rowdies to boisterous excursions.

"The order has gone out all along the line for the steamers to whistle no more than is absolutely necessary," reported the *Herald* in July of 1885. "There is very little need of whistling at all, and it is terribly annoying to those living along the shore, as it wakes everybody up too early in the morning and is forever breaking the babies out of their naps. The pilots of the private boats are just as bad if not worse than those on the public steamers, about tooting whistles."

Even the well-to-do estate owners were causing some consternation among the locals when they began to consider the needs of the estates over the needs of the public. In 1884, for example, local papers were outraged at the outbuildings that began cropping up along the shoreline. "The lakeshore belongs to the people," wrote the *Herald*, "and it ought to be kept completely free from sheds and the like. Coal houses are a necessity, but it is not necessary to have the whole shore covered with them. One house can be built enough for all the boats, and if the Board has got any sand in its crop it will order all of them down."

The Board's "crop," however, apparently hadn't a grain of sand, as more and more buildings began to appear on the shoreline. In fact, by the turn of the century, most of the camps and resorts were gone, bought out by wealthy men and women wishing to create large, private estates where the public was no longer welcomed—except, of course, along the Shore Path. In 1906, according to the *Lake Geneva Herald*, with a wealthy few owning most of the lands around Geneva Lake, shoreline property was now worth $40 a foot, valuing the entire shoreline (not even considering the summer estates built on the lands) at about $4,222,000.

COURTESY OF SUE MORTON

# THE PRIVATE YACHTS

Nearly a century-and-a-half later, pleasure boating still lives on strong on Geneva Lake. Yet the Golden Age of the private steam yacht (which began in earnest in 1874, when *Gertie* was brought to the lake on the new Chicago and Northwestern Railroad for owners G.L. Dunlap and Julian Rumsey) was certainly like no other. These boats not only provided a truly elegant passage—whether taxiing an estate owner or running errands, entertaining guests on busy day trips or settling them down for moonlit cruises before bedtime, these private yachts were not only majestic, streamlined and luxurious, but each was carefully crafted for her owner.

When *Daisy* was built by Napper, owner L. Z. Leiter (Linden Lodge) wanted only copper fastenings, but there were no copper washers to be found. Leiter, being the industrious man he was, made his own, by drilling out the centers of shiny copper pennies. The smokestack of the *Passaic*, designed by George Warrington in 1899 for Richard T. Crane (Jerseryhurst), was painted in Crane Company colors: orange with a black band. And the *Time*, built in 1897 for Samuel Allerton (Folly), was built with elements representing Father Time.

Many of the yachts' interiors were fashioned with high-quality woods, such as varnished mahogany, and contained fine furnishings, including engraved dishes, ornate furniture, and brass or silver fixtures. *Whileaway*, built for Henry H. Porter (Maple Lawn) in 1891, had a round skylight and stained-glass windows, and the *Hathor*, built in 1898 for Martin A. Ryerson (Bonnie Brae), had a buffet that could accommodate the most important of guests, such as Henry Ford and John Rockefeller. *Gertrude*, thought to be one of the prettiest yachts on the lake, boasted a bright red smokestack and a gilded bust of a curvaceous woman with lovely golden tresses.

The best entertainment was equally important to the cruising set; *Aloha* (formerly *Ethel Mary*), owned by Tracy Drake (Aloha Lodge), was often seen cruising the lake after sunset, with Caruso or Farrar singing out from the phonograph on board. L. E. Myers enjoyed poker games in the cabin of his *Allegheny* (formerly the *Normandie*) during the 1930s; while *Louise*, built in 1900 by the Racine Boat Company for John J. Mitchell (Ceylon Court), was pure luxury, with guests ushered aboard by a gold braided captain, while a steward prepared and then served hors d'oeuvres in the cabin.

However, steam yachts were not without their share of troubles. Since fires were often banked and left overnight so the vessels would be ready for immediate use in the morning, errant sparks or cinders often dropped onto the deck or shot out through the smokestack onto the canopy and could easily set a yacht aflame. And if a steam yacht avoided fire, it was certainly subject to other elements—such as water and wind, which brought about decay.

Yachts were often given elegant, romantic names to match their designs, such as *Passaic* (after vacation spot Passaic Falls), *Tula* (the daughter of Montezuma) or *Hathor* (the Egyptian goddess of love and joy). But just as often, they were named after their owners or other family members, as in the case of *Louise* (after John J. Mitchell's wife), *Normandie* (after owner Norman Harris) and *Daisy* (after L. Z. Leiter's daughter). Sometimes, the names were purely whimsical, as in *Whitecap*, *Time* and *Whileaway*.

Once in awhile, the given name of a steam yacht fell by the wayside, as a nickname took over. *Ethel Mary*, designed by William Bates and built in 1875 by Napper for George C. Walker, was commonly known as *Green Rabbit*, perhaps because of her bright green exterior, topped by a black smoke stack with white trim. In 1880 *Shadyside*, Judge T. F. Withrow's yacht, although quite seaworthy, had an engine that shook the hull to such an extent that it was known by some as *Shakyside*. Perhaps most colorful was *Normandie*, known during the late 1930s (ironically during the era of Prohibition) as the Floating Booze Bazaar.

Even though renaming a boat is traditionally considering a maritime taboo—destined to bring nothing but bad luck—Geneva Lake vessels regularly went through several renamings. *Gertrude*, as one example, designed and built around the turn of the century by George Warrington for E. A. Potter, came to be known as *Garcia*, *Minerva* and, finally, as *Doreen*.

Whether name changes or changing times, not many of the old gals survived; some were lost due simply to the ravages of time and decay; others to economic downfalls and world wars. Some yachts, however, did go through several iterations before succumbing to age. *Tula*, *Daisy*, *Whitecap*, *Topsy B.*, *Thetis*, *Whileaway*, *Bendemere*, *Princess* and *Lorelei* (all, strangely enough, ones that maintained their original names) were among those that did stints as commercial passenger vessels on the lake before meeting their demise.

Still others went on to have very different purposes from their original functions. *Topsy B.*, built by Napper for George B. Barnard in 1888, was later owned by Wisconsin Transportation Company, and later still, was hauled out to Highway 50, becoming a roadhouse called The Ship. She lasted until 1960, when the road was widened. *Gertrude*, after several owners, was purchased in 1954 for $100 by a group of enterprising teenagers who formed a club to raise money for her restoration through $10 memberships. They made enough to get her launched, then moored her 500 feet from shore, providing an excellent place for club members and visitors (who had to be rowed to the site) to hang out. The next summer, unfortunately, she sank at her mooring.

*Polaris* (originally *Olivett*), was one of three similarly styled boats designed by George Warrington in 1898 (the others were *Hathor* and *Tula*), and still cruises the lake as a small charter vessel. *Louise* was fitted with a gasoline engine and sold in 1930 to the Wisconsin Transportation Company. After an eight-year re-conversion back to a steam launch in the 1970s, she began cruising once again as a steamer and still blows her whistle on charter excursions today. The other remaining yachts from the steamer days—*Matriark* (formerly *Passaic*), *Ada E*, *Hathor* and *Normandie* are still owned privately.

COURTESY OF THE KENOSHA COUNTY HISTORICAL SOCIETY

# THE PUBLIC'S TRANSPORT

Because there were few—if any—good roads around the lake in the mid-to-late nineteenth century, it became necessary for transportation between one community and another to occur over water. There were a couple of early attempts at public transport—*Ariel*, brought here in 1843 from Michigan, and *Atalanta*, which arrived in 1858. But *Ariel* was left to decay when a dam broke during the flood of 1850 and she was washed right out of the lake; *Atalanta* caught fire and was destroyed in 1860.

Everything changed with the construction of *Lady of the Lake*, a side-wheel steamboat built in 1873 by John W. French for Ed Quigley. When Quigley's vinegar works factory burned down, he decided to turn his attention toward a different kind of business, public transport. He commissioned an eighty-two-foot-long steamboat (lengthened later to ninety-eight feet) that could carry some two hundred passengers, thus reliable public transportation on Geneva Lake was born. The very next year, French built the *Lucius Newberry* steamer for Oscar Newberry—with room for 700 passengers. As the story goes, the *Lucius Newberry* was commissioned in response to Captain Quigley failing to pick up Oscar Newberry (Lucius's son) during a storm when he was on the lake in a small boat. The outraged son vowed to build an even bigger boat to run *Lady* off the lake.

Of course, there turned out to be room for both vessels and many more. But the *Lucius Newberry* was something to behold; 115 feet long, with separate wash closets for ladies and for gentlemen, two stairways leading to the upper deck, one on either side, and a forty-one- by twenty-one-foot dance platform that had a Georgian pine wood floor. There was even a place for a full band of musicians! In the cabins were wall panels with oil paintings by local artist John Bullock, plus Brussels carpeting, plate-glass mirrors and an upright piano. The ship's bell was a large bronze bell from an old Mexican cathedral confiscated during the Mexican American War in 1846–1848.

The first real transportation company on the lake was Anchor Line, established when John A. Wilson bought *Lucius Newberry, Lady of the Lake*, and other smaller steamers. Wilson, a temperance activist, had the bars removed, but hired a band for summer excursions, and had his officers and crew outfitted with the type of uniforms that you might see aboard Hudson River steamers.

The Anchor Line was sold several times: first to C. A. Noyes in 1886, then to John E. Burton in 1887. Three years later, Burton's farm manager, Wesley Johnson, purchased the company and renamed it the Lake Geneva Steamer Line. "Captain" Johnson, as he would be fondly known the rest of his days, also served several times as mayor of Lake Geneva and was director of the First National Bank. Unfortunately, the company's two original steamers were not long for the lake; the year Johnson purchased the company, *Lady of the Lake* was destroyed at her pier by sources unknown, and the *Lucius Newberry* caught fire while tied to the public dock. She had to be cut free so that other boats moored nearby would not catch fire—and she drifted, aflame, along her regular excursion route. Just one half hour later, she had burned to the water line and sunk. Divers discovered her remains 90 years later, including the clapper of the bronze ship's bell.

Despite those tragedies, the Lake Geneva Steamer Line kept the business going with a wide variety of other public boats and was always busy with regularly scheduled cruises and charters. Some of their steamers included: *Commodore, Alert, Majestic, Harvard, Geneva, Bavaria,* and *Aurora*. Boats such as these were often chartered by parties from camps on the lakeshore, hosting dances or concerts, or simply daytime cruises for socializing.

Meanwhile, Tilford ("Til") Stuyvesant had been building boats on the lake since the late 1800s (see page 46), and decided, in 1911, to try his hand at building and operating larger sightseeing vessels, under the name Lake Geneva Motor Boat Line. His most popular boat was *Walworth*, built in 1916, a 74-foot long streamlined steamer that carried mail and passengers around the lake for nearly 50 years.

*Walworth* was not the only boat with a unique purpose. *The Ripple*, built in 1880 by Walter Jewell, delivered newspapers to lake residents until 1911 and also towed fishermen in rented boats out to their fishing spots, then back to the dock later in the day. *Robert W.* was a small steamer owned and operated by the Y.M.C.A. camp, built around 1884. Her nickname was *Holy Tom*. And the *Cornelian*, owned by Cornelian Dairy, delivered dairy products to lakeshore residents in the late 1800s. She was later bought and used by Steve DeBlase, a local grocer, to deliver fruits and vegetables, and became known as the *Banana Boat*.

By 1918, Stuyvesant and Ernest Liechty had joined forces to create the Wisconsin Transportation Company, purchasing the Lake Geneva Steamer Line and merging it with the Lake Geneva Motor Boat Company. They operated the business until 1957, when they sold it Russell Gage. Gage called his new company Geneva Lake Excursion Corporation. He painted the boats a variety of bright colors, gave them new names, and in 1963 added to the fleet the excursion boat *Lady of the Lake II*, an accurate replica of a Mississippi River paddle wheeler, with double decks and twin smokestacks. In 1965, *Walworth II* mail boat was also added to the fleet, and in 1972, *Belle of the Lake*, a replica of the original *Lady of the Lake*, was built, offering fine dining, an open-air bar and a Mark Twain dinner cruise.

# NERO AND THE TRIB

*The Tribune Company of Chicago, has made arrangements with Eph Sanford to handle their papers here and around the lake. The Tribune is the great paper of Chicago and its many patrons of Lake Geneva must and will be supplied with the paper of their choice...*

~ *Lake Geneva Herald*, July 1895

The men and women who built their estates around Geneva Lake in the latter part of the 20th century were used to getting what they wanted: the finest architects, the best gardeners, the fastest horses. Most were people of action and savvy, self-made success stories; titans of business, politics, and philanthropy. So, it is little wonder that their link to the pulse of the big city and the ever-changing world outside their hidden summer havens, *The Chicago Tribune*, would have been seen as a daily necessity.

The dilemma, however, was that in 1895, no trains arrived in Lake Geneva until well past the time the broadsheets were expected to arrive. Likely, no newspaper to read with their morning coffee made these millionaires surly, so stacks of the *Tribune* were bundled up hot off the early morning press every day (including Sunday) and tossed aboard the Chicago, Milwaukee and St. Paul railroad. Up the rails to the north, the bundles were thrown off at Western Union Junction, then tossed aboard a Racine and Southwestern freight train which would carry them west, on to Springfield, Wisconsin.

It was here that Captain Eph Sanford, having roused himself well before the sun even threatened to rise, took over, hauling the newspapers by horse and wagon to the docks of Lake Geneva where the steamer, *Wilbur F.* was ready and waiting to begin its early morning delivery to camps, clubs, hotels and residences around the sleeping shores.

CONTINUED ON PAGE 59

# PROFILE: JOHN BURTON

John E. Burton was born in Hartford, New York in 1847. At the age of twelve, something happened to the young man that would leave an indelible mark in his life. Having learned that Abraham Lincoln's campaign train would be stopping in nearby Utica in 1860, the young Burton made a half-day's trek to the station for a glimpse of the famed candidate. Fighting enormous crowds, Burton shimmied up a telephone pole that brought him close to the rear of the train from where Lincoln addressed the crowd. Hanging upon his every word, the young man would take away from the experience a lifelong devotion to Lincoln, eventually becoming a "profound Lincoln student and one of the country's foremost collectors of Lincolniana, and the owner of a staggering amount of books, manuscripts, documents, portraits and relics."

COURTESY OF THE GENEVA LAKE MUSEUM

When he reached sixteen, Burton attempted to put his devotion to Lincoln and his cause into practice by enlisting in the Union Army, but his father caught up with the eager young lad and brought him home where he completed his scientific studies at a seminary. In 1868, after graduating at the head of the class, he took a teaching position. The following year Burton married Lucretia "Dell" Johnson and, after a brief stint teaching in Illinois, he and his wife headed to Wisconsin, where Burton became head of the Lake Geneva Schools in 1870. Together they had four children: Howard, Warren, Kenneth, and Bonnie.

Burton continued to administer for the schools for a short time, but then changed course. Burton was a man who looked to different avenues for investing, including, but not limited to: publishing; commercial, agricultural, and residential real estate; insurance sales; and mining—the latter of which would both make and break him before his life was over. With award-winning skills as an orator and excellent "people skills," Burton was a whiz at not only selling insurance (writing the first $100,000 policy in Wisconsin) but in finding hundreds of investors in Wisconsin's speculative ore mining industry.

In a few short years, Burton would accumulate a fortune. In 1898, however, Burton's business empire would come crashing to the ground when the mining industry was hit hard by a lengthy depression. With his financial resources spread far and wide, Burton was forced to liquidate everything. His greatest concern was for his mining investors. "Mining is a gamble," he was quoted as saying. "I gambled $1 million in the ground that held ore. What my investors gambled on was my word. I have to pay them back." And Burton did just that, selling his personal holdings to pay back as many investors as he could.

In good times and bad, Burton's kindness, compassion, and integrity was well reputed. In his diaries of 1885, for example, Burton recorded a client's inability to make an insurance payment. After hearing the man's story, he not only entrusted the man to repay him, but also bought his client new shoes, a train ticket, gave him ten dollars and sent him on his way to a job in Sheboygan.

Sadly, in 1915, Burton fell upon hard times again and was forced to auction off his personal library, which included his most beloved collection of Lincoln memorabilia. So extraordinary was his collection that it took 106 boxes to ship the collected works to New York, where it would be put on the auction block. Today that collection can be found scattered across the country in both personal and museum collections such as the Smithsonian. Among his most prized possession to be sold was a copy of the Emancipation Proclamation, one of three or four revised copies signed by Lincoln, as well as a printed copy of the debate notes between Stephen A. Douglas and Lincoln, which contained margin notes handwritten by the sixteenth president himself.

"Without a trace of self-pity in his voice," recalled Alice Hackett, Burton's granddaughter in a 1971 *Standard Press* article, "he would tell me about his mines and his millions and how he lost them. But he was most expressive when he talked about Lincoln…Whenever you asked him about his Lincoln collection a great sadness came into his eyes… He felt the loss of [this] much more than he did his fortune."

COURTESY OF THE *CHICAGO DAILY TRIBUNE* ARCHIVES

Over the years, the delivery of the *Trib* would be honed to near perfection and would include the use of fast mail trains, an electric train and boys with ponies. More often than not, the operation ran as smooth as the placid waters of the lake. Yet there were times when the task proved downright treacherous as churning waters, wild winds and sheets of rain challenged even the most veteran of mariners to keep the engine stoked and the steamer afloat. Nevertheless, each day the *Wilbur F.* managed to sound the whistle announcing its approach and deliver its charge; for no matter what the weather or way, one thing remained certain... every subscriber must have a paper by breakfast.

"It would be difficult for the Geneva cottagers to get along without 'Eph,' as it would be impossible for Grover Cleveland to be President without having his fish tackle handy," reported the *Chicago Daily Tribune* in 1894. "...the toot of *Wilbur F's* whistle was the signal that gathered the dwellers along the shore at every pier to receive the usual Sunday literary treat. Piled up fore and aft in the Wilbur F. were huge bundles of Sunday *Tribunes*, which disappeared during the round trip with the same alacrity that the traditional hot cake is made away with."

For many years, another sure bet was the appearance of a very special newspaper courier—of the canine kind—on the docks of the Lefens' estate. His name was Nero and he was a small, black Cocker Spaniel who made it his unwavering duty to deliver that paper to his people come rain or shine.

"...from the boat he is seen with his jaws apart, his pearly white teeth making the shape of the vise-like [sic] receptacle into which the paper is grabbed," wrote a *Tribune* reporter in July of 1900, "and then he rushes off the pier, away off and over a sloping lawn to the veranda, where master or mistress is waiting on the faithful carrier."

"Nothing short of being chained to a post will deter the dog from performing his duty," the article continued. "The moment he sights the boat, whether he is chasing a bird or fussing with the cat, he postpones his sport, and then from the boat a black streak may be seen making down the sloping lawn to the pier. He rushes out as far as he can get, and takes The *Tribune* in his mouth with the accuracy of a skilled ball catcher."

For such devotion, Nero was well-rewarded, not only with a family's love, but his very own seat in one of Northwestern's northbound parlor cars.

## CISCO FISHING

*"...there is probably no event in the whole round of seasons that so effectually breaks up all business arrangements and so thoroughly disrupts all social ties as does the annual run of ciscoes at Lake Geneva. A farmer will leave his cornfield, a mechanic his job, a merchant his counter, and a woman everything but her fashion plate when it is announced that the 'ciscoes are running, and everybody flocks to the fishing grounds for the time."*
~*Lake Geneva Cisco*, July 16, 1881

Fishing has been part of the culture around Geneva Lake since man—and beast—first roamed its shores, so there is no doubt that it played a significant role during the lake's mid-19th century settlement, and even more so just prior to its rise as a popular resort, during which time gentlemen from Chicago came to the lake for the extraordinary hunting and fishing opportunities.

A fisherman and his catch, circa 1875.

As if drawn by the hum of the swarms, large schools of Cisco would then rise from the cool depths of Geneva Lake to feed on the cloud of insects. At the surface, the fish would be greeted by eager fishermen who would catch them hundreds at a time.

Because of the short-lived feeding frenzy, the coming of the Cisco became an event on Geneva Lake. As soon as the first school was sighted on the surface of the lake, telegraphs would be sent in all directions and within hours the lake would be a-swarm with fishing vessels. Daily newspaper reports would inform fishermen of the hot spots. "The water was fairly alive with them off Nightingale's," reported the *Lake Geneva Herald* in 1891, "and the newest beginner had all he could carry."

In fact, the Cisco became a much favored and easily scaled fish. "The flavor of its flesh," reported the *American Angler* in 1898, "flaky and creamy, is peculiarly sweet and appetizing, and can only be described by calling it of cisco savor, for no other fish, to our tongue,…has such a characteristic and pleasing taste." In fact, so favored was this small freshwater fish, it could summon one dollar per pound on the market—an aristocratic sum for the time—and was often found on the menus of Chicago's swankiest restaurants.

By 1906, however, something wasn't right with the Cisco. Thousands were seen dead and dying on the surface of the lake. And even though no particular disease could be seen, most of the fish were reported to be only two-thirds their normal size.

"One thing is certain," reported the *Herald*, "and that is the ciscoes have 'acted queer' for a number of years. In early years they were caught from the shore anywhere between the 10th and 15th of June. Of late years they can only be caught in deep water off Black Point and then as early as the last of May or the first of June. The flies were imported and when the local supply came, the fish had disappeared."

It is very likely that "man's hand" and his incessant need to intervene (such as importing flies as recorded above and stocking the lake with non-native fish) was the ultimate downfall of the mid-summer Cisco. In 1907 the local paper reported that fishing for Cisco had now commonly become a winter event that now attracted "about as much attention as the annual Sheridan Regatta—neither of them now cut much of a figure in Geneva Lake attractions." Yet the following June, the Cisco surprised everyone by reappearing once more and could be seen following the shoreline in large schools as they had for so many years. This reappearance, however, was short-lived. In the years following this event, the Cisco would rarely be seen during the summer and would more often be caught during the dead of winter, found only at depths of forty or

As the Chicago millionaires eventually established homes along the shores of Geneva Lake, they, too, were lured to the lure and were known to stock the lake with millions of fish from around the nation with the hopes of making this particular Wisconsin watering hole some of the finest sport fishing in the Midwest. Sadly, this meddling with Mother Nature would eventually lead to a dramatic change in the lake's natural eco-system.

What first attracted many to the waters was a tiny, native species, called the Cisco; a beautiful, silver-scaled fish about eight to eleven inches long, said to have first arrived here through subterranean passages from Lake Superior. These herring-like fish appeared at the lake's surface only a few days out of the year, usually in the full moon of June, just as the May Fly (which early on was known as the Cisco Fly) appeared and hovered over the lake in swarms.

COURTESY OF THE RON POLLITT COLLECTION

The lure of fishing on Geneva Lake dates back far before white settlement and continues to entice anglers to this day.

more feet. By 1937 their sighting was so rare, conservation regulations allowed fisherman to catch only 40 a day, or no more than 12 pounds. And flies were no longer the preferred bait, but beads—shiny, colorful beads. Taken from Christmas trees and dressmakers' shops, all kinds of beads were reported to attract the small—now scarce—silver fish to the line.

Despite the significant change in habits, Ciscoes would continue to attract fisherman who hauled their shanties to the ice-covered lake in vast numbers, "thicker than fleas on a hound dog's back," so it was once said.

Nearly ten years later, millions more Ciscoes were dying in the lake with little understanding why. At present, schools of the Cisco will occasionally appear at the surface of the lake and are often reported found in the stomachs of larger fish, but the anglers of today do not take nearly as much interest in the small, silver fish as their predecessors did and the once thriving population is certainly not what it used to be. The Wisconsin DNR is currently planning a study to determine just what the Cisco population is in Geneva Lake.

# THE FABULOUS 4TH OF JULY

As the summer popularity of Geneva Lake began to escalate in the 1880s, so, too, did Lake Geneva's tourism; and what better celebration to show off all the beauty and splendor of the lovely inland lake than illuminating it under the kaleidoscopic glow of fireworks on the Fourth of July.

"At the parks up the lake there were immense crowds who came from all directions," reported the *Lake Geneva Herald* in July of 1882. "And at an early hour all the roads leading to the lake were thronged with merry seekers after a holiday, and by noon, the parks were one mass of human beings struggling for pleasure."

Yet as long as there were shade trees, cool waters, and the promise of sunset and fireworks, the crowds would not be dissuaded from partaking in the festivities that must have been a sight to behold. Not only was the lake teeming with sleek steamers and straw hats, frilly parasols, flags flying, and children's laughter, but the lakeside residents made the event almost surreal.

"As far on either side of the lakeshore as could be seen," reported the *Herald*, "the grounds of the summer residents were illuminated with Chinese lanterns, and fireworks were sent up on every side."

In addition, nearly every vessel on the lake was decked out with colorful bunting of red, white, and blue, and strung with colored lights. The effect at night was stunning and one of the many reasons why the drowsy, but dazzled crowds remained well into the night.

Word would spread of the magical celebration and in the following years, the local communities and resorts would organize more and more events to entertain the Fourth of July masses. There were wheelbarrow races and yacht races, dashes and hurdles, tub races and foot races, ball games and marching bands, parades and picnics, and dances aplenty. And each year, the lakeside summer residents would—to the great pleasure of vacationers —affably try to surpass his neighbor in fireworks displays.

And, on occasion, the celebrations would fall victim to a bit of unbridled enthusiasm. "At 4 o'clock, the village cannon… was hauled to the lakeshore and 100 guns were fired," recounted the *Herald* in July of 1885, "each report echoing and reechoing around the lake until it sounded more like

COURTESY OF THE GENEVA LAKE MUSEUM

a prolonged peal of thunder than anything else. From that time on, the discharge of firecrackers and torpedoes was incessant and deafening."

But who could not help but get wrapped up in the festivities, when around every curve of the lake's shoreline there was gaiety, good-natured fun and glorious scenes depicting a nation of prosperity and plenty.

"As one passed these gorgeous country seats… crowning the graceful hilltops, almost concealed amid the luxurious foliage," wrote one newspaper reporter of his Fourth of July excursion around the lake in 1885, "some snowy white, but most of them in brilliant colors, and the landing thronged with beautiful women in snowy robes and dazzling wraps he could easily fancy that he had suddenly been wafted away from earth to Arcadia or Eden."

And when the parades and patriotic speeches were concluded, the sun began to set and the quaint boathouses and windmills, grand mansions and flower gardens began to fade into the darkness, then Geneva Lake came alive with light, music, and merriment.

"On the whole the celebration was a memorable one," the *Herald* correspondent concluded, "and everyone who participated in it reached the conclusion that Lake Geneva was the place of all places to spend the Fourth of July and the rest of the summer."

## THE MID-SUMMER FAIR

*Each year the cottagers seem to take more interest in the development of their farms, and many of the Chicago residents have blossomed into remarkably good farmers, making a large share of the expense of maintaining their summer homes, and besides having the enjoyment of rural work.*
~*Lake Geneva Herald*, September 19, 1885

As the grand estates and thriving resorts began to settle in to summer life beside the shores of Geneva Lake in the 1880s, a vital component to their comfort involved farming much of the vast acreage included in each lakeside property. So it seems only natural that the estate owners—these men of action and leaders of industry—would eventually surrender to the urge to compare his great garden harvests and breeder's prowess with that of his neighbors. These "bragging rights" actually began in the early years of settlement when during the summer months, green-thumbed residents regularly visited the offices of the local paper—harvest in hand—to show off to the editor the finest of their home-grown crops. However, as the Chicago millionaires came on the scene, their competitive natures took the agricultural game to an entirely new level.

Whether growing for the family table or the farmers market, these gentleman farmers could afford the best and, like their sumptuous summer homes, were hardly shy about showing off a bit.

So, when in 1904, the Lake Geneva Fresh Air Association needed more funding to continue their efforts to bring impoverished Chicago children to the lake each summer, the idea for an agricultural competition was proposed. One can only guess; it was happily embraced by the affluent farmers who now had just the showplace they needed.

The Levi Leiter (Linden Lodge) estate, currently held by Levi's son, Joseph, was the setting for what would come to be known as the "Mid-Summer Fair." Benches and tables, stalls and stages were erected, committees organized and crops readied for the event. "…16,000 feet of wire were strung and 300 lights used," reported the *Lake Geneva Herald* "and the result was a grand success—the grounds and tents were as light as day."

There would be pony cart rides for the little ones, music, homemade candy, a palmist, a housekeeping booth (where items such as brooms and dusters would be sold), vaudeville performances, ladies' needlework exhibits, a Victor talking machine, a Japanese tea house and garden where tea was served "by ladies and children in native costume, a popcorn man, a peanut man, a fish pond, and many other sideshows" for the crowd's pleasure.

The event even offered an automobile race from Chicago to Oconomowoc and a chance to peer at the full moon of midsummer through the lens of a telescope at Yerkes Observatory.

And then, of course, there were the competitive exhibits—cattle, horse, sheep, poultry, fruits, flowers and vegetables—with entire families of nearly every lakeside estate (as well as farming families from all around the area) involved in both the event's organization and/or competitions.

Mrs. Mitchell (Ceylon Court) organized the flower exhibits where the Selfridge's (Harrose Hall) displayed orchids from their greenhouses. Mrs. Nathaniel Sears (Glen Fern) would oversee the vegetable displays; and, of course J. H. Moore (Loramoor) would not only organize the horse show, but reigned supreme with his magnificent collection of show horses.

And when the fundraising began in earnest, the affluent estate owners stepped up to the plate, bidding large sums of money for the exhibited items. All in all, it was an enormously successful event attracting about 7,000 visitors who helped raise $5,000 for the Fresh Air Association's Holiday Home.

The following summer, more was added, such as land and water sports competitions, clowns, and souvenirs; while an even greater number of contestants and exhibitors signed up for the fair, which would again be held on the grounds of Linden Lodge.

Fair organizers emphasized that the event was "not for the professional gardener. He is barred. It is for the man or woman who attends his or her own garden…" Yet one can only assume that the Fair's judges might have looked the other way (on more than one occasion) when the more prosperous participants signed up, knowing full well that staffs of gardeners helped maintain the vast lakeside estates.

A good-natured spirit was to be reported everywhere during the two-day annual event, as was made very evident when auction sales skyrocketed as estate owners opened their wallets for the cause. J. H. Moore, reported the *Lake Geneva News*, paid $205 for two bunches of grapes and Otto Young (Younglands) paid $250 for another few bunches of grapes grown on the R.T. Crane (Jerseyhurst) estate. "A tray of fruit from S. B. Chapin's (Flowerside) garden was knocked down to R.T. Crane for an even hundred and a goat went to J. H. Moore for $150."

When the average worker earned under $500 a year, these auction sums were staggering. And even though fair organizers (most of whom were the lakeside elite) said this event, as Charles Wacker (Fairlawn) explained in a newspaper interview, was for the "encouragement and congeniality between the summer folk and the local residents and of real farm interests" it must have been an extremely frustrating task to compete against these titans of industry and their vast resources.

Yet the fair would continue to thrive for a number of years. In 1907 the grounds of Loramoor were offered for the event. And even though the profits from the fair seemed to dwindle as the years passed, this affair would eventually be the impetus for not only the formation of the Lake Geneva Gardeners and Foremens Association (dedicated to promoting local horticulture and conservation), but the founding of Horticultural Hall (where the event was moved in 1912 and eventually evolved into two annual events: the Lake Geneva Garden Show and the Holiday Home Rummage Sale), as well as the establishment of the Lake Geneva Garden Club.

"If I were to choose a profession in life," Charles Hutchinson (Wychwood) was once quoted as saying, "it would be one of three and that of gardener is among the number. I place in the same category the minister of the gospel, the teacher of children and the cultivator of flowers…The profession of a gardener is a noble one. You may rightly rejoice in it."

And rejoice the gardeners of Lake Geneva did—and continue to do over a century later.

COURTESY OF SUE MORTON

# PROFILE: JOHN BULLOCK

COURTESY OF THE DORIS M. REINKE RESOURCE CENTER

One of the only known photos of the photographer/painter, John Bullock, which is thought to be taken by his son.

John Bullock was born in England in 1835. Before discovering his love of oil painting, he apprenticed as a potter. Bullock came to America in 1858, creating portraitures in Philadelphia. His career path as a painter was set—that is before the invention of the solar camera changed his life. Bullock turned his attention to making daguerreotypes and made a successful business of photography throughout the Civil War before a longing for his art returned, which eventually took him to Chicago.

In 1872, following the Great Chicago Fire, Bullock came to Lake Geneva to make some sketches. One fine August day that year, the *Lake Geneva Herald* recorded: "Some nineteen of the Lake House guests chartered the *Clara* and with J. H. Moore as captain, started with a healthy breeze for the head of the lake. Mr. J. Bullock, the well-known artist, was on board with sketch book and pencil, outlining the matchless scenes at every tack of the vessel, these are being painted and offered for sale in Chicago…"

Bullock found the southern Wisconsin region so charming, he decided to make Lake Geneva his family's permanent home. He opened a studio in 1875 and soon gained a reputation for taking some of the finest photographic views of Lake Geneva, which were eagerly sought by tourists—so much so that his studio was finding it hard to keep up with the demand. Yet despite the fact that he had the potential for a profitable business, Bullock often ignored his photography studio for his true passion: painting.

Though his paintings were also profitable, he often refused to sell them. Bullock did accept the occasional commissions, however, including painting the interior of the *Lucius Newberry* steamer. Bullock was charged with creating twenty-three scenes of Geneva Lake on the vessel's paneled cabin walls. "Mr. John Bullock, during the past fall, has painted some exceedingly beautiful views in oil of bits about Lake Geneva," wrote the *Herald* in 1890. Bullock also had one of his paintings exhibited at the 1893 Chicago World's Fair.

In 1907 Bullock returned to Chicago, where he would spend his final years. Upon his departure, the local paper wrote of his enduring love of Geneva Lake: "He saw its beauties when it was calm as a mirror and when its surface was lashed to a fury by the strong winds of the southwest; he saw the exquisite coloring of the maple trees which line the shores when they were touched by the early frost of Fall and delighted to place them on canvas so that others less favored than he with artistic ability could enjoy the beauties he saw."

Bullock died in 1912 at the age of 77 and returned to Lake Geneva one final time to be buried in Oak Hill Cemetery. Over the years, the artist's paintings, many of which have remained in the hands of local collectors and museums, have become excellent historical chronicles of early Lake Geneva.

# Lake Life in the 20th Century

COURTESY OF WISCONSIN HISTORICAL SOCIETY, WHI-1800

One of the greatest impetuses for change around the lake was, of course, the arrival of the automobile, which would not only have great impact on local lifestyles (residents and visitors would no longer depend solely on boats to provide delivery and transport), but would also create an increasing tourist business as the country became more and more mobile. This exciting change would certainly be wrought with growing pains as newspapers from the early part of the 20th century illustrate in their attempts to mediate the rising conflicts between the horse and horseless carriage.

"...this year there seems to have entered a spirit of recklessness among the chauffeurs," reported The *Herald* in June of 1906, "which is liable to cause trouble, unless it is curbed. While our citizens and officers wish to allow all the privileges to automobiles—and they are on our streets by the score every day—yet there comes a time when forbearance ceases to be a virtue and a continuation of reckless driving...will cause an effort to enforce the speed of 12 miles an hour —which is fast enough for any man while in the city limits. We would advise all owners of automobiles to bear this in mind, for they will have no kick coming when they are pinched."

And those who chose to shun the auto for another year were also subject to some chastising and continually urged to educate their horses to the new contraptions they would in all likelihood cross paths with on a daily basis.

"Don't delay it in the hopes that the auto will pass out of use," stated The *Herald*, "because it will not. You will meet more of them than ever on the road this year...So don't delay taking every precaution to prevent runaways and also don't let the man behind the wheel impose upon you."

COURTESY OF JEANNETTE STOLTZFUS
Young John Fleming Jennings on his grandfather's new car at Villa Thekla (now the Lindens.)

# THE ONSET OF WAR

Life along the shores of Geneva Lake would eventually settle in to its new technologies and new ways, but only for a few short years, until the onset of World War I, when the nation's feeling of plenty was being marred by the country's entrance into the European conflict. Rationing of foods and other goods was soon affecting everyone's lives—and the community of Lake Geneva was no exception. In May of 1917, a proclamation was sent from the Governor of Wisconsin to the state fish commission to begin work on catching fish from local lakes to sell to the public. So every night that summer, a long net was strung from the Broad Street bridge over Geneva Lake where carp and suckers were caught and sold at five cents per pound. One evening, in just forty minutes, the State Game Warden in charge had sold 372 pounds of fish.

Yet each day and every week, the daily sacrifices being made by the people of Lake Geneva were tragically overshadowed by the sacrifices made by the many young men (and women) who lost their lives during the short-lived but devastating war that left fifteen million people dead—sixty-seven of which came from Walworth County.

Early one morning, in November of 1918, news reached Lake Geneva that the armistice had been signed and that the "cruel and devastating war had ceased." Word spread through the town and along the shores of the lake until people began joyously rallying in the streets, sounding bells and whistles, calling for the Lake Geneva Band to play. By dawn, the streets were filled with hoards of happy people. That evening, a spontaneous, torch-lit parade, led by the band, wove its way through town to the lakeshore where a young soldier, William F. Trinke (who would go on to become a State Senator, see page 72) addressed the crowd about what peace would mean to the many men fighting overseas. At some point during the celebration, an automobile delegation from Williams Bay arrived in Lake Geneva, dragging "the Kaiser" in tow. Afterward, an enormous bonfire was lit at the side of the lake, warming the jubilant throngs.

Before the ashes of the bonfire were cold, the simple pleasures of life beside the lake were already showing signs of reappearing. Just below the newspaper report announcing the end of the war, a short item was run about the Secretary of the Wisconsin Food Administration announcing that flour and sweetened condensed milk would be available to the public once more. With almost child-like glee, the newspaper reporter concluded, "This means that the people will have fresh candy for Christmas."

COURTESY OF THE FONTANA PUBLIC LIBRARY

# THE TWENTIES THAT ROARED

In the years that would follow, lives around Geneva Lake would remain somewhat peaceful; that is, until the increasing rattles of the now very popular automobile could be heard from one end of the lake to the other. Undeniably the motor car had much to do with the lake's continued rise in popularity, which was helped in great part by the construction of concrete highways stretching from St. Louis to Chicago.

"There are many charming sylvan retreats within a brief automobile ride from town which lure the motorists from home for the traditional week-end outing," wrote Madame X in the July 28, 1929 *Chicago Tribune*. "The one that this tourist would put at the top of the list is lovely Lake Geneva in Wisconsin's gently hilly country at the south end of the state. It is reached by a variety of excellent roads. The drive from Illinois' broad and fertile prairies up to Wisconsin's more picturesque landscape with its countless little lakes, provides an interesting variety for the nature lover."

As roads all over the country continued to be lengthened and improved, cross-country touring became all the rage and Lake Geneva became well known for offering cool summer breezes and a shady spot for camping. So it was that by the 1920s, each summer and every day, thousands of tourists rambled around Geneva Lake, setting up camps along nearly every spare inch of public land along the shores.

"Everyday from the first of June to the first of October sees cars, big and little," wrote Paul Jenkins in *The Book of Lake Geneva* in 1922, "laden with camping outfits and khaki-clad and sunburned folk, pausing to scan the roadsides around the lake for possible camping spots."

# THE LEAN YEARS

In the decade following the great stock market crash of 1929, residents around Geneva Lake did their best to get by and get on with their lives. Sadly, it was during these lean years that many of the grand old estates and their farms began to be sold and subdivided, likely spurred on by margin calls demanded and fortunes doomed.

Yet even as Geneva Lake's "Golden Age" seemed a thing of the past, lake residents and visitors did their best to keep life around the shores as interesting and entertaining as possible. The local movie theaters did a great deal to help people escape their woes and worries, as movie stars such as Jean Harlow, Lionel Barrymore, William Powell and Myrna Loy brought fantasy, romance and adventure to the silver screen.

The Public Library also saw a dramatic increase in patronage, as people looked for an inexpensive way to pass the time. "The library is filled with people these days," reported the *Lake Geneva News Tribune* in May of 1932, "most of them studying to better themselves in their own lines of endeavor or for new professions and crafts. A majority of them are young men, shabby but clean."

Outside of these institutions, however, local farmers were facing the lowest prices seen in a generation. Important local commodities, such as milk, livestock, chickens and eggs continued to fall month by month and farmers were seeing prices nearly 50 percent below those of a decade earlier.

The Civil Works Administration (CWA) which was established by the New Deal during the Great Depression to give jobs to millions of unemployed, was doing its best to give local residents a sense of purpose. In May of 1934, nearly $63,000 was being spent on eleven CWA projects in Lake Geneva—most of which involved building bridges and new construction. Yet one of the greatest Depres-

© KAYLA COLLINS

sion era accomplishments for Lake Geneva residents was the local funding and construction of the recreation center on the shores of Geneva Bay in 1932. Built for a whopping $85,000, the civic center (first known as Northport, but renamed Riviera the following year) opened its doors to an eager public on September 1, 1932. One thousand people were reported to attend its first informal opening (men were charged ninety cents and women, sixty cents), which featured Ralph Williams and his Orchestra. The grand opening occurred the following spring and featured Wayne King and his Aragon Ballroom Dance Band.

Yet signs of hard times were still everywhere. In addition to a rash of robberies being reported on nearly a weekly basis throughout the first half of the 1930s, "Hobo Jungles" as the local newspaper called them, were cropping up all around the area—and not simply men in search of work (as many transients had been in the year or two prior), reported the paper, but seamier characters looking to sponge off the kindness of locals.

And the summer tourist trade was dismal. Most hotels were operating on a reduced scale, many cottages didn't even bother operating at all, concession stands and restaurants, boat services and retail stores were operating at a loss —even the new Riviera couldn't keep its head above water.

COURTESY OF THE LIBRARY OF CONGRESS, PRINTS & PHOTOGRAPHS DIVISION. FSA/OWI COLLECTION. LC-USF33-001752-M5

Two young "mibs" practice their game, excited by the Western Finals of the National Marble Tournament.

Hoping to keep spirits high, city officials tried to keep the riff-raff out and public entertained with a variety of events sponsored throughout the year and the years following. In 1934 lakeside residents got wrapped up in the Western Finals of the National Marble Tournament during which time 100 young men (mibsters, as marble players are known) from around the region came to the beaches of Lake Geneva to compete in the four-day event in June.

The marble champs were put up at the elegant Hotel Geneva and competed each morning in Ringer Stadium, which had been constructed on the public beach next to the Riviera, leaving the afternoon free to enjoy the summer splendors of the lake. Two locals, fourteen-year-old Gordon "Butch" Johnson and ten-year-old Allen Bailey—both from Lake Geneva—had also made it to the Western Finals which meant the home crowd was rooting at a fever pitch for their resident "mib kings" to make it to the national finals to be held in Ocean City, New Jersey at the end of the month. Alas, the local favorites just missed the finals, beaten by two boys from Tennessee.

"Most of the boys away from home for the first time," reported the *Regional News*, "will go home with splendid and stirring tales to tell their parents and their less fortunate neighborhood pals. They'll also carry home a healthy coat of Wisconsin's best tan."

By 1936 signs that the economy was on an upswing began to appear around the lake. "For the first time in six years, smiles have replaced worried frowns on the faces of merchants in Lake Geneva and the lake region," reported the *Regional News*. "…This summer of 1936 has been one of intense activity and the persistent ringing of cash registers, the symphony of a successful season, has told a story that hasn't been heard for many long years."

In fact, the paper went on to report, sales were up nearly 100 percent over the average of the past few years (1932 proving to be the all-time low); professional services were starting to show signs of profit—even Lake Geneva's hotels began to fill with guests.

"For the first time in several years," E. T. Nussbaum, one of Hotel Geneva's owners was quoted as saying, "guests at our hotel accept our prices without question… Many fine folks from Cincinnati, St. Louis, and other distant points have been coming this year and these people are spending freely, tipping liberally, and seem not to be constantly aware of what their vacation is costing them."

It would be a slow recovery for the communities of Geneva Lake—and the country—but hope was strong and the coming years held promise. The next few decades, the people of the lake communities would certainly face new challenges, including another World War, civil unrest and the growing pains inevitable in any developing collective, yet life along the shores would continue to respect much of its colorful past and work toward a future that would add many more compelling stories to the annals of Geneva Lake's very long and venerable history.

# PROFILE: WILLIAM TRINKE

When William Trinke was orphaned at the age of 14 with the tragic loss of both his parents, he was forced out of school and into adulthood. But from early on, it was clear that Trinke was a man who would not give up—no matter what obstacles were thrown his way. Barely a teen, he worked as a farmhand, construction laborer, and eventually began a painting business, interrupted only when the United States entered the trenches of the First World War. At the age of 17, Trinke enlisted in the 1st Wisconsin Cavalry, serving with the 32nd (Red Arrow) Division in France. The young cavalryman, however, served only two months when he was injured after being thrown from a horse and forced to return home.

Upon his return to Lake Geneva, Trinke re-established his painting business and began the restoration of his family's home, which he soon sold for a sizeable profit. Seeing how lucrative real estate could be, the young veteran began his own real estate business and, over the next decade or so, created a successful business venture which he sustained even as the country headed into the Great Depression. Although the real estate business suited him and he prospered by it, Trinke admitted that he was always a bit intimidated by the fact that his education had only reached the sixth grade.

"I built up sort of an inferiority complex," he was quoted as saying in a 1935 *Milwaukee Journal* interview. "Somehow, I resolved no matter how long it would take I'd get the education that I should have completed years before I ever started a business."

Trinke first began to pursue his dream with correspondence courses, but later moved his wife, Altha (Hooker) Trinke and their daughter to Milwaukee, where he began extension coursework with the University of Wisconsin; while at the same time studying on his own the grade school and high school coursework he also needed.

"There was a strange paradox of having to write a theme in Freshman English," wrote the *Journal* reporter, "while at the same time struggling to differentiate between an adverb and adjective in a grade school grammar course."

Trinke admitted during the *Journal* interview that the first two years were the most difficult years of his already difficult life. In fact, he told the reporter that he lost 15 pounds in his first few months as a student. But Trinke persevered and would not only complete a major in Political Science, but would ultimately go from sixth grade to a bachelor's degree in a phenomenal four years. And, upon completion of his B.A., Trinke would once again move his family to Madison where he would earn a law degree from the University of Wisconsin in 1937, at the age of 40.

Trinke would open a law firm back in his hometown of Lake Geneva and practice there until his retirement in 1979, as well as continue his real estate endeavors, developing 11 subdivisions, including one which still bears his name, Trinke Estates, Geneva Bay Estates, and Geneva Manor Subdivision on the grounds of the old Leiter estate.

As if this wasn't enough to keep him busy, Trinke also served as director of the First National Bank for more than 25 years, as president of the Walworth County Bar Association, was a member of the State Bar Association of Wisconsin, served as the State Commander of the American Legion from 1945–46, and would serve three terms as a Wisconsin State Senator. It was during his senatorial tenure that Trinke proposed a rather controversial piece of legislature which would bar Chicago area visitors from using public parks and beaches in southeastern Wisconsin during summer weekends. The boating committee to which he proposed the measure to keep "Chicago freeloaders" off the lake flatly refused.

COURTESY OF THE GENEVA LAKE MUSEUM

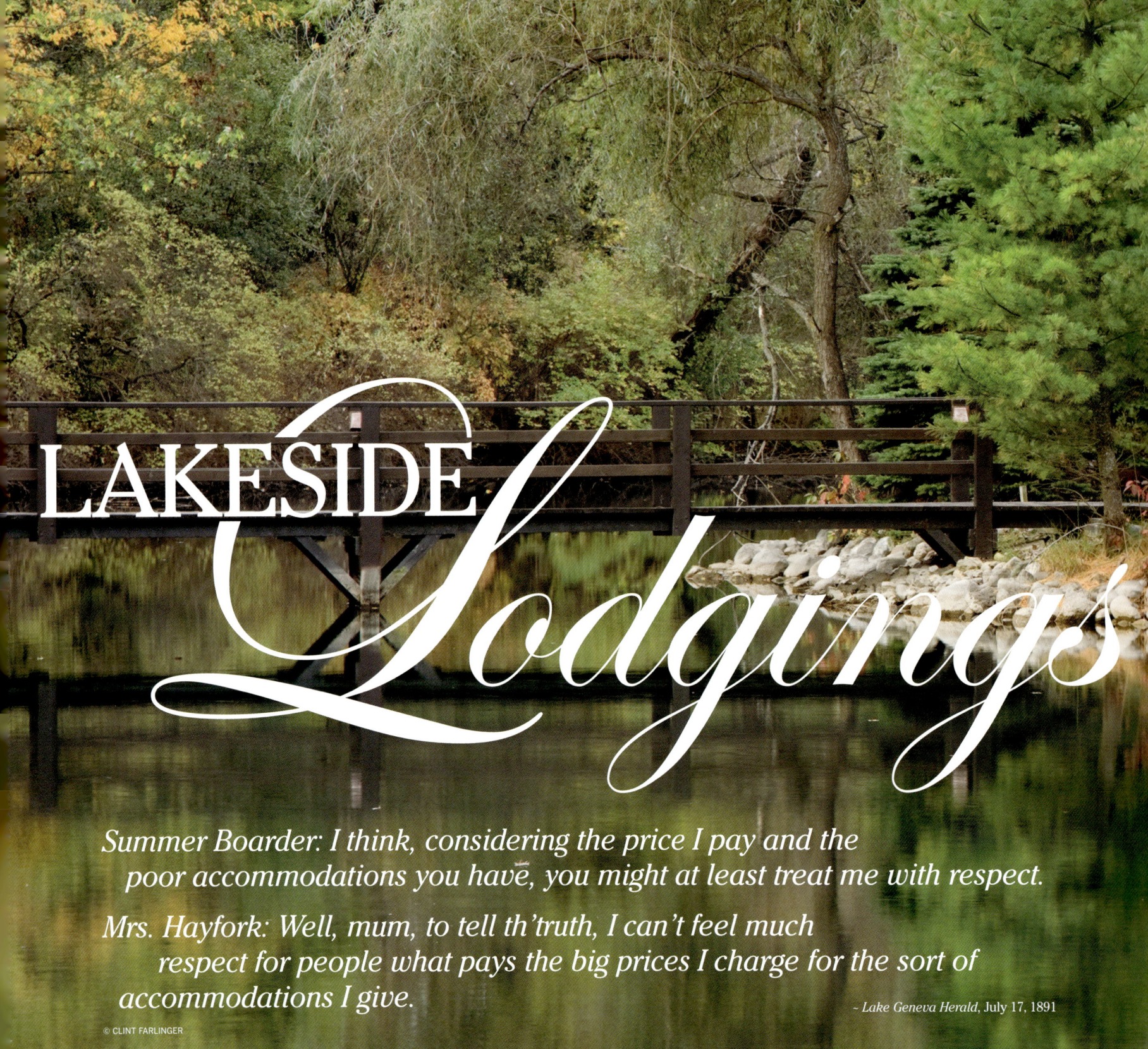

# LAKESIDE *Lodgings*

*Summer Boarder: I think, considering the price I pay and the poor accommodations you have, you might at least treat me with respect.*

*Mrs. Hayfork: Well, mum, to tell th'truth, I can't feel much respect for people what pays the big prices I charge for the sort of accommodations I give.*

*~ Lake Geneva Herald,* July 17, 1891

© CLINT FARLINGER

Over the years, different hotels and resorts—under many different names and run often by many different owners—would come and go along the shores of Geneva Lake. Some, such as Kaye's Park, flourished for many years; many more did not. Opening accommodations to weary travelers and summer tourists often involved long, thankless hours: rising before dawn to light fires and begin preparations for hearty, homemade meals; hand-washing linens; arranging boat excursions and tea parties, hops and social events—even tending to the needs of clientele opting to rough it at small campsites available at various resorts.

Being a hotel/resort owner also meant there were young men in need of a few innocent flirtations and ladies in need of chaperoning, old women in need of a cozy chair and old men wanting to find that secret fishing cove. There were babes in need of a quiet napping place and young lovers in need of a shady spot to spoon—and every guest arrived with great expectations that their summer holiday at the famed Midwestern resort town would give them stories to tell back home for years to come.

For reasons such as these, it is little wonder that many hoteliers simply couldn't hack it.

## THE HOTELS

Before the onslaught of summer tourists and Chicago millionaires, the first accommodations to be built along the shores of the lake were mainly for early settlers needing a place to rest before beginning their own businesses and settling their own farms. The Geneva House, erected between 1837 and 1838 by one of Geneva's founders, Robert W. Warren, was built only after Warren first invited guests into a primitive log cabin, which was, to say the least, sparse in its amenities.

"In each corner of this sleeping room was a bedstead..." described another early settler, Solomon A. Dwinell, for the 1882 *History of Walworth County*, "it had but one leg, the rails at the other ends being inserted in the logs which composed the walls of the building. The bed was made of dried grass called 'prairie feathers' and laid upon shakes instead of cords… A slight covering for it to which the clothes of the sleeper were added, furnished a more desirable resting place than the wet ground on a cold stormy night… A comforter was spread upon us before morning in the shape of a mantle of snow, sifted through the shakes of the roof over our heads."

Robert's brother, Greenleaf S. Warren, also erected another one of the earliest hotels in 1837, which he called The Owl House. Built just a block from the water's edge, Greenleaf kept the inn for several years in direct competition with his brother. Robert, however, would eventually take over The Owl House, only to sell it a few years later (in 1845) to A. D. Colton who named the inn "Colton's Exchange." Colton fast gained a reputation for keeping a stellar country hotel, attracting visitors from near and far. One of its greatest claims to fame was in August of 1872 when Mary Todd Lincoln was a guest of the hotel, then known as the Lake House.

"Our village has been favored during this week past with a visit from Mrs. Abraham Lincoln," reported the *Lake Geneva Herald*, "who spent several days at the Lake House. We are pleased to report that she was very favorably impressed with our scenery and that we may hope to see her again."

Eventually, the hotel would be sold several more times and undergo a great many changes—both inside and out, yet it always remained a popular spot for summer visitors. In the spring of 1873, Orville Blakeslee purchased Lake House where he would remain as its innkeeper for many years.

"His long experience as hotel-keeper and steward of the lake boats at an early day," wrote the 1882 *History of Walworth County*, "had given him a well-earned reputation as an efficient landlord and a host who knows how to keep a hotel."

Although simple in their offerings, the first hotel accomodations to be established in Lake Geneva became not only places where one could rest their weary head, but community centers where, for instance, sermons could be offered. Yet, as the lake communities grew and visitors to the lake began to increase, so too did the need and desire for more elaborate hotel accommodations.

"An evening or so ago a small party of millionaires… took a trip up the lake," reported the *Chicago Daily Tribune* in July of 1879, "and Mr. Ayer proposed that if a stock company could be formed to build an immense hotel—one that would accommodate 1,000 guests or more—that he would take stock in it and guarantee to build a railroad from Harvard to the lake, and transport at his own expense all the material to be used in building, and for five years all the furniture to be used for the hotel. This was a magnificent offer, but as none of his companions took it up it still stands open."

Although the 1,000-room hotel has never come to fruition, many elegant and elaborate hotels, such as the magnificent Pishcotaqua Park House, the 200-room Whiting House and, as mentioned earlier, Kaye's Park Resort, offered summer vacationing on a grand Victorian scale, with sweeping verandahs and porches, picturesque parks and gardens, ponds and playgrounds, grand dining halls and billiard halls, croquet grounds and bowling alleys, cool lake breezes and, quite often, convivial company.

"The jolliest man in Geneva, is Colonel J. E. Huntoon of the Chicago Board of Trade, now at the Burton House," reported the *Cisco* in 1887. "He tips the scales at the modest figure of 315. The Colonel believes in living as he goes and having a good time generally. He uses about twenty good Havana cigars, and catches a long string of black bass daily, and tells a good story capitally. However, not-

COURTESY OF THE GENEVA LAKE MUSEUM

The Lake House was a popular hotel on the corner of Main and Broad streets in downtown Lake Geneva. Among its guests was Mary Todd Lincoln, who visited in August 1872.

withstanding his jollity, love of good cigars, and general 'good fishing qualities', Mrs. Huntoon discounts him at fishing, having the better catch every time."

By the mid-1880s, news of Geneva Lake's summer pleasantries spread fast throughout the Midwest and beyond, and soon hundred of thousands of vacationers were arriving each summer—all looking for a place to unpack and unwind.

In 1887, according to the *Cisco* (a short-lived summer publication), a summer vacationer could rent a furnished house in the village at prices varying from fifty to one hundred and twenty-five dollars. "Of course," the paper reminded tourists wishing to be near the sparkling waters and cool lake breezes, "the price depends greatly upon the proximity of the cottage to the lakeshore, but a good modern house of ten rooms will average $125 per month anywhere within a block from the lake."

Many hotels, such as Minier's, also offered campsites. "The camp is as full as it can be and all seem to be enjoying themselves," reported the *Harvard Independent* in 1883. "Mr. Minier makes frequent trips to the camp and keeps them well supplied with the necessities of life."

Every guest accommodation had something to offer the average tourist.

"Hotel LaSalle and Hotel de Repasz are both on the lakeshore," read a typical hotel ad in an 1881 *Cisco*. "They are commodious, pleasant, and accessible places offering home accommodations at reasonable rates. Bathing houses and suits in connection with the hotels. Boats, etc., are readily obtained. The terms range from $1 to $2 per day, according to length of stay and number of persons per room…"

During the height of the summer and the height of its popularity, hotels surrounding Geneva Lake were packed to capacity. Good money could be made, if one had the desire… not everyone, however, had the stamina.

For instance, John Lone first built his hotel, called "The Surf," in 1914, (later changing the name to Hotel Lone). Although his hotel was a successful one, in June of 1919, Lone would trade his hotel and property (estimated worth $24,000) "for a 160-acre farm with growing crops, fully equipped with horses, cattle and machinery." C. L. Irwin, owner of the farm, located in Waterford, Wisconsin, considered the trade an even one.

And not all the troubles of hotel ownership had to do with the clientele. The Lincoln Inn, a two-story structure with verandahs on both sides was another popular lakeside establishment, run by Bill Long who fast gained a reputation for fine food and service.

Sadly, in February of 1931, a bomb (which had been placed in a cellar entrance) detonated, demolishing the nearby Milano Cafe and causing severe damage to the hotel. A bus driver reported seeing a car parked in the alley between the two buildings about five minutes before the explosion, but no individual could be identified. No one was injured during the explosion, but windows were reported broken nearly a mile from the scene of the blast.

Though the café received the most damage, officials on the scene believed the inn was the intended target and rumor had it that the Chicago mobsters were behind the incident.

"Local gossip ran at fever heat," reported the *Milwaukee Journal*, "and the names of Chicago gang leaders were freely mentioned. It is common knowledge here that "Bugs" Moran and his wife have made Lake Geneva their stopping place several times and that other Chicago gangsters like the town. Last summer one hotel man complained "they have taken over my place and I can't do anything about it.""

COURTESY OF THE GENEVA LAKE MUSEUM

COURTESY OF THE FONTANA PUBLIC LIBRARY

# THE GREAT OUTDOORS

Often Geneva Lake-lovers were not interested in hotel accommodations, but found the opportunity of back-to-nature vacation living irresistible. Camping also provided the means for middle-class families to reside at the lake without emptying their wallets. Besides the noted economics of outdoor living, by the late 1870s, camping was also very much "in vogue."

There were several types of camps on Geneva Lake: those that were owned or sponsored by religious or community organizations (Holiday Home, Y.M.C.A, Camp Augustana); those that had a private owner who leased space, tents, cottages, or hotel rooms to summer dwellers such as Marengo Park; and those that were co-purchased by a "club" or group of people from a particular community—usually somewhere around Chicago (Chicago Club, Rockford Camp).

No matter who held the titles, the parks had certain things in common: a sense of camaraderie, group activities, and plenty of swimming, boating, and other sports. Many camps shared community cooking/dining, and laundry facilities —and even scheduled activities with neighboring camps.

COURTESY OF THE FONTANA PUBLIC LIBRARY

Warwick Park, located on Black Point, east of the popular Kaye's Park, was a 50-acre resort opened in 1880 by W. Anson Barnes. The rolling terrain made for picturesque surroundings and from its Observatory Hill, some 300 feet above the lake, the entire surface of Geneva Lake could be seen. For $2 per day—or from $8–$14 per week—guests could either pitch a tent or rent a cottage. Meals could be purchased in the dining hall for $7 per week, or patrons could do their own rustic cooking.

Oak Park, consisting of 20 or so families from the Illinois town of the same name, was a rather rustic camp located next to the Bon Ami Club. A jolly group of young people called the "Bashi Bazouks," (a Turkish term meaning a leaderless band of soldiers) was said to fill the park each August.

Nightingale Camp was named for Professor Augustus F. Nightingale (see page 81), who owned a bit of land between Kaye's Park and Harvard Club. The camp was also known by another name, due to the exuberance of its campers—"Camp Jolly." Nightingale and twenty or thirty friends spent several weeks each summer sailing, fishing, swimming, and otherwise taking advantage of the beautiful waters of Geneva Lake.

By the late 1800s/early 1900s, the tents and simple cottages were being replaced by more permanent structures with kitchens, baths, and screened porches. The feeling of the camp community, however, remained. Patrons often attended dances ("hops") or concerts at other camps; while combined cruises on the *Lucius Newberry* also provided opportunities for young people staying at various camps to get to know each other. One particularly exciting event in 1883 was a special cruise of the Fourth Regiment officers and band, who went around the lake serenading residents and stopping several times for on-shore dancing and refreshments.

# PROFILE: AUGUSTUS F. NIGHTINGALE

COURTESY OF SUE MORTON

Augustus F. Nightingale was born in 1843 in Quincy, Massachusetts, into a well-established family with its roots in the Mayflower Quakers. He attended Wesleyan University in Connecticut where he graduated as class valedictorian in 1866; and following this, would pursue a career in education for the remainder of his life. He first became a professor of Latin and Greek at Upper Iowa University, followed by a presidency at Evanston, Illinois's Northwestern University's Female College in 1868. In 1872 Nightingale became the superintendent of Omaha, Nebraska's public schools and making his mark there as a leader in new education ideals soon found himself back in Illinois, accepting the position as principal/instructor at the new Lake View High School in Chicago.

Nightingale's work at Lake View would eventually gain him a good deal of attention and would earn him the appointment as Superintendent of the Chicago school system in 1890 (and eventually the Cook County school system in 1902). During his tenure as Superintendent, Nightingale became instrumental in not only raising the standards in the public school system and revising and perfecting the school laws of Illinois, but also in establishing secondary schools throughout Cook County, Illinois, and beyond; becoming the chairman of the National Education Association in 1895. Nightingale would be on the University of Illinois's Board of Trustees from 1899 to 1905 and its president from 1902 to 1903 and would also receive several honorary degrees: a Master of Arts in 1869, a PhD in 1891 and a Doctor of Laws in 1901.

When this leader in education looked for a retreat from his responsibilities, he looked north to Lake Geneva. Here, during the 1880s he built his lakeside home that historical accounts claim he named Altruria based on a late 19th-century novel by William Dean Howells, *A Traveller from Altruria*. Set in a fashionable summer resort on the East Coast, the novel is about a stranger who comes to experience the truth behind America's proclamation that "all men are created equal," only to find his own country, Altruria, far transcends every aspect of life in America—be it economic, social, political, and moral.

The novel certainly must have meant a great deal to Dr. Nightingale who was a man committed to social causes and a potent force in shaping public thought and action—not only in his professional life, but also in his personal life. In the book, *Family Secrets: Crossing the Color Line*, by Catherine Slaney, it is revealed that Nightingale's daughter, Florence, married a young, African-American doctor by the name of Wilson Ruffin Abbott II during a time when such a marriage was not only unheard of, but social dynamite, especially to a family such as Nightingale's with its high social profile.

However, Abbott, a highly qualified and respected heart and lung specialist in Chicago, would assume a white identity throughout his life; and even though he kept ties with his relatives and Chicago's black community by volunteering his services on the city's south side, Abbott would never go public with his true ethnicity.

Florence and Wilson had a son, Gus, who would eventually be raised by Augustus and his wife, Fannie, following Florence's death when Gus was only six years old. The young doctor would marry a second time and bring another boy into the world, who tragically drowned at three years old while visiting the Nightingales in Lake Geneva. After this terrible accident, Dr. Abbott would not be seen visiting the Nightingales at their summer home again.

Dr. Nightingale passed away in Chicago in 1925, leaving behind a remarkable legacy. "In almost every field of work from the primary to teaching the classics in a university, from grade teacher to superintendent of high schools, from instructor in Greek and Latin to college president," stated his *Chicago Tribune* obituary, "he has left the mark of an earnest student and apt instructor, an intelligent organizer and a judicious director."

# CISCO BEACH CAMP

**BUILT:** 1880 AS PISHCOTAQUA PARK, 1890 AS COOKE'S PARK, 1926 AS CISCO BEACH CAMP, AND 1946 AS CAMP AUGUSTANA

**ORIGINAL OWNERSHIP:** unknown; 1890 John Cooke; 1926 Chicago Inner Mission of the Illinois Conference of the Augustana Synod (Lutheran).

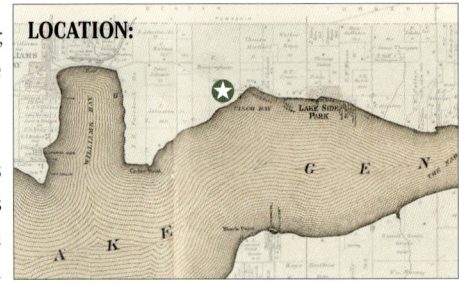

**LOCATION:**

**WHAT'S IN A NAME:** As with some of the other camps on the lake, Camp Augustana was known by various names over the years, beginning with Pishcotaqua, an Indian name that means "sparkling waters." When John Cooke purchased the property, it became known as Cooke's Park. The grounds were christened Cisco Beach Camp (because of the abundance of cisco fished in the lake) when the Augustana Synod of the Lutheran Church in Chicago took the property over in 1926. Finally, in 1946, the camp became incorporated and owned and operated by the Illinois Conference Luther League. It was at this time the camp became known as Camp Augustana.

**PROPERTY DETAILS:** Cisco Beach Camp, later called Camp Augustana, was a camp for children from Augustana churches in Chicago and Rockford. There were several buildings, including the main building (now the home known as Ara Glen), where the youngsters stayed, as well as additional dormitories; twenty-five small cabins on the hill that were rented to families, summer cabins for employees (including three administrators' homes), a dining hall, and a chapel. Basketball and tennis courts provided sports activities for children, as did the beach that had its own pier for rowboats and was perfect for swimming.

Chapel on the Hill now owns part of the original campgrounds, while nearby Knollwood and Ara Glen subdivisions make up the remainder of the property purchased from the Augustana Synod.

The present Chapel on the Hill Christian Arts Center was a barn when Cisco Beach Camp was established. The main camp office was in a white farm house on Highway 50 and Cisco Beach Road. The old dining hall is still standing and now functions as the current parish hall.

**HISTORIC NOTES:** Evidence of a Native American campsite was found on the property, including hearthstones of fireplaces, flint arrowheads, grooved axes and pottery fragments.

In 1880 Pishcotaqua Park was established as a resort, with Pishcotaqua Park House, a large, four-story hotel that offered a bowling alley, shooting gallery, billiard hall, playground, and mineral spring. The hotel and park was purchased and run by John Cooke and family beginning in 1890, until the hotel burned down in 1892. Cooke then converted the billiard hall into a residence for his family, called Ara Glen.

This site, once enjoyed by campers and visitors to the area as early as 1880, is now property of Knollwood Subdivision.

© CLINT FARLINGER

Children and families looked forward to camping at Cisco Beach Camp each year, where the fishing was good and the atmosphere was relaxing.

By 1926 Ara Glen was up for sale and fifty acres were purchased for $75,000 by the Augustana Synod. Sixteen of these acres were made into Cisco Beach Camp and the rest sold off and subdivided into Knollwood subdivision. The $75,000 was raised by creating seventy-five $1,000 shares that were purchased by men in the Bethlehem Lutheran Church—all of whom made their money back at a profit when the subdivision was created and sold off.

Another summer camp, Villa Immanuel, was operated right next door by The Immanuel Woman's Home Association, who sold their property to Camp Augustana in 1955 for $68,000, so that Augustana could expand.

By 1977 the synod had moved its camp facilities to Oregon, Illinois, and Camp Augustana was sold to developers Lavern Twist and Jack Huml. The property was then divided into eighteen single-family lots (known as Ara Glen subdivision) and the remainder was sold to Chapel on the Hill, a non-denominational community church. The main building of the camp was remodeled back into a private residence.

When the main building, Ara Glen—first a billiard parlor, then a family home, then a camper's residence, then a family home again— was extensively remodeled by Frank Guido in 2001, a note from a worker who must have helped to construct the building was found on one of the original walls: "John Page, born September 27, 1834. Huron County, Ohio."

**HEART AND SOUL:** Dr. John Jesperson, the Executive Director of the Chicago Inner Mission of the Illinois Conference of the Augustana Synod, had a vision—to provide a respite for the sick and downtrodden residents of the city of Chicago. That's what inspired him to search for, and eventually find, the perfect property on Geneva Lake in 1926. While his vision didn't play out exactly as he wished (rather than sick and underprivileged children, the camp functioned as a respite for groups and organizations), the camping experience became a reality for many city youth who may not otherwise have had that opportunity.

There was always something interesting to do at Camp Augustana, whether that meant sports, talent shows, musical performances, or spiritual activities. Everyone attended Sunday services, and there were bonfires at night. Most campers stayed at Augustana for only a week or two, but many would remember the experience the rest of their lives. In fact, during the summer of 1969, camper Audrey Johnson Metzger remembers watching Neil Armstrong take his first steps on the moon from the cafeteria, where the counselors let them stay up far past their bedtimes.

# ROCKFORD CAMP

**BUILT:** 1886

**ORIGINAL OWNERSHIP:**
Mr. Joseph Stam and his heirs, ending with grandson Steven Stam, who died in 1975.

**LOCATION:**

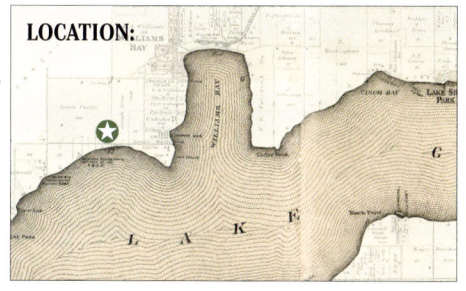

**WHAT'S IN A NAME:**
Rockford Camp was called so because the residents were friends and neighbors from Rockford, Illinois.

**PROPERTY DETAILS:**
Rockford Camp began, like many other camps on the lake, as a tent camp. Around 1900, the boundaries of the camp moved when the original leased property was divided in half—one half becoming Eleanor Camp and one half remaining Rockford Camp.

Smallish cottages were constructed, some quite primitive and without bathrooms—long into the age when they were common. One of the cottages was known as "Hickory Hut," because it had a large round hole in the front porch of the cottage so that a big hickory tree could continue to grow there.

**HEART AND SOUL:** What makes Rockford Camp unusual is that Joseph Stam and the campers pitching tents on his property in the late 1800s had a simple gentleman's agreement. Mr. Josiah Sloan Leonard and Mr. Morton Brown, both from Rockford, Illinois, came to Geneva Lake and were the first to approach Farmer Stam about renting his lakefront acreage. Because Stam couldn't farm the land closest to the lake, he wisely allowed the campers to erect their tents. He would continue to do so each summer for a small fee and a handshake.

Mr. Stam died around 1900 and his land was divided. His daughter, Mrs. Ethel Romare, sold her piece to Eleanor Camp (today known as Wesley Woods), which meant Rockford Camp had to move west a bit, to the portion then owned by Mr. Stam's son, Charles, who issued twenty-year leases to the residents of Rockford Camp, which continued to be renewed until 1975.

Camp life was Norman Rockwell-simple. Children in the camp walked to the nearby Stam farm to buy milk each day and every morning a boy from the grocery store in Williams Bay arrived to take the grocery and meat order. Later in the day, orders were delivered by horse and cart. Meals were cooked on a kerosene stove or men would heat large stones from the shore in a fire in the yard; and at supper time everyone broiled his or her own steak on the rock of their choice. Mealtimes at Rockford Camp were more like picnics in which the whole camp participated.

Water for washing was carried from the lake or taken from the rain barrel and men shaved with a mirror suspended from a nail in a tree. Families who lived in the smaller cottages without baths took their soap down to the pier to wash up.

Activities included walking or rowing expeditions to the Leiter Fish Hatchery, Yerkes Observatory, and the beautiful flower gardens of Ceylon Court. Rockford Camp families also visited the Williams Bay railroad station to witness the arrival of the "Millionaire Special," (the train that brought wealthy residents to the lake from Chicago), and strolled "the public's own" shore path. By mid-century, you could get a hot lunch at noon at Lee's in the Bay and in the evening folks sometimes brought a picnic supper out on the water, dining al fresco under the stars. There were also square dances each Wednesday night at nearby George Williams College Camp.

Rockford Camp children made the most of lake life, playing games such as "Tap, Tap the Icebox" and "Submarine Bomber." In the latter, the person who was "it" stood on the pier, while everyone else hid underneath. The object of the game was to swim out from under the pier without getting "bombed" by the person on top.

In 1975 Rockford Camp landowner, Steven Stam, died, and his daughters sold the land to a developer for $400,000. All the families had to move out by 1981. One house, owned by Pi Leonard (the name stuck when her mother called her "Sweetie Pie"), was donated to Wesley Woods and still stands today, renamed "Miller House." The remaining nine cottages were sold to investors who tore them down and built three private homes.

COURTESY OF SUE MORTON

# BELVIDERE PARK

**BUILT:** 1869 BUT WASN'T FORMALLY ORGANIZED UNTIL 1875

**ORIGINAL OWNERSHIP:** Mary Reed, who later sold to Mr. and Mrs. Marcus C. Russell (Russell Park). In 1875 it was owned by twenty-seven families from Belvidere, Illinois.

**LOCATION:**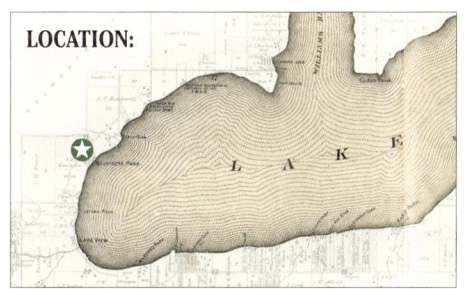

**WHAT'S IN A NAME:** Like many of the lakeside camps, Belvidere Park was named after the Illinois city in which its residents lived full-time.

**ALL IN THE FAMILY:** Judge Kohlsaat and his family, who began vacationing in Belvidere Park in 1890, eventually built a home (House on a Hill) on the nearby shore. Harry Wells, a young man who lived a few doors down, fell in love and married Kohlsaat's daughter "Dim." Later, Wells became an instrumental part of Fontana's community affairs, heading up Music by the Lake, among other activities.

**PROPERTY DETAILS:** The three and a half acres that made up the original Belvidere Park were purchased for $700 in 1875. After starting out as a temporary campground, the property (which would eventually encompass sixteen acres) would, in due course, have twenty-two cottages, spring houses, and a recreation building.

**HEART AND SOUL:** At the height of the season, there were often more than 100 people staying at Belvidere Park. It was reported to be the first club on the lake, originally part of Forest Glen Resort and then Russell Park.

Activities made life at Belvidere Park anything but monotonous. The *Lady of the Lake* excursion boat would often be docked at the pier, providing dancing in the evening or church services in the morning. One of the homes at Belvidere Park even had an organ, so church services were sometimes held there. The mothers in Belvidere Park and nearby Spring Haven formed an entertainment club in 1894 that served both camps. Readings, musical performances and moonlight cruises were some of the events sponsored by the club.

**HISTORIC NOTES:** There were indications of a Native American campsite and workshop found when the homes were built, including some 100 arrowheads discovered at the base of a large oak tree.

© CLINT FARLINGER

# FONTANA PARK

**BUILT:** 1875

**OWNERSHIP:**
George Smith (1839–1873),
Doric C. Porter (1873–1894),
Warren F. Furbeck (1894–1901),
Ida Richardson (1901–1911)

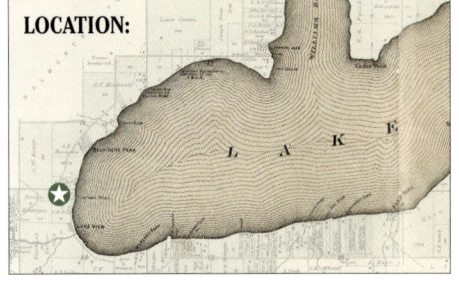

**LOCATION:**

**WHAT'S IN A NAME:**
Between the years of 1873 and 1894, what is now Buena Vista was known by several names: Fontana Park, Porter's Park, Montague & Porter's Park, and Porter & Montague's Park. By the time W. F. Furbeck purchased the camp in 1894, it was known as Buena Vista, Spanish for "beautiful view."

By 1894 the property was commonly known as Buena Vista. Furbeck closed the park to the public the next year, and then sold it to Ida Richardson of New Orleans, Louisiana, after the market crash of 1901.

Albert Cotsworth was hired to manage it, with instructions to "preserve the wildness," and around this time, architect Henry Lord Gay was hired to design the curved streets of Buena Vista. In the 1940s Chicago Industrialist Robert Tarrant's "cottage," Brooklawn, was said to be the largest and most upscale residence at Buena Vista. Tarrant's three sons (Robert, Edward, and John) even had their own dining room on the first floor and a complete set of rooms upstairs for their sole use, including a library, recreation room, and bedroom—all decorated in a nautical theme, including wide planked floors, portholes for windows, and ship's lanterns for light fixtures.

Another home at the very top of the park, called the Crow's Nest, was built by Willis S. Herrick and offered a commanding view of the lake and Herrick's lovely gardens.

When the property was subdivided after 1901, only thirty of the one hundred lots were sold by 1911. The remaining properties were due to go up for auction in August of that year, but relatives and former renters bought up most of the properties before they could be auctioned off to strangers. The Buena Vista Lot Owners' Association was then formed in January 1912.

**PROPERTY DETAILS:** Originally a summer tent-cottage colony, operated by partners Doric C. Porter and Guerdon Montague, Buena Vista's tent-cottages had wood floors and wood halfway up the walls. The campgrounds also offered a large dining hall and a livery stable for horses. Known as one of the more beautiful camps, the park had fountains installed throughout the grounds and a community springhouse that had been built over one of the mineral springs on the property, so that campers could take advantage of what were thought to be medicinal waters.

When half of the property was subdivided into lots at the turn of the century, it was with the stipulation that much of the land must remain natural. The homes that were subsequently built were not your ordinary cottages—they were considered quite upscale for the times and were arranged in crescent formation from the house at the highest point—600 feet above lake level, all the way down to Geneva Lake. Today, much of Buena Vista retains its parklike atmosphere, with wide open spaces, hilly terrain and a large brook running through the property.

**HEART AND SOUL:** Because the spring waters here were thought to have medicinal properties, the park—under all of its various names—was visited by people looking for restorative water cures. A large, tumbling brook was one of the park's chief attractions, and water from it was piped into fountains throughout the park, including two elaborate beauties built in the interior of Brooklawn—one in the entrance hall and one in the garden room.

By the late 1930s, the Chipmunk Club was in place and thriving at Buena Vista. This was a "social, sports & general jollification association" that was set up to encourage fun activities for the children.

**HISTORIC NOTES:** The former village inhabited by Chief Big Foot was likely the largest Potawatomi settlement in southern Wisconsin. In fact, early maps of the lake referred to it as "Big Foot's Lake." It is reported that Chief Black Hawk visited Chief Big Foot and spent several days urging him to join forces against the settlers prior to the Black Hawk War in 1832. Big Foot, however, remained neutral. The burial site of Chief Big Foot's son was on the property, and at one point, Montague & Porter built a railing around it to protect it from tourist damage.

COURTESY OF FONTANA PUBLIC LIBRARY

# CHICAGO CLUB

**OWNERSHIP:** Englewood Club, aka Geneva Lake Encampment Association of Englewood, Illinois (1878), Bon Ami Club (1878). Both consolidated as Chicago Club in 1893.

**WHAT'S IN A NAME:** Both Englewood and Bon Ami club members hailed from Chicago, therefore, when consolidation occurred in 1893, their city's name was chosen for the new venture.

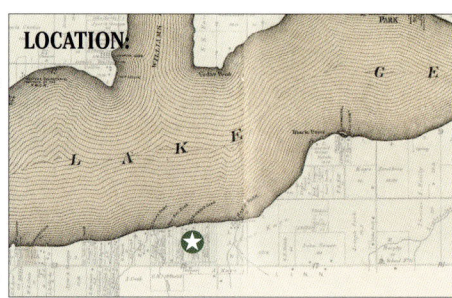

**PROPERTY DETAILS:** Early tents of both Englewood and Bon Ami Club residents were fourteen by twenty-four feet, four-room tents, with two rooms on each side and a passageway through the middle. By 1885 many were enlarged with the addition of a small frame structure that included a living room and bathroom. Even though the first cottages contained only living and sleeping rooms, they did not skimp on details. Many had fine interior finishes, such as open staircases of polished black walnut or mahogany. Since the cottages were seasonal, they were heated only by fireplaces.

All club members ate their meals at the clubhouse, a large, one-story frame building with a huge dining hall, kitchen, parlor, laundry, and ice house. Nearly at the water's edge, the clubhouse's wide veranda jutted out toward the lake. Surrounding the clubhouse and homes was a large picturesque park with old oak and maple trees that extended all the way to the lake. The club had swimming, croquet, and rowboats.

In 1890 a larger clubhouse was built—a forty by 100 feet, two-story structure with bedrooms on the second floor for guest overflow. A set of tracks ran from the clubhouse down to the lake, so that a horse-drawn railroad cart could be used to haul supplies from boats to the camp.

By the 1920s, most of the original cottages had been torn down and the newer homes were built with their own kitchens. The clubhouse was eventually torn down in the late 1920s due to lack of use and by the 1930s, all of the homes were outfitted for year-round use. Today, all the original cottages are gone, but four homes that remain on the Chicago Club property date to the late 1920s or early '30s, with the exception of one that burned, but was reconstructed to appear identical to its sister homes. All of them are white, clapboard homes trimmed in green; and there are tennis courts, maple trees and a large wooded park area extending to the lake.

© CLINT FARLINGER

© CLINT FARLINGER

**HEART AND SOUL:** Bon Ami Club was a literary group formed in 1874 in a westside Chicago neighborhood. They were known to plan various camping trips to locations between Chicago and Lake Superior, and finally purchased property on Geneva Lake in 1879. Memberships in the club were eagerly sought, but only twenty-five families were allowed in at any one point. The initiation fee was $10 and yearly dues $5.

The Englewood Club, on the other hand, began with the Englewood Baptist Church, who gave their minister, Reverend F.G. Thearle, the task of finding a suitable property on which members could camp. In 1879, he traveled to Geneva Lake and found a 10-acre site west of Kaye's Park. Membership was limited to 50 families.

By 1893 Bon Ami and Englewood memberships had both dwindled, so they combined into The Chicago Club. Bon Ami sold their land (fifteen acres) for $25,000 and their residents moved over to the former Englewood Club property. Then, sometime early in the 20th century, Chicago Club became a corporation and the homes were transferred to private ownership.

At the Chicago Club, the wide veranda of the clubhouse was the perfect place for the "rocking-chair brigade," a row of ladies who were seemingly relaxing with needlework, but who were also keeping a sharp eye on the youngsters. Hops were held in the dining hall and members of the club also went to dances at Kaye's Park, plus parties and concerts at Nightingale's.

In 1977 Jim Riley of Chicago heard the Chicago Club property was up for sale. Having heard good things about it, he bought it, sight unseen. He called a number of friends and offered the four homes on a first-come, first-serve basis. Four friends bought the homes (also sight unseen) and today the club is operated as a condominium association.

COURTESY OF SUE MORTON

# MARENGO PARK

**BUILT:** AROUND 1881

**ORIGINAL OWNERSHIP:**
Miss Bissell and Miss Reed

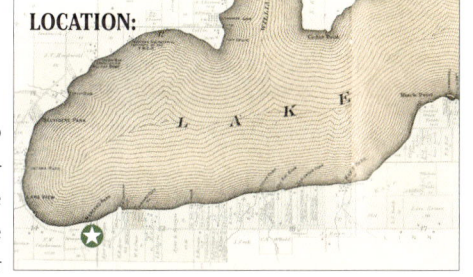

**WHAT'S IN A NAME:**
Originally called Marengo Park because of the cottage-owners who hailed from the Illinois town of the same name, the park was later referred to as Frascati Park for reasons unknown.

**PROPERTY DETAILS:** The hotel (Marengo Park House) was opened in 1881 by two ladies who came to the lake from Toledo, Ohio, Miss Bissell and Miss Reed. It was a large two-story building surrounded by towering oaks. The building was modeled after a Southern plantation home, with broad porches on which guests could relax and mingle. Cottages on the property were owned by people from Marengo, Illinois.

A wide variety of amenities made Marengo Park a desirable place to spend the summer: bathing houses; boat houses; a laundry and a wide, beautiful lawn that held rustic benches, swings, and croquet grounds. A platform for dancing and lovely flower beds created a delightful ambience for evening activities in the park.

**HEART AND SOUL:** In the early 1880s Billy Wood's sloop was seen delivering loads of lumber and other building materials to the park, perhaps in preparation for the new owners of Marengo Park House, who completely overhauled the hotel for the season.

The grounds of the park directly faced Fontana and it was a lively place in the evenings, with hops that frequently took place on Tuesday and Friday evenings on the outdoor dance platform.

**HISTORIC NOTES:** Marengo Park had a reputation for new owners, sometimes on an annual basis. Here are some of them:
1881–82: Misses Bissell and Reed
1883–84: Mr. B. F. Wright
1889: Misters Miller and Banta
1890: I. V. Hollinger
1894: Misters Watters and Parkhurst

COURTESY OF GENEVA LAKE MUSEUM

# EDGEWATER PARK

**BUILT:** 1923

**WHAT'S IN A NAME:** Edgewater has proven to be a popular name at the lake: another Edgewater Park can be noted on old maps of Geneva Lake's south shore, between Button's Bay and Fontana; and yet another Edgewater Park exists today in Williams Bay.

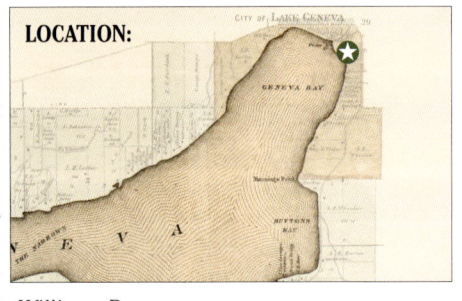

**LOCATION:**

**PROPERTY DETAILS:** What distinguished The Edgewater Park Tourist Camp from other camps on the lake was the transition of large homes (built between the mid-1800s and the early 1900s) into hotels. C. O. Lindquist opened Edgewater Park as a tourist camp on the lakeshore in 1923, and surrounding hotels included, at various points in time: The Edgewater Beach Hotel, The Antlers Boarding House, the Lakeside Hotel, The Elizabethan Inn, The St. Moritz, and, much more recently, Pier 892 Hotel and Bella Vista Suites. Most of the original homes in the area were Queen Anne style. The Charles Minton Baker house, which was built around 1857, or earlier, was one of those early homes.

**HEART AND SOUL:** The Edgewater Beach Hotel, originally a Queen Anne-style home, was the first house in the district to rent rooms to tourists. The proprietor of the property, located on Wrigley Drive in the 1920s, was Madame Juliani. By 1939 twelve new homes were proposed as a subdivision of the property occupied by the Edgewater Beach Hotel.

Redwood Cottage, another Queen Anne-style home, was built in 1885 for the widow Emily Baker. It later became a dormitory for the Lake Geneva Seminary for Young Ladies, then a residence for patients of the Oakwood Sanitarium. In 1926 the 17,000-square-foot structure became known as Lakeside Hotel; followed by the St. Moritz Hotel in 1949, Gilbert's Restaurant, and most recently returning to its roots as The Baker House.

This area of Lake Geneva seems destined to remain a beacon for tourists. Several hotels remain located at this historic site, as well as the Eleven Gables bed and breakfast and Pier 892 condo properties.

**HISTORIC NOTES:** In 1872 the Wisconsin Historical Collections recorded the existence of a linear mound (more likely referring to the panther mound recorded nearby) near the Baker home. Fireplace stones, arrowpoints and other Native American implements were collected from various points around the tourist camp and hotel properties.

© CLINT FARLINGER

# THE SANITARIUMS

Lake Geneva was not only a retreat for those with the health and vigor to enjoy. Its sparking, spring-fed waters were also used to calm the nerves and promote healing for the sick.

Dr. Oscar A. King of Chicago, who sought to have bills passed in the Wisconsin Legislature governing such institutions, founded the Lake Geneva Sanitariums in 1883, then called Oakwood Springs Sanitarium. After competing with other cities, including Janesville, Beloit, and Palmyra, Lake Geneva's beauty, nearness to Chicago and free water supply to the sanitarium grounds and buildings won out—due mainly to the efforts of James B. Heg, then owner and editor of the *Lake Geneva Herald*.

Oakwood Sanitarium was completed in 1884–85 and opened for patients on May 13, 1885. It was designed to be used for the "treatment of disease of the brain and nervous system, including nervous diseases of children, impediments of speech, nervous prostration, motor and sensory affections of the nervous systems, mild cases of mental diseases, nervous affections of the eye and ear, also, gynecological cases when complicated by nervous derangement."

The sanitarium was built on sixty-three wooded acres that provided extensive views of the lake and the city. The rolling hills made for easy walking for patients of Oakwood. Cutting across the corner of the property was a swift silvery ribbon of the White River, which formed a twenty-acre lake that was twenty feet at its deepest within the sanitarium grounds.

Built at a cost of $80,000, and touted as fireproof, Oakwood had a decadent hotel feel. It was five stories high and had fifty rooms with semi-private parlors and kitchens to ensure every client felt as though they had their privacy. The staircase was made of marble and mosaic tiles, and fireplaces were constructed of imported marble.

After an addition to Oakwood was built in 1889, two other locations were acquired: Lakeside, founded in 1893, was the former Hotel Luzern (built in the 1860s). Lakeside Cottage, added in 1896, was the former residence of Robert Baker (see page 148).

Patients enjoyed the Lake Geneva area and its natural amenities all year long. They played lawn games, went for a swim, a stroll, or fishing in the summer.

When Hotel Luzern was built in the 1860s, it had 42 rooms, a private pool and a miniature golf course. In 1893 it became part of Oakwood.
COURTESY OF THE GENEVA LAKE MUSEUM

COURTESY OF PEG WILLIAMS

Lakeside and Lakeside Cottage (pictured above) were utilized for the "care and treatment of medical and general sanitarium cases."

In the winter they'd go sledding, iceboating, ice skating, and so on. And when the weather was inclement, they would enjoy recreation indoors. Some such guests included Lillian Russell, Ashton Stevens, Mary Gridley Bell, who donated $100,000 to the "new" Lake Geneva Public Library, and a rumored stay by Greta Garbo.

In 1901 the three sanitariums were housed under the renamed umbrella, Lake Geneva Sanitariums, and run by Dr. King and his two brothers, Albert and Reiley. Dr. King died in September 1927, leaving his wife to run the facilities. A few years later, financial problems caused the facilities to close. Oakwood closed sometime in the early 1930s. Over the next two decades, the property had been vandalized and subject to at least three fires. Neighborhood kids came to view it as haunted. The remains of Oakwood were razed in the 1970s.

# PUBLIC DOMAIN

*"The village park is daily and every evening a scene of joy and life. It is full of happy young people from early morn until dewy even [sic], and there is nothing of so great value to the village as that same park. In the name, therefore, of the young folks of the village, from toddler of two or three years to the young man of downy moustache, from the wee miss with her dolly, to the spit-curled young lady with a 'feller,' we beseech the Village Board to cut the grass in the park and keep it cut. Cut it early and often…"*

~*Lake Geneva Herald*, June 2, 1882

Public parks began being developed around Geneva Lake in the early part of the 1870s, as more and more interest was shown in the lake as a tourist spot. One of the first public parks developed around Geneva Lake was Lake Shore Park which was established in September of 1872. Under the direction of A. E. Lytle, the park was built between the two bridges south of town and included gravel walks and a fish pond fed by the lake.

As time went on, more public playgrounds began to be established near the lake's eastern shores. Some were simple, untouched spaces of green, others were developed into elaborate lakeside sanctuaries offering day visitors a place to rest in the shade, sip from a fountain, stroll along the lakeshore, picnic, swim, and pursue other summer pleasures.

Established in 1874, Lake View Park, located about two miles south of Lake Geneva, was a perfect example. Situated on level ground and offering an abundance of young trees, the park was equipped with fountains, benches, swings, picnic tables, an ice cream and confectionary store, a dance hall, and stables —all for the convenience and pleasure of the public. Even some of the earliest estate owners, such as Shelton and Geroge Sturges, Nathaniel Fairbank, and Levi Leiter allowed the public to enjoy parts of their grounds as "driving parks."

However, in just a few short years, with the number of pleasure-seekers on the rise, estate owners became far less welcoming to the summer throngs.

"Mr. L. Z. Leiter has at last found a way whereby he can keep the general public from the grounds of Linden Lodge," reported the *Lake Geneva Herald* in April of 1884. "He has lately bought a Jersey bull for which he paid $1,800 and which has the run of the grounds, and which is said to be the ugliest brute in town. People are even afraid to pass along the road as there are only a few slender pickets between them and the animal."

Over the next two decades, some small lakeside plots were donated, set aside or simply proved to be undevelopable and, by default, were open to the public, such as Flat Iron Park (originally known as Willow Park) and Baker Park in Lake Geneva, and Reid's Park in Fontana (the first parcel of which was donated by George M. Reid in 1890).

In 1894 Mary Sturges also donated a significant piece of Lake Geneva lakefront to be used as a public park, including the old Farr Cottage (which the family had occupied for many years) to be used as the city's public library. Today, this public promenade, known as Library Park, is one of the jewels of the lake.

By the turn of the century, however, most of the public parks were purchased for private development. In fact, by the time Kaye's Park closed in 1901, there were virtually no public parks along the lakeshore. It wasn't until 1926 that complaints by regional newspaper editors about the lack of public recreational areas along the lake, prompted a movement to purchase land for public use.

It wouldn't be until 1930, however, that Fontana finally established Fontana Park and Public Beach, and not until 1946 that swamp land at Button's Bay was purchased and developed into Big Foot Beach State Park. And although Williams Bay established its first public park in 1934, it would not be until 1966 (after the Chicago and Northwestern Railroad ceased operations to the lake) that Williams Bay was able to open its first lakeside park with the establishment of Williams Bay Public Beach and Boat Dock.

The one true constant that has allowed the general public access to Geneva Lake has been the Shore Path which, from time immemorial, has welcomed all to explore the beauty of this magnificent inland lake.

© CLINT FARLINGER

# Geneva Lake Map

As summer pleasure-seekers began to fill the shorelines, there would be one true constant—that of change—which would transform the water's edge from season to season, one generation after the next.

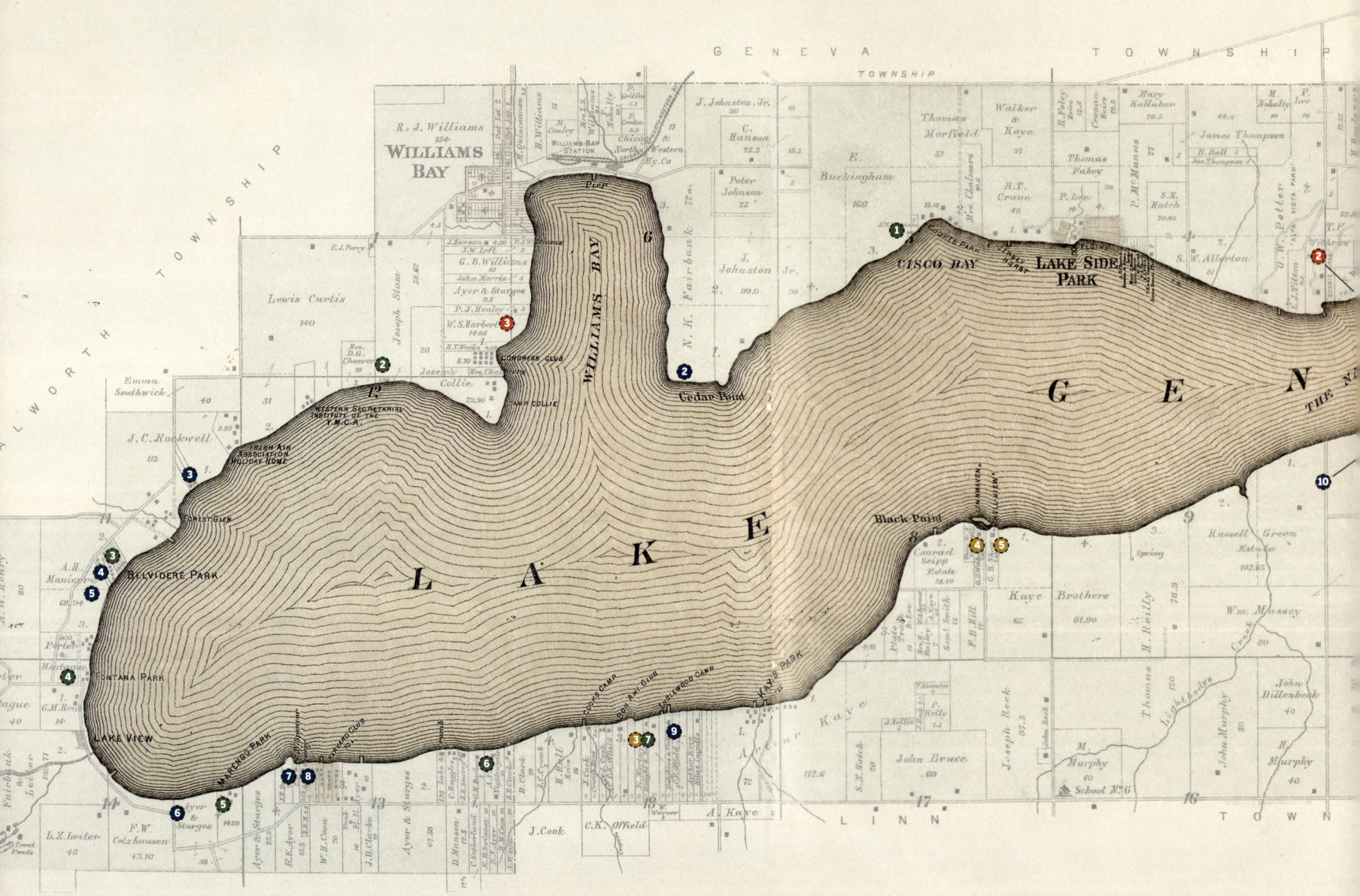

## KEY

**LOCATION:**
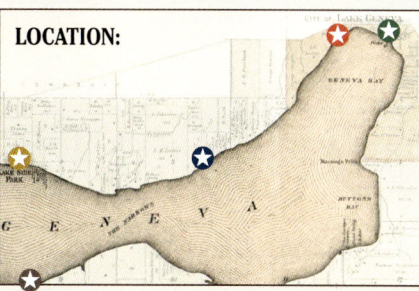

Use the locator map to find approximately where along Geneva Lake's shoreline that estates, clubs, associations, camps, and public places (included in this book and identified by their original names) were established.

### ● ESTATES (EXTANT)
1. The Orchard
2. Alpine Villa
3. Sunny Hill
4. House on a Hill
5. Pinegate
6. Ferris
7. Rainbow Point
8. Hazeldore
9. Oak Shores
10. Cotswold Cottage
11. Allegheny
12. Boyd Farm
13. Fair Oaks
14. Willow Landing
15. Redwood Cottage

### ● ESTATES (RAZED)
1. Gaylynne
2. Folly
3. Tre Brah
4. Allview
5. Sumachs
6. Negawni
7. Knoll

### ● NOT TO BE FORGOTTEN
1. Briarwood (RAZED)
2. Waldeck
3. Our Home (RAZED)
4. Linn Haven (RAZED)
5. Hill View (RAZED)
6. Anchorage (RAZED)

### ● CAMPS / PARKS / INN
1. Cisco Beach Camp
2. Rockford Camp
3. Belvidere Park
4. Buena Vista
5. Marengo Park
6. Nightingale
7. Chicago Club
8. Edgewater Park
9. Lincoln Inn

© WISCONSIN HISTORICAL SOCIETY, WHi-26017

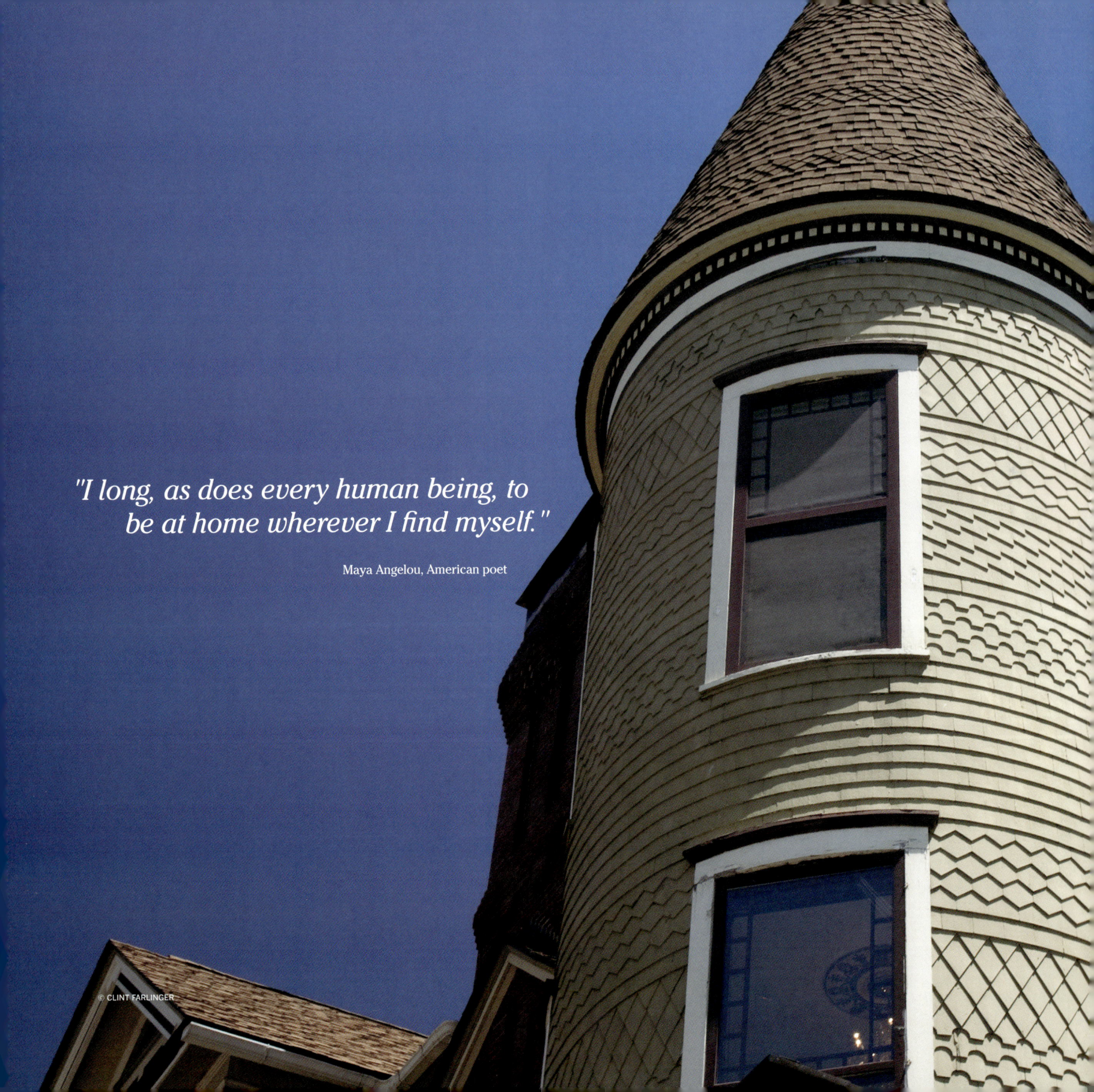

"I long, as does every human being, to be at home wherever I find myself."

Maya Angelou, American poet

# THE *Places* & THE *People*

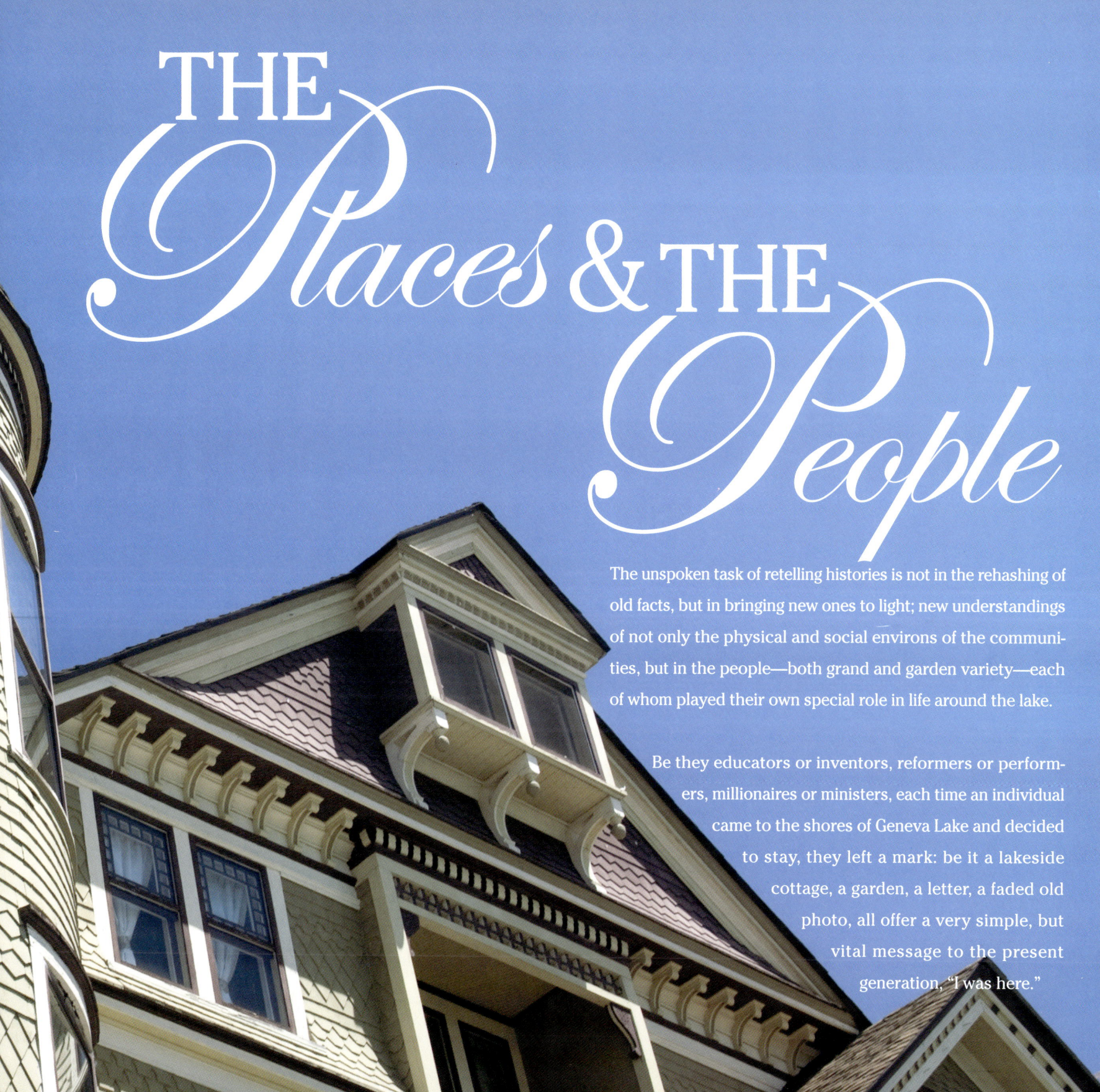

The unspoken task of retelling histories is not in the rehashing of old facts, but in bringing new ones to light; new understandings of not only the physical and social environs of the communities, but in the people—both grand and garden variety—each of whom played their own special role in life around the lake.

Be they educators or inventors, reformers or performers, millionaires or ministers, each time an individual came to the shores of Geneva Lake and decided to stay, they left a mark: be it a lakeside cottage, a garden, a letter, a faded old photo, all offer a very simple, but vital message to the present generation, "I was here."

COURTESY OF THE SCHLESINGER LIBRARY, RADCLIFFE INSTITUTE, HARVARD UNIVERSITY

# THE ORCHARD

**BUILT:** 1898

**ORIGINAL OWNERSHIP:**
William Francis "Frank" and Ethel Sturges Dummer

**LOCATION:**

**ALL IN THE FAMILY:**
Ethel's father was George Sturges (Snug Harbor); her uncles were: Shelton Sturges (Maple Lawn) and Buckingham Sturges (Fairfields); and her sister was Rosalie Hubbard (Rehoboth).

**PROPERTY DETAILS:**
The Orchard was designed and built by architects Pond and Pond. The house itself is 7,000 square feet and has no insulation. When it was owned by the Dummers, half of the forty acres were wooded; the other half had a farm, barn, fruit trees, an ice house, and a field for making hay for their horses. By the hand of a Scotch carpenter, with the help of some eager young girls, there was also a two-story playhouse built and enjoyed by generations of children. Having always had a hankering to use tools, Ethel pitched in as well and helped saw sideboards and worked on window casings.

**HEART AND SOUL:** Frank and Ethel married at Snug Harbor in 1888 with 100 loving witnesses looking on—including the many relatives from the Sturges clan who had homes in Lake Geneva. After their honeymoon, they had their Chicago home built on the site where her grandfather, Solomon Sturges's home had burned down in the Great Chicago Fire. They built The Orchard ten years later, which became known as Dummer's Hill.

"There was no electricity back then," says granddaughter Ethel Fisher of her memories from The Orchard. "We used oil and kerosene lamps." Many extended family gatherings took place, especially since sister, Rosalie's, children were about the same age. "The adults played on the long grass tennis courts. We kids loved to take hay rides… row boats and canoes. We used to walk down to Snug Harbor and Rehoboth to use the lake," recalls Ethel.

"We'd ride the horses, pick the fruit, berries, and veggies," says granddaughter Polly Vaughn, "have spider web parties, go to Aunt Rosalie's; there'd always be a picture puzzle on the table for us to do in our spare time." The many Sturges offspring continued to enjoy going back and forth between the estates until they were grown.

© CLINT FARLINGER

# PROFILE: ETHEL STURGES DUMMER

Ethel Sturges Dummer was born in 1866 into one of the wealthiest, civic-minded families in Chicago. She was a social welfare leader, a philanthropist and author whose work—both behind-the-scenes and leading the charge—changed the lives of thousands of women and children. Throughout her life she attempted to establish equal rights for unwed mothers and their children as well as end the sexual double standard, introduce mental hygiene, and make enormous strides in the field of social work.

The daughter of George and Mary Delafield Sturges of Chicago, Ethel was just a child when the Great Chicago Fire ravaged their home and the family was forced to flee to Lake Geneva. The family later moved to Snug Harbor, a large, lakeside home, where they summered for many years afterwards. Ethel was one of nine children. Of them, only seven survived to adulthood.

When she was still young, Ethel began to notice the difference between sexes, particularly when her dad told her she couldn't climb trees anymore—that girls had to wear dresses. At first schooled at home with her siblings, Ethel later attended The Kirkland School, a private preparatory school in Chicago. Though she loved many of her teachers, Ethel soon noticed that her brothers' textbooks were far superior and she later admitted that her "unconscious jealousy of her brothers' opportunities may have been the source of her feminism."

Ethel believed that if a woman's eduction was "merely for our pleasure, it would be unnecessary, for not knowing what hidden treasures were within our reach, we should have been happy in our ignorance and missed nothing. But with each taste of knowledge comes a corresponding responsibility, a certain debt which must be paid by sharing the benefit derived therefrom with others and using the learning acquired to aid and instruct fellow workers."

In 1888 Ethel married one of the Sturges' legal advisors and a man fifteen years her senior, William Francis "Frank" Dummer. A shining star in his own right, Dummer had passed the bar exam without attending law school.

Frank, as he was called, developed a close friendship with the entire Sturges family during one of their son's long illnesses—especially Ethel. When their engagement was announced, a friend asked if it had been a long engagement. Ethel's mother replied, "Yes, but the two of them were almost the last to discover it." Their wedding ceremony was held at Snug Harbor. Ethel and Frank had four daughters: Marion (1890); Katharine (1892); Ethel (1895), nicknamed "Happy"; and Frances (1899). They also had a son who died in infancy.

COURTESY OF THE SCHLESINGER LIBRARY, RADCLIFFE INSTITUTE, HARVARD UNIVERSITY

Ethel Sturges Dummer (1886–1954) in her garden at The Orchard.

Ethel's early interests in reform were influenced by leaders such as Ellen Gates Starr, Mary MacDowell, and Allen B. Pond. Her interest in child welfare reform led her to join the National Child Labor Committee and the Chicago Juvenile Protective Association. In 1908 Ethel also became a founder and trustee of the Chicago School of Civics and Philanthropy, and later the University of Chicago School of Social Service Administration. During the Great Depression, she also helped finance the private studies of adolescents in need.

Ethel not only provided financial support, but donated her time, intellect, and ideas; one being Boole Blocks, a mathematical teaching aid named after one of Dummer's intellectual heroes, which she and her daughter Ethel "Happy" Dummer Mintzer (Director of the Francis W. Parker School in San Diego), worked together to promote. Ethel received an honorary Doctorate from Northwestern University in 1940 and went on to sponsor child development courses there. Her writings include *Why I Think So—The Autobiography of an Hypothesis* (1937), *The Evolution of a Biological Faith* (1943) and *What is Thought?* (1945).

COURTESY OF PEG WILLIAMS

# GAYLYNNE

**BUILT:** 1877 | **RAZED:** EARLY 1980s

**ORIGINAL OWNERSHIP:**
Henry Lord Gay

**WHAT'S IN A NAME?**
Gaylynne was named for Henry Lord Gay and his sister. It was renamed Italian Waters by H.C. Lytton.

**LOCATION:**

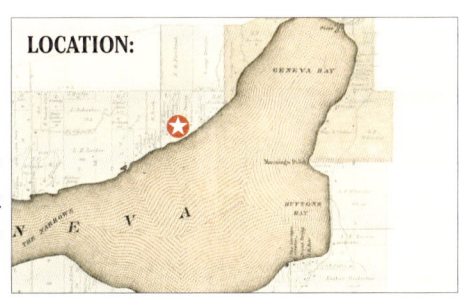

**PROPERTY DETAILS:** In 1882 Henry Lord Gay sold the estate to his sister and brother-in-law, Mr. and Mrs. John Johnston, Jr. They sold the estate to Mr. and Mrs. Henry Lytton in the late 1890s/early 1900s. After subsequent ownerships by E.K. Boisot and Arthur Leath, William Wrigley, Jr. purchased the estate in 1927. Wrigley added the property on to his vast lakefront holdings, now totaling 250 acres.

Gaylynne, designed by famed architect Henry Lord Gay and added onto by John Johnston, Jr., rose to three stories in 1882 and was considered "an ornament to the north lakeshore and a comfortable home."

It was indeed an ornament, as many people enjoyed passing by it for a look. An excerpt in the June 29, 1888, *Lake Geneva Herald*, extolled: "The grounds are beautifully laid out in walks, lawns, flowerbeds, etc. The house is of tasty design with large airy rooms and elegantly furnished. Back of the house from the lake was the garden, which under the faithful and skillful care of Mr. Charles Lee is almost a wonder to behold…There, with the aid of a hothouse, we found cauliflower which measured seven inches, beets six inches in diameter, strawberries six inches in circumference, tomatoes vines three feet high, onions four feet high and peas and flat leafed turnips fit for use, potatoes going out of blossom and all other vegetables in the same advanced state of perfection."

**HEART AND SOUL:** Henry C. Lytton, who would own the estate after the Johnstons, started off in the business world making fifty cents a week and eventually rose to become the president of a large clothing store, first called The Hub, then Lytton's. He was generous to his employees—reportedly offering them checks to act more dilligently—and was free with his advice: "save, save, save." Lytton was also a big believer in print advertising and sales gimmicks. He regularly took out ads in the local newspapers and promoted events with great flair. As one story goes, Lytton tossed free overcoats from the roof of his store to attract customers.

COURTESY OF THE LAKE GENEVA PUBLIC LIBRARY

# FOLLY

**BUILT:** 1884 | **RAZED:** 1925

**ORIGINAL OWNERSHIP:** Samuel Waters Allerton

**ALL IN THE FAMILY:** Agnes Allerton's sister, Reinette Lester McCrea, owned Blacktoft just down the shore.

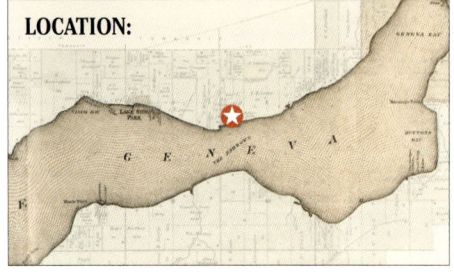

**PROPERTY DETAILS:**
Designed by Henry Lord Gay, Folly was built of redwood and was an amazing four stories tall, including a tall tower. The grand mansion sat on twenty-six lakeside acres. The Allertons loved Folly and had extensive gardens on the grounds, including a greenhouse full of roses that had 30,000 blooms per season. It is said that after dark, every room in the house was lit up to serve late-night users of the lake.

**HEART AND SOUL:** Allerton always considered himself a hard worker. When asked about this by the *Chicago Tribune*, he replied: "When I was a boy and lived on a farm I was considered the best boy to work in my county. I had a small interest in the farming and this individuality gave me the courage to work for something of my own. With self-denial I saved $3,200 and established a character that enabled me on my name to borrow $5,000 more. In this way my credit as a worker was worth more to me than the money that I had worked twelve years to earn. No boy can succeed unless he can build up a character and credit."

When, in 1903, 400 lawn mowers, gardeners, and florists employed in private parks organized a union and demanded recognition, Allerton responded that as he has "always been a farmer, he will cut his own grass rather than be dictated to by a union as to whom he shall employ."

Allerton's second wife, Agnes (Johnstone), was a woman's suffrage advocate. In 1902 she established West School in the Lake Geneva area to teach both boys and girls the domestic sciences during the summer months—cooking, sewing, canning and so on.

Allerton died of diabetes on February 22, 1914. Upon his death, he bequeathed nearly $20 million to his wife, children, and grandson, as well as a tidy sum to one of his servants for her many years of faithful service. When Mrs. Allerton died on December 19, 1924, she donated Folly's entire household to Holiday Home Camp. Mrs. Edwin Frost, wife of the Yerkes' astronomer, took charge and removed everything from the home and sold it to raise money for the camp. The year following his stepmother's death, son Robert Henry Allerton had Folly torn down.

# PROFILE: SAMUEL ALLERTON

COURTESY OF THE NEWBERRY LIBRARY

Samuel Allerton was born in Duchess County, New York in 1829. Samuel's father (Samuel Allerton, Sr.), a tailor and general store merchant, invested unwisely and lost nearly everything by the time Samuel, Jr. was twelve years old. The baby of nine children, young Samuel attended school during the winter for a few years and then began working on a farm. When he was just 18 years old, he had saved enough money to invest in some livestock and began to breed and raise his own cattle. By the age of 21, the enterprising young man had amassed a small fortune and with this, headed west where he purchased a cattle ranch in Piat County, Illinois, close to the Illinois Central mainline to Chicago. Allerton saw great promise in this young, urban center and soon used this growing lakeside metropolis as the base for his ever-expanding livestock interests.

In just a few short years, Allerton would be owner of several successful stock farms and by 1860, with a sudden sharp decline in hog prices, would—in one fell swoop—corner the market by purchasing every hog in Chicago. Profits from that investment not only constituted the foundation of his fortune, but the complicated financial transaction would cause Allerton to become an early advocate of establishing better Chicago banking facilities, as well as large, centralized union stock yards near railroads and packing plants. The hog transaction would lead Allerton to found the First National Bank of Chicago, and, in 1866, he would also join forces with John B. Sherman to organize Chicago's famed and infamous "Eighth Wonder of the World": Chicago's Union Stock Yards. Allerton would eventually be a principal in five of the burgeoning nation's stock yards, including the Pittsburgh Union Stock Yards, and owner of the Allerton Packing Company.

As one of Chicago's wealthiest and most influential citizens, Allerton's accomplishments would also include: Director of the First Trust & Savings Bank, the National Safe Deposit Company, the Weaver Coal & Coke Company, and the North Waukegan Harbor & Dock Company; vice president of the Art Marble Company; Director of the Chicago City Railway Company; and he was on the Board of Directors for the Columbian Exposition, Chicago's World's Fair in 1893. That same year, Allerton's professional prowess was so admired, he was persuaded to accept the Republican nomination for mayor, but would be defeated by Carter H. Harrison in a close race.

"Mr. Allerton has achieved rank among the millionaires of the country and attained social and political distinction by the sheer force of his sterling integrity, intellect and practical energy," the German Press Club of America wrote about him in 1901.

Allerton was married twice; first to Paduella W. Thompson in 1860, with whom he had two children, Kate Bennett (born 1863) and Robert Henry (born 1873). Then, when Paduella passed away in 1880, Allerton married her sister, Agnes, in 1882.

When Allerton passed away in March of 1914, he left an estate worth an estimated $20 million; which included 12,000 acres of Mississippi Valley, Ohio, and Wyoming farmland (including "The Farms" in Monticello, Illinois, once regarded as the "model livestock farm of the world"); significant Chicago real estate; and principal shares in the First National Bank of Chicago, as well as the Pittsburgh Union Stock Yards Company.

COURTESY OF THE LAKE GENEVA PUBLIC LIBRARY

# ALPINE VILLA

**BUILT:** 1894

**ORIGINAL OWNERSHIP:**
Herbert Alpine and Ida Louisa Merriman Beidler

**PROPERTY DETAILS:**
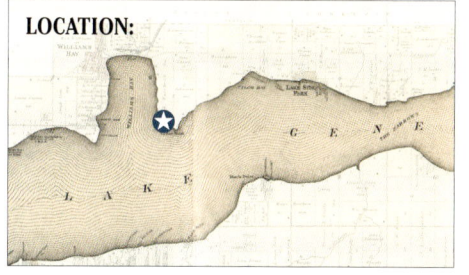
In 1890, Beidler and his wife bought 121 acres of land along the northern shore of Geneva Lake—the current location of Cedar Point. They retained the shore lands and sold off the remaining acreage. Eventually, however, they sold off lake lots as well. In 1894 the Beidlers built their lakeside sanctuary, Alpine Villa. Within ten years the second story of this residence was expanded. It was at the time that the home's cupola was placed on the ground, now used as a gazebo for the house next door, the estate's carriage house. Alpine Villa's gardener's home also remains standing as a private residence.

**HEART AND SOUL:** Beidler was born in Chicago on August 22, 1861. He moved with his family to Muskegon, Michigan, until autumn of 1876, and then went on to receive a higher education in New York. After a brief exploration of the West, Beidler headed to Chicago where he began working as a draughtsman for the Ellithorpe Air-Brake Company. On January 20, 1887, Beidler married Ida Lousia Merriman, who was born in Chicago in May, 1862. He later became the vice president of the company and after it was dissolved, formed a new manufacturing company, of which he became president. Ida Lousia died on October 6, 1916. Beidler followed nearly eight years later, on August 31, 1924. By then he had remarried, and was survived by, his widow, Mrs. Ann E. Beidler.

In 1925 Alpine Villa and its remaining property was sold to developers who subdivided lots into what is now Cedar Point. For almost 60 years, the Beidlers' home belonged to the Edward Moore family. Richard and Bonnie Hulina bought Alpine Villa in September of 1994. With no insulation in the home and only one small furnace, the Hulinas spent nine months replacing heating, plumbing, electrical, roofing, siding, windows and landscaping while retaining its original charm.

**HISTORIC NOTES:** In Lake Geneva, Beidler was an avid yachter. He was the co-founder of the Geneva Lake Yacht Club which, for a time, was headquartered at his lakeside home. For a time, he also served as president of the Lake Geneva Country Club.

©CLINT FARLINGER

CHICAGO PUBLIC LIBRARY, SPECIAL COLLECTIONS AND PRESERVATION DIVISION. CCW.1.236

# ALBERT W. HARRIS & KEMAH FARM

Albert Harris, the son of Chicago banker, Norman Wait Harris, was a man who committed his life to making his own mark instead of resting on the laurels of his father's—and family's—successes and he did so with energy and enthusiasm until his death at the age of 91 years old.

"As a financier, philanthropist, and government advisor," read his *Chicago Daily News* obituary, "his voice was a powerful one in shaping the city's history."

Yet far beyond his business acumen, A.W. Harris had many passions that would make for an exciting and colorful life that often reads like a novel—a western novel in particular. In 1910, as one example, at the age of 42, Harris made the trip of a lifetime, driving a prairie schooner (otherwise known as a covered wagon) from Los Angeles, California, through southern Utah to his farm in Williams Bay, Wisconsin—1,700 miles with just himself, a couple of horses, and his beloved Chesapeake Bay Retrievers. He wrote about the experience in his book, *Cruise of a Schooner*.

One of Harris's greatest passions was for horses. He not only competed in gruelling endurance races into his early fifties, but was one of the last Chicagoans to let go of his horse and buggy. In fact, for Albert, his horses were always a beloved part of his family. Ned, a Standardbred, bay gelding—which was the very first horse he purchased in 1891 for life with his new wife—would even be the subject of a book.

The Wisconsin farm he journeyed to in a covered wagon was his 140-acre Kemah Farm overlooking Geneva Lake, which Harris had purchased in 1902 from descendants of Captain Israel Williams. The Harris family used the Williams farmhouse until 1938, when the old house was razed and in its place a new white, clapboard cottage with crisp white shutters and a gray shingled roof, designed by Robert Seyfarth (a well-known Chicago architect who designed many homes along Chicago's North Shore), was built in its place.

In addition to the new home surrounded by ancient oaks, hickories, and maples, Harris also added a pool (fed by a local spring), sweeping lawns with vistas of both Geneva Lake and Lake Como, gardens, tennis courts, and, of course, acres of green pastures for his beloved horses.

Kemah (a Native American word meaning "in the face of the wind") Farm was where Harris could unabashedly pursue his passion for horses and the great outdoors. He stocked the farm with Hereford cattle, dogs, Mustangs, Indian ponies, and eventually would come to breed a famed line of Arabian horses, which still bear his name, Harris Arabians.

In fact, A. W. Harris's name is synonymous with Arabian horses in America. He would not only become known as one of its best known breeders (and was reportedly the first to breed in the Midwest and one of the first to breed in the country), but also would help to promote the Arabian Horse Registry in America (acting as its director from 1924–1949) in order to maintain the official registration and ownership records for purebred Arabian horses, as well as foster the preservation and improvement of the breed. He would also be president of the Arabian Horse Club of America (now known as the Arabian Horse Association) from 1939–1949 and would publish several books on the breed, including: *The Arabian Horses of Kemah* (published in 1922), *The Blood of the Arab, the World's Greatest War Horse* (published in 1941), and *The History of Arabian Horse Club Registry of America* (published in 1950), which is still cited regularly.

Among the many publications penned by Harris, *The Ponies of Kemah*, a promotional brochure written in 1906, describes the benefits of his horse training facilities in Williams Bay:

"…just a few minutes walk from the Williams Bay station of the Chicago & Northwestern Railway…we have splendid pastures, with spring brooks running through them; woods,…and warm spacious barns for the winter. The Williams Bay station…lies just across the road from the south line of the farm, where in summer there are numerous pleasures of all descriptions, and automobiles are as numerous as the boats, so that the experience our ponies get before leaving Kemah, in the way of sights and noises, cannot be improved upon for training. And no country roads carry any more automobiles in summer than do those around Lake Geneva."

Beyond his love of horses, Harris also focused much of his energies on his community. Among his philanthropic accomplishments, he founded the Chicago Community Trust in 1915, the second organization of its kind in the country devoted to promoting and funding civic affairs, education, health, and social services and culture. Thanks to Harris's firm belief in the power of philanthropy and his initial endowment of $600,000, the Chicago Community Trust has grown to be the fourth largest community foundation in the country today.

Among his favorite social organizations was the Chicago Boys Club. In January of 1953, Harris—then in his late eighties—donated Kemah Farm to the organization, which helped (and still helps) underprivileged youth. Kemah Camp was not only a place where the city's kids could escape from their urban confines, but where many disadvantaged youth could learn valuable leadership skills. The gift included thirty acres, the family's summer home on the lake, five outbuildings, and a collection of buggies and equine trappings. The Harris family then moved their horse facilities to their remaining acreage situated beside Lake Como. After Albert's death in 1958, his son Norman (a well-known breeder of Anglo-Arab horses) would continue breeding horses at Lake Como until he passed away in 1965.

Although Albert certainly loved the waters of Geneva Lake, his heart was always on land and in the saddle. Looking from the windswept hilltop of Kemah Farm down toward the lake, Albert Harris was once heard to say with an enormous sense of pride, "Down there they go by boat. Up here, we go by horse."

COURTESY OF THE EVANSTON HISTORY CENTER

# PROFILE: ELIZABETH BOYNTON HARBERT

"Not the woman question, but the human question." This was the famous slogan originated by Elizabeth Boynton Harbert during the suffrage movement. Not satisfied with the role of women as second-class citizens from an early age, she was a moving, powerful voice that led others to follow her toward change. In her lifetime she wrote and published three books, several essays and articles; composed songs; edited two women's publications, one of which she founded; and was a member and/or president of several committees for change, including World's Congress Auxiliary, World's Unity League, National Household Economics Association, Iowa's Woman Suffrage Association, the Women's Club of Evanston, Illinois, and many more.

She and husband, William, owned Tre brah, on the western shore of Williams Bay, where, when they weren't relaxing, they would hold meetings on a variety of philanthropic, human rights topics.

Elizabeth Morrison Boynton Harbert was an author, lecturer, social reformer and suffragist born ahead of her time in Crawfordsville, Indiana, on April 15, 1843 or 1845 (there is disagreement as to which is the actual birth year). Elizabeth went to school at a Western Female Seminary at Oxford, Ohio, which by then was considered not only a right, but also a necessity for those who were charged with rearing America's young, clean minds. After all, the reasoning went, women spent their whole day with the children and could not be left ignorant, filling children's minds with said ignorance.

In 1862 Elizabeth graduated with honors from John Covert's Terre Haute finishing school in Indiana. She went on to college at Asbury (now DePauw) University in Greencastle, Indiana. Elizabeth also applied at the all-male Wabash College where she was denied admission due to her sex, but was given special permission to attend lectures. The injustice of being turned away from a school that had significant academic merit was so upsetting that an indignant Elizabeth earned her first paycheck of $10 from the *New York Independent* by writing about it.

Elizabeth soon became active in the Women's Suffrage Association of Indiana. It was there that she would eventually meet her future husband, William Harbert. After being released, at an emaciated 97 pounds, from a Libby prison during the Civil War, William briefly attended law school in Greencastle, but withdrew to own and operate a shoe business in Terre Haute with partner William T. Stone.

Elizabeth and William Harbert enjoyed the fine view and good conversation in their lakeside home, Tre brah.

Meanwhile Elizabeth earned another degree from Ohio Wesleyan University in 1864. Three years later she published her first book, *The Golden Fleece*.

In 1866 William and his partner sold their shoe business and enrolled in the University of Michigan's School of Law. After earning his degree two years later, he moved to Des Moines, Iowa. Elizabeth and William married on October 17, 1870, after which she joined him in Des Moines and, the following year, published her second book, *Out of Her Sphere*, a work of fiction themed around the societal pressures and expectations facing women of the time.

While in Des Moines, Elizabeth joined and was elected president of the Iowa Woman Suffrage Association. She also had her first child in 1872, a boy whom they named Arthur. Two years later, daughter Corrine was born. While raising her children, Elizabeth maintained her active role in the suffrage movement. She even succeeded in getting the Republican party of Iowa to put a purely women's plank into their state platform. Elizabeth was also the first woman to design and secure the adoption of a women's plank by a political party.

In 1874 two big things happened in the Harbert household, they had baby number three: another daughter, Boynton Elizabeth; and they moved to Chicago. By 1876 they made their home in Evanston, Illinois. Here, Elizabeth, would continue her unrelenting efforts in suffrage and other interests, including religion, music, and philanthropy. She also co-founded and presided over the Illinois Social Science Association in 1877, an organization formed "to suggest plans for the advancement of industrial, intellectual, social educational, and philanthropic interests..."

Elizabeth pursued her writing as well, this time for *Chicago Inter-Ocean* and was soon hired to be the editor of a section, called "Women's Kingdom," which she performed admirably for eight years before quitting due to its "anti-prohibition, anti-suffrage editorial board."

After leaving *Inter-Ocean* in 1884, Elizabeth founded and edited her own monthly women's newspaper, called *The New Era*. Shortly thereafter, she became a founding member of the Illinois Women's Press Association (IWPA), dedicated to the "advocacy of suffrage and the advancement of women in the professions..."

It was around this time that Elizabeth and William built their new cottage in Williams Bay, which they named Tre brah—Harbert spelled backwards—where they enjoyed the cool lakeside breeze buffeting off the high shoreline. They also got together with like-minded neighbors and visitors, such as Dr. Alice Stockham of the Vralia Camp and R. B. McMullen of Maples, and the famous suffragette, Susan B. Anthony, who arrived here during the summer of 1886 for meetings about suffrage, strategy and other human rights topics.

Back in Evanston, Elizabeth was elected to the board of the Evanston Girl's Industrial School and organized the Women's Club of Evanston (1889), where she served as president for seven years. Elizabeth was also elected president of the National Household Economics Association and published her third book in 1892, *Amore*, a philosophical love story.

In 1906 the Harberts moved to Pasadena, California, where their youngest daughter, Boynton, followed in her mother's footsteps as a civic leader. Daughter Corrine joined them as well. There, in Pasadena, Elizabeth continued her suffrage efforts and was voted vice president of both the Woman's Civic League of Pasadena and the Southern California Woman's Press.

Less than three months from seeing Elizabeth's life's work as a suffragist come to fruition, William passed away at the age of 77. Elizabeth, a tireless torchbearer for the suffragist movement, lived to see the day the 19th amendment was passed on June 4, 1919. Before her death on January 19, 1925, she was given an honorary Ph.D. from Ohio Wesleyan.

COURTESY OF JUDY VOSE

# SUNNY HILL

**BUILT:** 1901–1902

**STYLE:** DUTCH COLONIAL REVIVAL.

**ORIGINAL OWNERSHIP:** J.J. Mogg (1901–1929); Edward and Amma Blomeyer family (1929–present)

**LOCATION:**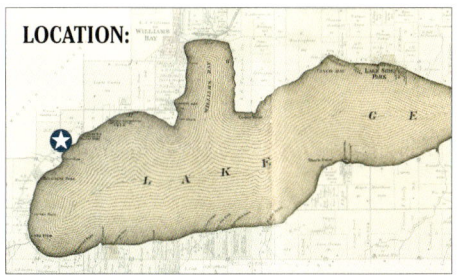

**WHAT'S IN A NAME:** One day Amma saw a house she wanted on Geneva Lake and told her husband. "I found us a house on a sunny hill… Honey, you can't have your boat on Lake Michigan, but you can have a boat on Lake Geneva."

**ALL IN THE FAMILY:** Millard "Grandpa" Mogg built the house for his daughter in 1901–1902 in what's now known as the Sunny Hill Historic District. He lived just west in Angel's Flight (c. 1904). Also in that district were Bromley Hill (1893–97), and the Roberts House (1893–97).

©LAURA SIMPSON

**PROPERTY DETAILS:** Sunny Hill is a Dutch colonial revival with architectural elements such as a gabled roof with Flemish eaves. There is also a small, front-gabled, vernacular caretaker's house made of clapboard near the edge of the property that in recent years was updated with a bathroom and heat; a four-car garage with an apartment overhead for the driver; and a laundry house.

**HEART AND SOUL:** "Grandfather lived there every summer after they bought it," says Blomeyer's granddaughter, Judy Vose, "and there were winter parties there. Guests would fly in, land on the ice, have dinner and leave.

"We came almost every week and we'd fish, walk the lake [sic], swim, boat, sail, ('everyone sailed in those days'), row boat, play in the woods, play cowboys and Indians. It was the era. You were expected to stay outside and amuse yourself." After Edward died in the early 1960s, Amma passed Sunny Hill on to her son.

COURTESY OF KEN AND TONI HARKNESS

# HOUSE ON A HILL

**BUILT:** 1905        **STYLE:** ENGLISH COTTAGE

**ORIGINAL OWNERSHIP:**
Judge and Mrs. Christian C. Kohlsaat and descendents.

**WHAT'S IN A NAME:**
The land upon which the Kohlsaats wished to build their summer home was steep, rising 200 yards up from the shore. So, using mules and wagons, the builders notched a landing in the hillside, forever branding the Kohlsaat's home the "House on a Hill."

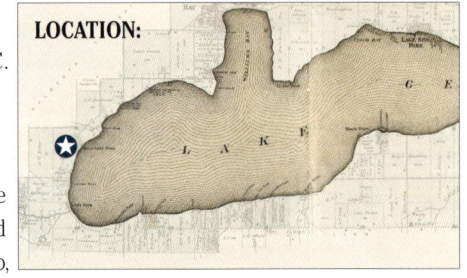

**ALL IN THE FAMILY:** The Judge and his wife had four children: three daughters and one son. Upon Judge Kohlsaat's death, the home was left to his unwed daughter, Edith. Edith eventually passed the house to her niece, Cynthia Kohlsaat Harkness. The house is now owned by Cynthia's son, Ken Harkness.

**PROPERTY DETAILS:**
This beautiful home was patterned after Rydal Mount, the home of England's illustrious poet, William Wordsworth, in England's Lake District. The Kohlsaat family visited England around 1900, touring the district and instantly falling in love with Wordsworth's home. They returned to the States with sketches of the famed cottage and hired Eben E. Roberts to begin the process of designing their own home; with the addition of clothes closets, bathrooms, and service quarters. More than 100 years later, it has retained the same architectual integrity. Alterations include opening the kitchen to the butler's pantry and incorporating the bathroom on the service porch into the interior.

Behind House on a Hill once stood an old barn and a turnaround drive for horses and carriages. Edith built a sitting room above the barn, and installed a piano, a kitchen, two bedrooms, and a loft area. She filled this refuge with beautiful antiques and countless books on poetry, languages, and wildflowers.

**HEART AND SOUL:** Judge Kohlsaat and his family began visiting Geneva Lake in the 1890s and stayed in cottages at Belvidere Park. The Judge and several other gentlemen were so enamored of Geneva Lake that they eventually purchased lots to the west of Belvidere Park. Choosing straws by lottery, Judge Kohlsaat drew the longest straw and chose the plot with the highest elevation.

Edith was a wonderful gardener, and very involved in social events at the lake. A lover of music, she was a member of the Fontana Community Church and often enjoyed music with friends at the church and at her home.

© KAYLA COLLINS

COURTESY OF MARTHA ATKINSON

# PINEGATE

**BUILT:** 1903        **STYLE:** PRAIRE-STYLE

**ORIGINAL OWNERSHIP:**
Sanford S. Vaughan and descendants

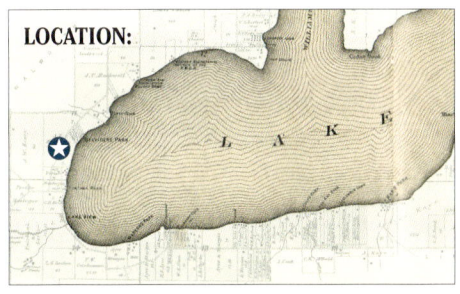

**WHAT'S IN A NAME:**
When Pinegate was built, there were pine trees framing the entrance to the property. Some remain to this day.

**ALL IN THE FAMILY:** Upon his death, Sanford S. Vaughan passed the home to his son, Howard A. Vaughan. Pinegate is now owned by Howard's daughter Martha Vaughan and her late husband, George Atkinson.

**PROPERTY DETAILS:**
Located next door to House on a Hill, Pinegate was built on one of several equally sized lots bought by a group of gentlemen who summered together at Belvidere Park. Each lot offered lake frontage and extended to the other side of what is now North Lake Shore Drive. In 1900 the men drew straws to determine who received ownership of the lots that varied in topography.

©KAYLA COLLINS

Sanford S. Vaughan, owner of a hand tool manufacturing company in Chicago, lived in a prairie-style house in Oak Park that had been designed by architect Eben E. Roberts, a Wright-school architect. So, when it came time to build his summer home, Vaughan was influenced by the style of his Oak Park home and decided to build a similar structure at the lake.

Built in 1903, Pinegate's exterior was originally red stucco with expansive eaves. Along with the main house, a horse and carriage barn and pump house were built. In the 1940s, the barn (no longer needed for horses) was converted to a guest house that is still in use today. The pump house, also still standing, has become a tool shed.

Also in the 1940s, the house was winterized by installing new doors and windows; some of its original design was lost in the renovation. In the 1990s a garage and additional living space were added to the rear of the home. Today the fifth generation of Vaughan children summer in Lake Geneva as well. "I honor the fact that there is a generational love affair with Lake Geneva," says Mrs. Atkinson.

COURTESY OF MILLICENT FERRIS

# FERRIS HOUSE

**BUILT:** LATE 1800s

**ORIGINAL OWNERSHIP:**
Unknown; Henry Lakin Ferris established by 1904

**ALL IN THE FAMILY:** Three generations of the Ferris family enjoyed this house. After selling the home, descendants of the family remained in the area, purchasing houses in places such as Buena Vista and Elgin Club.

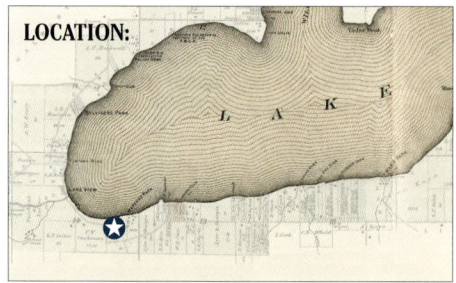

**LOCATION:**

**PROPERTY DETAILS:** Wrought iron still found on the estate was forged by Ferris's own company. The lampposts flanking the portico were among the first oil lamps used in Harvard, Illinois.

**HEART AND SOUL:** Married to Millicent Moser, Henry Ferris was a cousin to George W. G. Ferris, inventor of the famed Ferris Wheel. Henry was an inventor in his own right, too, patenting a hay carrier he devised in 1883 while working at his creamery near Alden, Illinois. In his lifetime, Harris had approximately 250 patented inventions. As news of his invention spread, men sought Ferris out, hoping to form a business venture. In the end, Ferris set up shop in the basement of Charles E. Hunt's hardware store. And so began Hunt, Helm, Ferris and Company. Incorporated in 1902, the company would eventually become known as Starline. In addition to farm equipment, they also manufactured "cannon ball vehicles," such as children's wagons, scooters, and pedal cars. They also made a bicycle they called a "Ferris Wheel."

© CLINT FARLINGER

# RAINBOW POINT

**BUILT:** 1926

**ORIGINAL OWNERSHIP:** The descendants of William H. Emery.

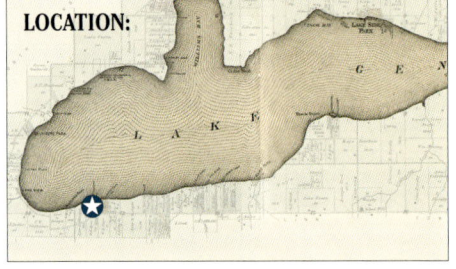

**LOCATION:**

**WHAT'S IN A NAME?** Ida Emery Ullmann, who built the two original homes with her sister-in-law Mrs. John Emery, was an avid gardener. After filling in the swampland to create the Point, she rimmed the edges with an expansive garden that measured 200 feet long and eight feet deep. This "rainbow" of colors delighted Geneva Lake visitors from every angle. Ida kept at least two gardeners on staff throughout the summer. Every fall, they would dig up the flowers and take them back to greenhouses in Elmhurst for the winter.

**ALL IN THE FAMILY:** Rainbow Point has been in the Emery/Ullmann family since the 1920s. The property was purchased by two of William H. Emery's children to create a summer compound for all to enjoy.

**PROPERTY DETAILS:** In 1926 two similar homes were built at Rainbow Point, each with white cedar-shingles and green shutters with carved cut-outs of shamrocks and evergreens. Today the compound includes these two homes, two cottages, and two guest houses.

Using dirt excavated from the building sites and the road, swampland was filled in to create the plateau of Rainbow Point.

**HEART AND SOUL:** The Emery family was well known in Elmhurst and Chicago in the late 1800s as the founders and owners of Chicago Rawhide (established 1867), manufacturers of buggy whips. With the invention of the automobile, they began to manufacture oil seals and belts for machinery. The business (which still flourishes today) remained in the family until the 1980s.

At one time, the Emerys owned nearly 200 acres of land near Duck Point (by Lake Geneva Country Club). Of the Emery's four children, one son established a home on the north side of the lake, and two others built homes at Rainbow Point. According to great-great-grandson Joe Pringle, his mother, Jody, has spent every summer of her 81 years at Rainbow Point, beginning when she was only 10 days old. In 2006 the family held an 80th birthday party for Rainbow Point, attended by more than 150 relatives from across the country. The compound is still owned by Emery descendants in the Ellis, Kinnick, Pringle, and Ullmann families.

© CLINT FARLINGER

COURTESY OF THE LAKE GENEVA PUBLIC LIBRARY

# HAZELDORE

**BUILT:** 1880

**ORIGINAL OWNERSHIP:**
Mr. Spencer (1880s);
B.A. Eckhart (1930–1936);
Frederic Greer (1936–1972)
Michael and Kay O'Malley (1972–present)

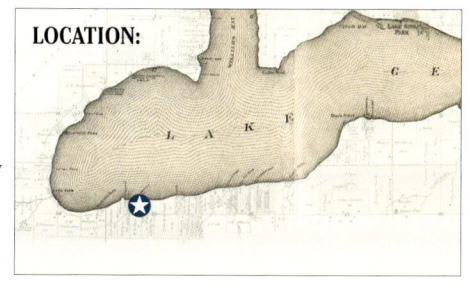

**LOCATION:**

**PROPERTY DETAILS:**
Hazeldore is one of the few true summer homes left on Geneva Lake. The house is comprised of three separate buildings under one roof connected by verandas: the owners' house, the summer kitchen, and the servants' quarters.

The house is known for its beautiful woodwork, created by a Connecticut cabinetmaker imported to work on the home for a reported one dollar per day. His fine craftsmanship can be seen throughout the house, particularly in the walnut and tiger maple-inlaid stairway and the living room ceiling. The ceiling is a mosaic of narrow pieces of wood in the shape of two octagons or giant spider webs. All the rooms are paneled, including the upstairs bedrooms. Another notable centerpiece of the home is a large brick fireplace in the living room.

Few changes have been made since Hazeldore was built. It still has a summer kitchen. Electric lights were installed in the 1930s to replace the delicately etched oil lamps, and two picture windows were added to improve the view.

© CLINT FARLINGER

**HEART AND SOUL:** Hazeldore was built in the 1880s by a gentleman named Spencer, one of a group of wealthy St. Louisians who considered buying all of Lake Geneva to preserve as a private resort. Spencer reportedly walked around the lake over a two-year period in search of the perfect site to build. He chose a plot revered by the Potawatomi as one of the cooler spots on the lake.

Spencer sold the home to the Bernard A. Eckhart family in 1930. Bernard's son, Percy, recalled the long trips in his father's surrey from Chicago to Lake Geneva, which would take two days, with a stopover in Wauconda. For the young boy and his family, the journey was well worth it. As the story goes, Percy's dog, Rex, was such a fan of the lake that he was known to hide in the woods behind Hazeldore when he saw the bags being packed to return to the city.

Frederic "Tombstone" Greer bought Hazeldore in 1936, spending every summer there with his wife and their daughters, Kay and Ann. In 1972 ownership passed to Michael and Kay Greer O'Malley and their two daughters.

As a boy, Frederic and his family lived for a time in an adobe hut in Tombstone, Arizona. His father, Dr. Joseph Greer, treated many of the Native Americans including, as legend has it, Geronimo, the leader of the Apaches. When Dr. Greer traveled into the hills to give aid to an Apache, the troopers warned him of "wild savages," saying his young son Frederic would end up under a tombstone if they continued. The nickname stuck and remained with him for life.

COURTESY OF THE LAKE GENEVA PUBLIC LIBRARY

# OAK SHORES

**BUILT:** 1915

**STYLE:** ENGLISH TUDOR

**ORIGINAL OWNERSHIP:**
Judge Slatery; J.M. Johnson; Edward J. and Minnie Nieubuurt and family (1950–1985)

**PROPERTY DETAILS:**
During the 1950s, Nieubuurt and his wife, Minnie, spent a year or so fixing up the estate's main residence, which included completely refinishing woodwork and repainting. It seems the previous owners had painted the interior walls, but hadn't bothered to move the furniture in the process. The original exterior of Oak Shores was red brick with white stucco and brown trim. The main house also had five fireplaces.

Following work on the main house, Nieubuurt began to turn some of the outbuildings on the estate into livable cottages. According to his grandson, Jim Smith, the caretaker's home was easy, but Nieubuurt also turned the chicken house, the well house, and the ice house into homes; then he built more from scratch, including a log cabin. Many are still part of the Oak Shores subdivision.

**HEART AND SOUL:** Edward J. Nieubuurt was a home builder in Chicago and had a cottage in Camp Sybil, just a short walk away from Oak Shores, which was enjoyed by the family in the summer. Still holding the papers on many of the Chicago homes he built during the depression, Nieubuurt took a horrible financial hit. Fortunately, Nieubuurt had many friends who stood by him, and in 1950, he was able to borrow enough money to buy the estate that would become known as Oak Shores.

The home on the lake was enjoyed every summer by the Nieubuurts and their four children and grandchildren. Minnie passed away in 1965. Ed died tragically in 1975 at the age of 79, killed by a drunken driver as he was on his way back to Chicago after a weekend at the lake. His children sold the house in 1985.

© CLINT FARLINGER

© CLINT FARLINGER

# COTSWOLD COTTAGE

**BUILT:** 1939

**ORIGINAL OWNERSHIP:**
Kunklie family 1939–1946

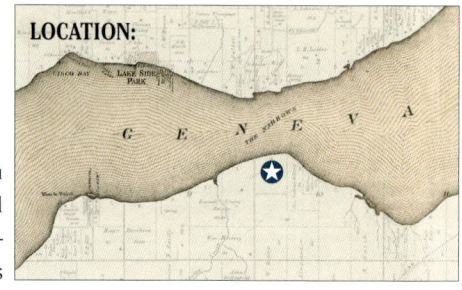

**LOCATION:**

**PROPERTY DETAILS:** In 1939 the Kunklie family, from Elgin, Illinois, hired famed Hinsdale architect, Harold Zook, to design a small cottage to be built on a beautiful south shore stretch of Geneva Lake. The home is a great example of an English cotswold cottage. Its large tudor beams, expansive windows facing the lake, and sweeping archways define the two bedrooms, living room, and den. The kitchen cabinets also showcase Zook's attention to detail and his love of nature with their charming wood carvings of squirrels, owls, and geraniums.

The house stands in its original form, unchanged other than the concrete shingle roof that replaced the original wood shingles. Built with two concrete-poured foundations fortified with steel "I" beams, the home could easily be standing 100 years from now.

**HISTORIC NOTES:** Zook, a student at the Armour Institute (now known as the Illinois Institute of Technology), had apprenticed for Howard Van Doren Shaw and opened his own architectural firm in Chicago in 1924. Zook is well known for his instantly recognizable homes, resplendent with detailed woodwork and hardware, patterned brick and stonework, and multiple rooflines.

COURTESY OF PEG WILLIAMS

# ALLVIEW

**BUILT:** 1905–1906

**ORIGINAL OWNERSHIP:**
John B. Grommes (1904); who then passed the estate to his heirs and son-in-law, Frank A. Rehm, who directed the development of the estate and would reside there until 1945.

**LOCATION:**

**WHAT'S IN A NAME?** The estate was named thus because it stood on a prominent point, affording magnificent views in all directions, "whether one is standing on the broad stone veranda on the north and looking across the bosom of the lake into Geneva Bay," wrote the local paper in 1906, "or from any of the windows to the south over the peaceful country surface…or from the upper windows where the eye takes in the entire west sweep of the lake."

When the estate later came under the ownership of Mrs. John Carpenter Clarke, it was renamed Windmoor.

**PROPERTY DETAILS:** Designed by Richard E. Schmidt of Schmidt, Gardner and Martin in Chicago (designers of the Montgomery Ward Building, the Michael Reese Hospital Building and other notable Chicago buildings), the English-style main residence was constructed for $50,000 by local contractor Charles LaSalle. The walls of the basement and porch were constructed of native boulders; while the first floor was continental paving brick, and the second and third floors were constructed of half-timber panels with pebble dash.

Allview outbuildings dating to the early 1900s include a reservoir that held water pumped from the lake and a coach house (pictured above), a potting shed, a lodge, and the caretaker's cottage (pictured opposite).

Before Allview was constructed atop the twenty-seven acres purchased by Grommes for $20,000, he had the hilltop dug up and moved to fill in swampland at the bottom of the hill. Then he built his home complete with a kitchen that included a butler's pantry, ice chest and cooling room; servant apartments; a screened dining room; a service elevator; a reflection hall with beamed ceilings, tinted walls, and a fireplace; a billiard room; and a library.

"From either side of the main entrance," described a local newspaper account, "broad staircases in white enamel with mahogany extend to a broad landing commanding a grand view of the country and from this other staircase takes you to a similar living room on the second floor."

The house was also heated for year-round use and had its own electric light and power plant, as well as hot and cold running water on every floor.

The estate's acreage (including the wetlands Grommes had filled in) were also developed by famed landscape architect Jens Jensen into a rolling landscape of drives, walks, newly planted groves, as well as a fruit and vegetable garden, and a poultry farm, which, at one time, had some 700 chickens in residence. Some remnants of Jensen's original landscaping remain today.

The top floors of Allview were removed in the early 1950s (which included a library, grand double staircase, and a third floor ballroom), by the estate's third owner, Merril L. Bengston, a Chicago machine tool manufacturer, who turned the once graceful manor into a modern ranch-style dwelling with just seven rooms. The old beams and lumber removed from the upper floors were then used to build another small ranch-style house nearby. The main home has since been razed, but the caretaker's cottage (designed by Hugh Garden, an accomplished Prairie School architect) still remains along with other outbuildings.

**HEART AND SOUL:** Born in Schoenberg, Prussia, in 1844, John B. Grommes came to this country (ultimately to Chicago) and eventually made his fortune in wholesale wine and liquor merchandising with his company Grommes & Ullrich (established 1870), which manufactured liquors with names beautifully reflecting the signs of the times, such as "Great Union Pure Rye," "Pullman Palace Car Rye," and "World's Fair."

He had three daughters: Frieda (Mrs. Armin W. Brand), Clara (Mrs. Frank A. Rehm), and Bertha (Mrs. Alfred Brand). He died at his beloved Lake Geneva estate in 1922.

COURTESY OF THE GENEVA LAKE MUSEUM

# ALLEGHENY

**BUILT:** 1925        **STYLE:** AMERICAN COLONIAL

**ORIGINAL OWNERSHIP:**
Lewis E. Myers

**WHAT'S IN A NAME?** Allegheny was named for Myers's birthplace, Allegheny, Pennsylvania, near Pittsburgh.

LOCATION:

**PROPERTY DETAILS:**
Designed by Howard Van Doren Shaw, this columned American Colonial estate is three stories tall and white with black shutters. The twenty- by forty-foot living room has an original woodblock-printed wallpaper depicting an Italian landscape. The panoramic wallpaper was first printed circa 1900–1912 and inspired by Italian painter Mongin's *L'Arcadie*. Two hundred and forty woodblocks (using ten colors) were used to complete the scene. In recent days, the wallpaper has been reprinted in grey and sepia using the original woodblocks. The living room also has a wall of windows that offer spectacular views of the expansive lawn and lake.

© CLINT FARLINGER

Allegheny's game room is a step back in time with its Early-American design, including its warped wide-board floor—pegged instead of nailed; its ancient hand-hewn, oak-beamed ceiling; and its black, hand-wrought iron door hinges. The fireplace in the billiard room also has a practical bake oven and a nearby niche to hold logs; while the third floor of the estate still contains a ballroom.

In addition to the main house, Allegheny's verdant thirty-six acres (designed by landscape architect Jens Jensen) also has a coach house, as well as the original greenhouses, where Lewis Myers once raised his beloved orchids, which gained both local, national, and international attention.

**HEART AND SOUL:** One wintry day in January of 1940, when the weather was twenty below zero, a fire hit Allegheny and was heading for the greenhouses where Myers housed his treasured orchids. As the fire raged, nearby farmers and neighbors pitched in to help save the more than 200 rare and unique specimens, rushing to their rescue and taking them to their homes. Most of the orchids were saved and kept in suitable environments until they could be safely moved to the nearest greenhouse, owned by the Button Brothers.

After Myers died in 1945, E.C. Styberg, Sr. bought the estate. With the exception of enclosing the dining porch and fireplace closures, Styberg and his son, E.C. Styberg, Jr., have kept the home as it was originally designed. In 1985 Styberg donated the development rights of twelve acres through a conservation easement with the Geneva Lake Conservancy.

**HISTORIC NOTES:** Lewis Edward Myers began his career with the Edison Electric Light Company in Pittsburgh in 1886. In 1890 he transferred to Chicago to run the office of the Detroit Electrical Works. Myers also helped build his fortune in electricity, inspired, no doubt, by his friendship with Thomas Edison. In 1916 Myers purchased a local electric company which would later become known as the Wisconsin Power and Light Company. As a result of his interest in electricity, and friendship with Edison, Myers had many Edison artifacts, including a replica of the first electric light bulb, personal notes and autographed photos of the famed inventor.

Myers founded the L.E. Myers Construction Company in 1891, which still operates today as a contractor of electrical utility construction projects nationwide.

COURTESY OF SUE MORTON

# GENERAL JOHN W. BOYD ESTATE

**BUILT:** LOG CABIN 1843, ENLARGED BY BOYD IN 1870　　　　**STYLE:** COLONIAL

**ORIGINAL OWNERSHIP:**
Percy Baker Farm 1843–1867; General John W. Boyd and descendants (1867–present)

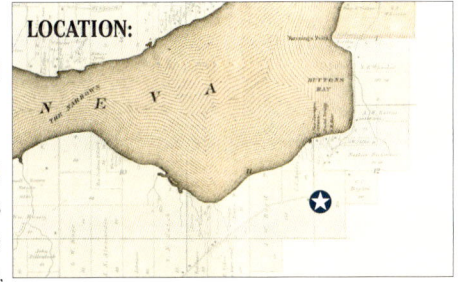

**LOCATION:**

**ALL IN THE FAMILY:** Boyd and his wife, Persis Buell Mudge, had three daughters. Two of their daughters (Francis and Alice) never married and lived in the home until their deaths. Their third daughter, Louise, married Nathan Dickinson, a young man from another prominent local farming family (Walcowis Farms). Together, Louise and Nathan built the now-razed Lake Geneva estate Ivy Lodge less than one-half mile from her childhood home.

Nathan Dickinson was a son of Albert Dickinson, who owned the Albert Dickinson Seed Company in Chicago. The business faced an uncertain future after the Chicago Fire destroyed their building. But the family prevailed because of the swift and hard work of his children. His son Albert became President, Nathan became Treasurer, Charles assumed the role of vice president, and daughter Melissa became the secretary. The family travelled all over the world in search of new seeds. By the 1890s, the Albert Dickinson Seed Company was the largest seed company in the country.

COURTESY OF SUE MORTON

Persis Boyd enjoys a quiet moment with the children of Nathan and Louise Dickinson.

**PROPERTY DETAILS:** Since General Boyd first came to Lake Geneva, four generations of his family have lived in his home, and it remains virtually unchanged. In fact, his portrait still hangs above the large brick fireplace in the living room, surrounded by countless antiques, books, and artifacts collected by the family over many years.

General Boyd's great-granddaughter, Sue Dickinson Morton, now resides in the family home with her husband, Bob, and operates it as a bed and breakfast. The home, a charming, white-gabled colonial house, stands on five and a half acres of land at the intersection of South Lake Shore Drive and Pilgrim Church Road, better known to locals as Boyd's Corners.

Still standing behind the home are the original barn and carriage house. The beams holding up the roof of the barn are trunks of tall pines, and the main supports are large white oak beams, all culled from the property. The carriage house was brilliantly constructed with a second floor. Using a pulley system, the Boyds could store their many carriages on the second floor of the structure, leaving the first floor free for other uses. One of General Boyd's sleighs now resides in the Geneva Lake Museum, and a carriage was given to the Webster House Museum in Elkhorn.

**HEART AND SOUL:** In 1843 a young farmer named John W. Boyd arrived in Wisconsin from New York. Much of the soil on the east coast had gone fallow, and surveyors had deemed the land around Geneva Lake as prime soil for growing wheat.

John W. Boyd was the son of a New York community leader and political legislator. John followed in his father's footsteps in Wisconsin. He received his commission as Major General of the Wisconsin Territorial Militia by Governor Dodge in 1847. That same year, Boyd initially bought the Percy Baker Farm which included a small log cabin built in 1843 and 130 acres of land on the south and east side of Geneva Lake (which over time grew to 320 acres). With the help of builder Alexander Button, Boyd spent three years enlarging the log cabin, and moved his family into their new home on New Year's Day, 1870. Boyd's success at farming helped establish Wisconsin as America's wheat basket. General Boyd was not only a very successful farmer, but an avid student of the science of crop production, raising of livestock, and farm management.

**HISTORIC NOTES:** In addition to being a kind and generous family man, General Boyd is well known for his active political life. Raised as a staunch Democrat by his father, who served in the state senate of New York, Boyd left the Democratic party in the 1850s to support Lincoln and the anti-slavery movement. A profile silhouette of Boyd shows his strong likeness to the man he so admired; he was tall and thin with jet black hair and piercing blue-grey eyes.

Boyd was an active participant in state and county politics as well. He attended the state's first convention in 1846 and helped write the state constitution. He then served eight years as Walworth County's State Senator beginning in 1848. The Geneva Lake area likely would not have seen its popularity and expansion if not for Boyd's efforts in bringing the railroad to the area in 1871. The introduction of the railroad made this beautiful rural farming country accessible to families from as far as Chicago and Milwaukee. Locally, he helped found the Lake Geneva Seminary in 1864, where all three of his girls attended school.

Sometimes referred to as "Wisconsin's Abraham Lincoln," General Boyd left a large and lasting impact on Lake Geneva, and is a shining example of the pioneering spirit that built strong communities, states, and nations.

©KAYLA COLLINS

# NEGAWNI

**BUILT:** 1902 | **RAZED:** 1960

**ORIGINAL OWNERSHIP:**
Arthur Kaye (1873–1889); James Van Inwagen, (1889–1908) H.M. Byllesby (1908–1915)

**LOCATION:**

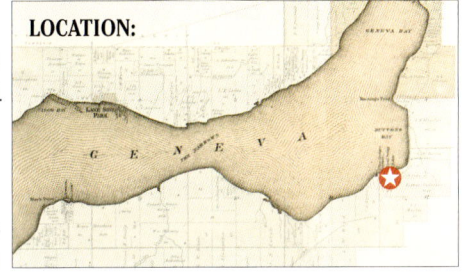

**WHAT'S IN A NAME?**
The property was known as a frequent camping ground of the Potawatomi, so it was no surprise that Van Inwagen named the estate "Negawni." Countless residents spun stories as to the origins of the name, convinced it had great Native American meaning. The truth was much more interesting: it was "Inwagen" spelled backwards. When Henry M. Byllesby purchased the property, he first renamed it Arrowglade in honor of the many arrowheads left on the property by the Potawatomi. In 1916, he would change the name to Holly Bush in honor of his native home in Lincolnshire, England.

**PROPERTY DETAILS:** In 1889 James Van Inwagen of the Tiffany Pressed Brick Company of Chicago purchased five acres of shore property from Arthur Kaye for $6,500. He then hired well-known architect Henry Lord Gay to build a gracious country home with a traditional open veranda from which to enjoy the lake views.

In 1908 Van Inwagen sold the estate to electrical executive Henry M. Byllesby. Byllesby built the gardener's house (pictured at left) that year, and a greenhouse in 1910, both of which remain today as private residences. Then in 1916, he completely transformed the estate from an American country home to an English tudor showpiece reminiscent of the ancestral Byllesby home in England.

**HEART AND SOUL:** Byllesby so loved his time at Geneva Lake that every summer he held a company outing for his employees and their families there. A special train brought families from Union Station to the nearby Zenda station, and private automobiles would abscond them to the Lake Geneva Country Club for the day. Attendees enjoyed boat rides, golf, rowing, fishing, and other sporting games. He even brought an orchestra from Chicago so that guests could dance.

Byllesby died at 65 years of age, his health forever damaged by his experiences in the war. He was buried in Lake Geneva. Hundreds of mourners attended from Chicago, including 150 cadets from Northwestern Military Academy.

**HISTORIC NOTES:** Byllesby was a long-time associate and friend of Thomas Edison. At one time, he served as vice president and general manager of Westinghouse. He later founded H.M. Byllesby and Company, an electrical engineering firm, in Chicago. In 1919 Byllesby was chosen as president of the Chicago branch of the National Security League, an organization devoted to furthering universal military training and preparedness. He had served as a lieutenant colonel in World War I, specifically as a purchasing agent in Great Britain and Scandinavia for the American Expeditionary forces, for which he was awarded the English distinguished service award.

COURTESY OF SUE MORTON

# THE SUMACHS

**BUILT:** 1896

**ORIGINAL OWNERSHIP:**
Charles C. Boyles

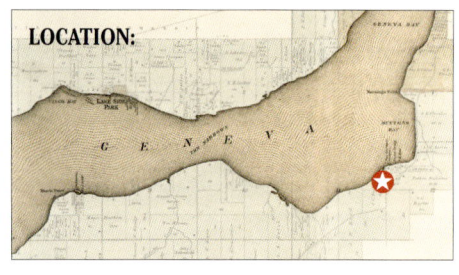

**ALL IN THE FAMILY:**
Boyles' second wife, Hannah Dickinson (whom he married in 1864), was the daughter of Albert and sister of Nathan Dickinson (Ivy Lodge).

**PROPERTY DETAILS:**
Charles C. Boyles, a businessman from Chicago, bought sixty-five acres of land on the south side of the lake near Button's Bay from General John Boyd and built his estate in the early 1880s.

Boyles loved farming and livestock, so in addition to a beautiful home, the property included a tenant's cottage and a number of large barns for livestock. During its heyday, the farm had working horses, driving horses, pigs, Black Leghorns, turkeys, and Jersey cows.

The farm was nearly self-sufficient and included plentiful orchards of apple, cherry, and hickory nut trees; vegetables and flower gardens; and currant, gooseberry, and raspberry bushes. Surrounding these were corn and alfalfa fields, and dense woods.

**HEART AND SOUL:** In 1883, when Mr. Gossage died, Boyles sold the business to Carson Pirie, Scott and Company and retired to Lake Geneva, where he lived with his wife for thirty years. In 1911 he sold the majority of his property to Henry M. Byllesby, who had also purchased the neighboring estate Negawni in 1908.

Boyles eventually retired to Winnetka, Illinois, and died in 1916 at 83 years of age.

**HISTORIC NOTES:** Charles Carroll Boyles was a partner of the Charles Gossage & Company, a dry goods business in Chicago. He was one of the first merchants ever to send circulars and mailings to his customers. He also invented duplicate slips, bound into little books, to keep track of transactions.

Mr. Boyles and his partner and mentor, Charles Gossage, insured their stock and buildings with strong British companies. So when the Great Chicago Fire swept the city, destroying every business in its path, the British firms were able to pay them in full for all they lost and Charles Gossage & Co. survived and thrived.

COURTESY OF THE LAKE GENEVA PUBLIC LIBRARY

# THE KNOLL

**BUILT:** 1885 REBUILT 1906 | **RAZED:** BY FIRE 1905

**ORIGINAL OWNERSHIP:** Samuel and Theodora "Dora" Rumsey Wheeler.

**LOCATION:**

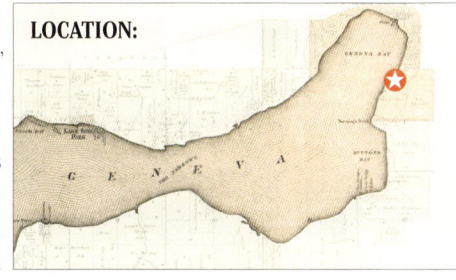

**ALL IN THE FAMILY:** Dora's father, Julian Rumsey, lived just south at Shadow Hill (until 1886). Sister Martha Rumsey Skinner lived further south at Willow Landing.

**PROPERTY DETAILS:** In 1906, the verandahed white house was designed and built by Samuel Wheeler after their first home on the site burned down. The family enjoyed the estate's seventy park-like acres, where they could often be seen riding their horses. To the surprise and delight of many, the home had eight bathrooms at a time when having just one was considered a luxury.

There was said to be a great library at The Knoll, and not just in the library itself. Books could be found in great quantities throughout the house, which offered a "wide selection of everything for the book lover," wrote the *Chicago Tribune*, "from *Pluchard's Lives* to *Gone with the Wind*."

Another feature Wheeler included on the estate was for the seamstress who lived with the Rumseys for more than forty years, Reka Freeze. When she came to do work for Dora, she slept at the farm, so Wheeler built a cinder path from the gate to the house so it would always be dry for her and for Fred Flemming, who used it to bring in the vegetables and milk from the farm. The path was named Fredreka Strassa.

**HEART AND SOUL:** Samuel Wheeler first married Amelia "Meme" Rumsey. She died, however, in 1887, and shortly thereafter, he married her sister, Dora. Together, they had three children. Their youngest, also named Theodora, married William P. Finney after they both matriculated from John Hopkins University with their medical degrees; Theodora specialized in epilepsy. Like her mother before her, Theodora went to Vasser before medical school. Later, when she had children of her own (Theodora, Pamela, William P. Jr., Ellen Rumsey, and Samuel Wheeler), her eldest daughter, Theodora, went to Vasser as well—the third generation of Rumsey women (starting in the 1860s) to attend the prestigious school.

The Doctors Finney kept The Knoll as their summer home. While there, Dora's favorite hobby was spending time at her Story Book Farm, a tearoom and gift shop across the road from their grounds that once served as the farmhouse at Shadow Hill. It had old-fashioned flower gardens and became a popular place for parties.

COURTESY OF THE LAKE GENEVA PUBLIC LIBRARY

# FAIR OAKS

**BUILT:** 1889

**ORIGINAL OWNERSHIP:**
James Sager Norton

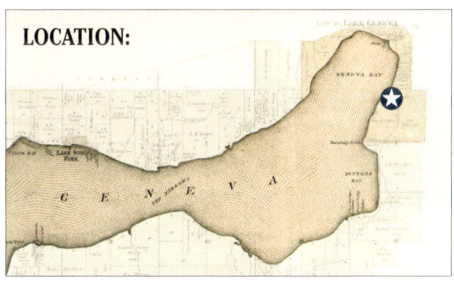

**LOCATION:**

**WHAT'S IN A NAME?**
The house has had two names: Fair Oaks, its most current name, and Summer Haven.

**ALL IN THE FAMILY:** Fanny Rumsey Norton's uncle, Julian Rumsey, lived at Shadow Hill. Cousin Martha Rumsey Skinner lived at Willow Landing. Cousin Dora Rumsey Wheeler lived at the Knoll.

**PROPERTY DETAILS:**
A three-story addition was built for Norton by local builder, Richard Soutar, in the fall of 1894, at a cost of $2,500–$3,000. Little has changed on the house since.

**HEART AND SOUL:** After Norton married Francis (Fanny) Rumsey, he bought land from Samuel Wheeler and built a cottage along the shores of the lake at a cost of $12,000. A terrible storm whipped across the lake, doing considerable damage to many properties in the Town of Linn, including Norton's. In addition to his lawn being torn up, his steam yacht, *Tattler,* was loosed and washed out into the lake.

After Norton died in September of 1896, the property was purchased the following year by Albert Keep, a successful young businessman and president of the Chicago and Northwestern Railroad until 1887, at which time he became Chairman of the Board.

In 1906 a fire broke out on the second floor of the estate. The cause of the fire was unknown and the only real damage (thanks to the quick actions of the Keeps) was caused by water and heat. Albert died the year following the fire, but his wife stayed on in the home, and was a beloved member of the community until her death in 1915.

The house then passed to Edmund. J. Doering in 1916, who kept it until 1924; then to O. P. Curran, Jr, who sold it to M. Karpen of Karpen Chicago Furniture Company. In 1937 Joseph E. Swanson purchased the estate and its ten acres, who passed it on to his son Ralph E. Swanson, who owned it until 1987. Bill and Judy Pollard bought Fair Oaks in 1987 and have restored the estate to its original appearance.

© CLINT FARLINGER

COURTESY OF SUE MORTON

# WILLOW LANDING

**BUILT:** 1872      **STYLE:** GEORGIAN

**ORIGINAL OWNERSHIP:**
Martha Rumsey Skinner (1890–1919);
Florence Reynolds (1930s–1995)

**LOCATION:**

**ALL IN THE FAMILY:** Martha Rumsey Skinner's father Julian Rumsey, had lived just south at Shadow Hill until 1886. Her sister, Dora Rumsey Wheeler, bought The Knoll south of Shadow Hill.

**PROPERTY DETAILS:** When Linda Learn and Andy Loughlin bought Willow Landing in 1996, there were ten bedrooms, two kitchens upstairs, and eight bathrooms in the approximately 6,000-square-foot home. By then, the house was in a great state of disrepair. Yet having dreamed of owning this house her whole life, Linda couldn't let this opportunity pass her by. No matter how scary the nighttime noises or how costly the remodel—which took an entire year to complete—it would become their slice of heaven. From enclosing the porch and adding a veranda; to removing the upstairs kitchens and combining the rooms to make five bedrooms, each with a bathroom; to extending the garage and redoing the drafty, leaky, moldy interior, there was no question in their minds about saving this lakeside treasure—even as the costs began to add up. As they remodeled, original pieces remained from when they bought the home, including the fireplace andirons, some bowls, a book, and an antiquated garbage can in one of the bathrooms.

**HEART AND SOUL:** Martha Rumsey, whose family had summered on Geneva Lake for several years, and whose father had won many yacht races with his beloved *Nettie*, married Nathan H. Skinner in October 1884. They lived together in Taunton, Massachusetts, until Nathan's death, after which Martha returned to live with her mother. In 1890 Martha bought Willow Landing, where she and sister Eliza lived until 1919. One of their favorite pastimes was racing boats.

In the mid to late 1930s Florence Reynolds bought the estate, where she raised her children. She rented out the estate briefly while she lived with her new husband in town, but in the end, came back to Willow Landing, where she lived until she passed away at 103 years old in 1995.

© CLINT FARLINGER

# A Letter to Emily Baker

Dear Emily:
It was a little less than a year ago while out for a Sunday drive with no particular place to be that a "right turn only" sign led Andrew and me unexpectedly to the magnificent place we now call home. As we pulled into the drive of your grand old Victorian, standing vacant and still, the sun was just setting, illuminating the cold, winter sky with its warm radiance. Perhaps it was just a reflection in the old, wavy glass, but as I looked back to the house, the windows of the turret glowed as if lit from within by an inviting fire.

Just then, I heard a voice. "Welcome to Emily Baker's summer cottage." The realtor, standing near the home's "For Sale" sign, invited us in. Stepping inside, we were immediately captivated by the home's grand interior, especially its unique and intricately carved fireplaces, (thirteen, we would find, in all) each original, with antique mirrors and mantles surrounded by brightly colored Mediterranean tiles. A massive wooden lion, hand-carved into the mantle, guards the largest of these, standing at least twelve feet high. In the mouth of the beast is a great ring (resembling a door knocker) reminding me of a Bible verse I learned in Sunday school so long ago, "Knock and the door shall be open unto you."

I continued to think of this verse as I climbed the great staircase and let my mind daydream about what it would be like to actually own a home of this magnitude. The realtor explained that the house, built in 1885, encompassed 17,000 square feet and had thirty rooms, each still boasting the original brass doorknobs and window closures. Standing on the landing of the second floor, we felt dwarfed under the three-panel stained glass window that hardly seemed weathered from the hundreds of winters it has seen come and go. As we continued up the staircase, Andrew took my hand and pointed again at the sun that could now be seen setting in every window we passed—a view created not merely by chance, but designed with purpose and respect for the beautiful lake that lay just beyond the panes. It was just about then that our purpose, too, became clear.

As soon as we were officially handed the keys, I began preparing the home for a new generation of guests; decorating each room guided by thoughts of you, Emily. Was this your place for lively entertaining and lavish lakeside parties, I would ask myself, or was it meant as a quiet retreat for you and your five grown children; a special and familiar place adjacent to your husband's childhood home?

I still pause each day at the entryway where your husband, Robert's, initials are inlaid in wood and I think of the sadness you must have felt when, at only 43 years old, he passed away, leaving you just shy of your twenty-fifth wedding anniversary. I read about what a great and respected man Robert was, both civically and professionally, working his way up from a store clerk in a Racine hardware store, to amassing great wealth through investing his earnings in the J. Case Company (where he was originally a bookkeeper). Serving as Racine's Mayor at the age of 35 and then several terms as a State Senator, the list of your husband's accomplishments were long for a life so brief.

Settling here from Vermont, Robert's father, Charles Minton Baker, was first enticed to the shores of Geneva Lake by the City of Lake Geneva, I am told, which offered the lawyer a large plot of lakefront land (part of which is now Baker Park in front of our home) where Charles could set up practice as Walworth County's first attorney. They say it didn't take too much enticing, for Charles was soon under the spell of this sparkling, spring-fed lake and moved his young family here by covered wagon

in 1838. The very next year your husband, Robert Hall Baker, was born. He must have told you many stories of his childhood by the lake and I can only imagine that was part of the reason you chose to build your summer home here.

So many questions, Emily. So many years.

While we were in the process of unpacking, a woman who introduced herself as Felice Pappas paid me a visit. Felice, whose parents once owned the home (known then as the St. Moritz), had grown up here and had come with her father, Peter, to share the history the home. I then learned it was Felice's mother who was instrumental in having the house put on the prestigious National Register of Historic Places in 1984, under the home's original name Redwood Cottage. I hung on every detail they told us, amazed to find out that in the home's 125 year history, the Pappas' were one of only two families (besides my own) to raise their children here. My son delighted in the news that he would be the first boy to actually grow up in the house and immediately asked Felice if she had ever slid down the long banister in the great hall. Felice smiled wryly and suggested there were likely a few others who could not resist the lure of the stair rail, especially considering the house was briefly used as a boarding school for the Lake Geneva Seminary for Young Ladies. The Baker House was also once part of a larger hospital complex, called Oakwood. Set up more like a hotel rather than a hospital, Oakwood was considered a "fashionable" sanitarium where the well-to-do could comfortably recuperate in its spa-like setting from everything from surgery to "light nervous disorders."

Peter also shared with us the time capsule he discovered in the floor: the Victorian shoe (presumably yours or your only daughter's), an Edison-style light bulb with the filament still intact, and the signatures of the home's carpenters on swatches of wallpaper. Not only did I now have a clear vision of your original design ideas, Emily, but also there I was, holding pieces of your personal history! We also recently met a man whose great-grandfather had installed the original inlaid wood floors each hand-cut piece made from five different varieties of wood, still in impeccable condition and a powerful tribute to the skilled artisans you once employed here.

Each new day we are learning more interesting facts about the home and are slowly weaving together the pieces of its rich history. Last week, our neighbors told us that they had purchased the Baker House's original pump organ and were gracious enough to offer us the opportunity to display it in the home once more.

Playing a part in the next stage of the house's history is both a privilege and a blessing, and it is in your family's honor, that we have renamed our home the Baker House, and have started a new house tradition. Every evening at sundown we put on vintage hats and ring a bell throughout the home signifying it is time to gather in the garden with family and friends to watch the glorious sunset. During this celebration we speak of the history of your family and of this grand, old manor, this graceful giant, and sylvan summer retreat; and then we raise our champagne-filled glass to the sky and toast to the "Summer Cottage of Emily Baker."

With Sincerest Thanks for the Lovely Home You Have Left Us,

Bethany Souza

# NOT TO BE FORGOTTEN

**ANCHORAGE** (Courtesy of Sue Morton)

**BRIARWOOD** (Courtesy of the Lake Geneva Public Library)

**OUR HOME** (Courtesy of Sue Morton)

**WALDECK** (Courtesy of the Lake Geneva Public Library)

**LINN HAVEN** (Courtesy of Sue Morton)

**HILL VIEW** (Courtesy of Sue Morton)

Captain Wiley M. Egan owned **Anchorage** from 1880–1922. The prominent Chicago businessman was president of the Board of Trade in 1867–1868, and was elected to the state assembly in 1871. For many years he was heavily involved in Great Lakes commerce and owned 25 different sailing and steam vessels.

In 1886, John Williams purchased land on which to build the lakeside estate, **Briarwood**, for himself and his family. Sadly, Williams died two years later of pneumonia. His wife, however, would enjoy the home for another twenty-four years, adding on to the estate and making various improvements over the years. She died in 1912. Both John and his wife are buried in Oak Hill Cemetery.

In 1886 G. B. Shaw purchased seven and a half acres of the recently closed Warwick Park and then purchased an additional five acres with his good friend Oscar D. Wetherall. Shaw would build **Hill View** the following year; while Wetherall built **Linn Haven** (a mirror image of Shaw's home) that same year. The properties were sold to Catherine Seipp (Black Point) in 1903, who had the homes razed, the land becoming part of Black Point's expansive estate.

Edward Norton purchased acreage from Arthur Kaye in 1890 to build **Our Home** on the south shore.

G. L. Paddock purchased nearly fifteen acres in 1892, and sold a 4.96 acre parcel to Francis Lackner (a Chicago lawyer) who built **Waldeck**. Colonel R.C. Clowry, president of Western Union Telegraph, purchased Waldeck for $25,000 in 1900 and would remain its owner until 1906. Edward Glennon, Vice President of New York Central Railway System, then bought the estate and renamed in Bendemere, remaining until 1941. When the estate was sold to Earl Dreschler in the 1950s, he changed its name once again, this time to Lakewood. Around the year 2000, the Wrigley family purchased Lakewood for their extended family.

> "*Right in the midst of millionaire homes and villas—in the exquisite and romantic Lake Geneva district—you can, for very little money, have your own summer home and live royally.*"
>
> I. Ferguson & Co. full page ad, *Lake Geneva News Tribune*, May 13, 1926

# LAKE GENEVA'S LITTLE SISTER

In 1837 Christopher Payne, the county's first official settler, moved his interests to Duck Lake—as Lake Como was first known—building a dam and a mill on Como's east end. The dam was said to have raised the level of the lake by six feet (to about nine feet) leading most to believe "Lake" Como, in essence, began life more as a watershed and wetlands. The original dam was washed away in a savage storm in the 1850s, but was rebuilt—several times over the following decades.

Within the next decade, farmers began to buy up the fertile land surrounding the newly formed lake (now about four miles long, a half a mile wide, with about eight and a half miles of shoreline), for $1.25 per acre. By 1846 the popularity and population of the area had grown; as had the harvests of the families farming the land surrounding Lake Como, who would produce 30,000 bushels of wheat that year and enjoy a general abundance for years to come. Although the fecund fields proved excellent farmland, the lands immediately surrounding Como were far too labor intensive to work, so the farmers began selling much of the shoreline to Chicagoans looking for summer retreats.

Very slowly, Lake Como would begin to attract its share of summer tourists and sportsmen. Yet it would not be Chicago's industrial tycoons who would claim the shoreline, but rather those individuals who fell into the category of industry's worker bees—the average Joe looking for his own modest summer getaway.

"Lake Como is preparing for a big summer," reported the *Lake Geneva News* in April of 1917, "Chicago workers have had a prosperous winter. We expect to get our share when the workers come to fish and rest." The newspaper went on to describe the busy business endeavors along the shores of Geneva Lake's pretty, little sister lake. New piers and bungalows were being built and fishing boats were being both built and readied for the season. Old Tom Pine's, a favorite watering hole, was also sprucing itself up and adding a grocer for the lake's summer residents and visitors.

Lake Como was not only becoming a modest weekend getaway for working-class Chicagoans, but had become a favorite among fishermen. "The lake is a real paradise for bait casters," reported the *Angler's Exchange* in the 1920s, "and is considered the finest black bass fishing in the southern part of Wisconsin."

"The advantages of fishing in this lake," the enticing news feature read, "are that anywhere you cast you are likely to get a strike—especially in the western portion of the lake."

During the early twenties, the small, shallow lake had only one hotel, Notter's Lake Como Hotel, which opened in 1921 by the Hermansen Family. The average Como Hotel resident was, according to Inar Hermansen, between his late thirties and early fifties and not a big spender, but had enough vacation money with which to enjoy his stay, which more often than not entailed a lazy day on the boat, casting lines into the water. And with its large ice house where the day's catch could be stored and a dinner bell announcing the start of the evening's meal echoing across the lake, the Lake Como Hotel was a fisherman's paradise.

A far cry from the lavish resorts and hotels along Geneva Lake's shoreline, the Lake Como Hotel was originally a house built by a man in the commercial ice business. Until the advent of refrigeration, ice was big business for Lake Como (see page 21) which had several large ice houses and direct railroad lines leading to and from Chicago along its shores. The main portion of the original hotel structure was a Danish Pavilion that had been part of Denmark's exhibit for Chicago's World's Fair in 1893. It was moved to the site at the turn of the century.

The Lake Como Hotel offered a mere thirty rooms, but they were neat, comfortable, modestly priced, and a train from Chicago would let passengers off just a few feet from the hotel's front entrance. However, unlike Lake Geneva's "Millionaires Special," which dropped its wealthy passengers dockside where their luxurious steam yachts awaited, Como's passengers were dropped at a train station which was, according to local accounts, a simple boxcar fitted with a small platform. The disembarking area was said to be so small that in order for passengers to detrain, they had to sit in a certain car in order to be let out onto the makeshift platform rather than into a ditch by the tracks.

Once off the train, visitors were greeted by a cast of local teens hired each summer to care for guests of the hotel. Soon the faces and families became familiar and the homey little resort was where families would return for gen-

A typical, relaxing summer day at Lake Como, where the prices are a bit higher than they were in the 1920s and the newspaper is not included.
© CLINT FARLINGER

In contrast to its "big sister," Geneva Lake, Lake Como was more of a quiet lake where working-class families came to swim, fish, and eventually, live.

erations to come. In fact, the community of regulars visiting Lake Como often gathered as one large family to dine, sun, fish, swim, row, play, or just plain recline.

During the early 1920s, Lake Como saw many summer cottages (many of which would eventually become year-round residences) springing up alongside its shores. Long, narrow lots (Como Beach Subdivision) were sold by the *Chicago Evening Post* for $50 (which included a subscription to the newspaper); and in 1926, for about 25 cents down, visitors to Lake Como were given the opportunity to become lakeshore landowners, with lots at North Geneva Highlands being offered for as low as $69.50. *The Chicago Evening Post* also erected a clubhouse in 1926 where Como residents could gather to socialize or meet as part of the Lake Como Beach Property Owners Association.

Many new Lake Como homeowners became disillusioned with their summer retreats when the weeds (cut down by the newspaper the year prior) began to overtake the shallow lake once again. As the water levels dropped, vegetation began to decay and fish began to die and things were not looking good for the future of the lake. Yet there still remained a loyal group of residents who held their land in high regard and worth fighting for. So, for the next several years they battled landowners and mother nature and finally raised enough money to build a new dam capable of maintaining the necessary water levels. The dam was completed in August of 1935 and a great celebration was held in the Clubhouse. (The clubhouse, which witnessed many good times over the years, underwent restoration in 1993.) In the years to follow, life beside the tiny lake began to settle in.

In the days of prohibition, both the northern and southern shores of Lake Como became the sites for several popular speak easies which not only attracted the non-teetotalling-types, but those who thrived on this blatant disregard for the nation's imposed temperance movement. As a result, the Lake Como Hotel also became a popular spot for another type of guest, which just so happened to be the power and wealth behind Chicago's underworld. Infamous gangsters such as Al "Scarface" Capone, George "Bugs" Moran, Jack "Machine Gun" McGurn, and John Dillinger, would use this quiet retreat as their cozy getaway from the rigors of terrorizing Chicago; while at the same time continuing to promote their interests in drinking and gambling. Rumor has it that during a raid of the hotel one evening (with sights set on "The Sewer," the bar located in the hotel's basement) several slot machines were dumped out of sight and into Lake Como where they are said to remain today.

In the wake of the Great Depression and Prohibition, life around Como began to settle in once again.

"Relaxing is a favorite pastime at Como," read a 1940s brochure. "Either by yourself or in the company of friends, there are comfortable chairs in the garden, by the lake shore or on one of the many verandas… If it's a sun-tan [sic] your heart desires, the new 150 ft. long sun pier with its special sun-sofas, is the ideal spot, and is the center of much [jesting] and gaiety among our summer visitors."

And when Lake Como's community was looking for mouth-watering BBQ or sundaes piled high with toppings, they might head over to the Blue Spruce Beer Garden, which would welcome people for several decades under different owners.

The Lake Como Hotel would meet new owners in the next few decades and undergo name and structural changes, first as the Red Chimney Inn and then becoming the now well-known French Country Inn after the Navilio family purchased the hotel in the mid-eighties.

The lake, too, as well as its residents, has faced the inevitable changes and challenges brought about by each new generation. The shoreline now overlooks Geneva National and its golf courses, Interlaken is now The Lodge at Geneva Ridge, and much of the east end of the lake is now under the control of the Wisconsin DNR, who is trying to effectively manage both its flora and fauna. Yet around the shores of Lake Como there still remains a quiet, modest community where friendly neighborhood bars invite guests to find a shady spot and order a cold one, where a quiet stroll along a nature trail helps one escape the rigors and reminders of urban life, and where, hidden in the peaceful shallows of this little lake, the day's catch awaits.

# INDEX

"The Farms" . . . 109
"The Sewer" . . . 154
18th Amendment . . . 27
21st Amendment . . . 27

## A

A Traveller from Altruria . . . 81
Abbott II, Wilson Ruffin . . . 81
Abbott, Gus . . . 81
Abolitionist . . . 10
Admiral . . . 22
Agricultural . . . 63
Albert Dickinson Seed Company . . . 138
Alert . . . 45, 57
Alice Hackett . . . 58
Allview . . . 131
Allegheny . . . 42, 54, 134, 136
Allerton Packing Company . . . 109
Allerton, Agnes . . . 108
Allerton, Robert Henry . . . 108, 109
Allerton, Samuel Waters . . . 37, 54, 108, 109
Aloha Lodge . . . 54
Alpine Villa . . . 111
American Angler . . . 60
American Colonial . . . 134
American Legion . . . 72
American Society of Landscape Architects . . 42
Amore . . . 115
Anchor Line . . . 57
Anchorage, The . . . 37
Anderson, Gilbert M. . . . 25
Andrae, Charles . . . 48
Andy Gump statue . . . 32
Angel's Flight . . . 117
Anthony, Susan B. . . . 115
Anti-Slavery Churchman, The . . . 15
Antlers Boarding House, The . . . 94
Ara Glen . . . 82, 84
Arabian Horse Association . . . 113
Arabian Horses of Kemah, The . . . 113
Architectural Review . . . 41
Ariel . . . 56
Armour Institute . . . 130
Armstrong, Neil . . . 84
Arrow . . . 20, 46
Arrowglade . . . 141
Art Institute of Chicago . . . 37
Asbury University . . . 114
Atalanta . . . 56
Atkinson, George . . . 121
Aurora . . . 45, 57
Aust, Franz . . . 42
Automobiles . . . 68
Ayer Estate . . . 11, 30
Ayer, Edward E. . . . 30, 37, 45, 46, 76
Ayer, Emma Auusta Burbank . . . 30

## B

Bailey, Allen . . . 71
Baker House, The . . . 94, 150
Baker Park . . . 99
Baker, Charles Minton . . . 149
Baker, Emily . . . 94, 149
Baker, Robert Hall . . . 149
Banana Boat . . . 57
Banta, Mister . . . 93
Barker, Terissa Ann . . . 8
Barnard, George B. . . . 45, 54
Barnard, Professor E.E. . . . 23
Barnes, W. Anson . . . 80
Bartlett, Adolphus C. . . . 23, 37
Bates, Alben F. Peter . . . 46
Bates, Benjamin . . . 46
Bates, William . . . 54
Bavaria . . . 45, 57
Baxter, Mary Short . . . 29
Beamsley, John . . . 21
Beauvais, Walter . . . 46
Beaux Arts . . . 40
Beebe, J.D. . . . 48
Beery, Wallace . . . 25
Beidler, Herbert Alpine . . . 21, 111
Beidler, Ida Louisa Merriman . . . 111
Bell, Mary Gridley . . . 97
Bella Vista Suites . . . 94
Belle of the Lake . . . 57
Belvidere Park . . . 87, 118
Beman, Solomon Spencer . . . 40
Bendemere . . . 54, 151
Bengston, Merril L. . . . 133
Bennett, Kate . . . 109
Berthelet, Arthur . . . 25
Bethlehem Lutheran Church . . . 84
Big Foot Beach State Park . . . 99
Big Foot Lake . . . 11, 88
Billie . . . 46
Billings, C.K.G. . . . 37
Bissell, Miss . . . 93
Black Hawk War . . . 11
Black Point . . . 29, 37, 46, 80. 151
Blackstone Theater . . . 41
Blackstone Hotel . . . 41
Blacktoft . . . 40, 108
Blair, Lieutenant Paul R. . . . 26
Blakeslee, Orville . . . 76
Blomeyer, Edward and Amma . . . 117
Blood of the Arab, the World's Greatest War Horse, The . . . 113
Blue Spruce Beer Garden . . . 154
Boat Builders & Designers . . . 45
Bogart . . . 40
Boisot, E.K. . . . 107
Bon Ami Club . . . 80, 90, 92
Bonnie Brae . . . 37, 42, 45, 46, 54
Book of Lake Geneva, The . . . 30, 69
Boyd, General John W. . . . 137, 138, 142
Boyles, Charles Carroll . . . 142
Brand, Mrs. Alfred (Bertha) . . . 133
Brand, Mrs. Armin W. (Frieda) . . . 133
Briarwood . . . 151
Brick Church Cemetery . . . 48
Brink, John . . . 14, 29
Bromley Hill . . . 117
Brooklawn . . . 88
Brooks, Elymas . . . 20
Brown, Charles . . . 29
Brown, Morton . . . 85
Buckingham, Alvah . . . 17
Buckingham, C.P. . . . 17
Buena Vista . . . 88, 122
Bullock, John . . . 56, 65
Bureau of Lighthouses and Lightships . . . 46
Burke, James . . . 23
Burton House . . . 76
Burton, John E . . . 20, 21, 57, 58
Butternuts . . . 37
Button, Alexander Henry . . . 8, 48, 138
Button's Bay . . . 8, 21, 94, 99, 142
Byllesby, Henry M. . . . 141, 142

## C

Caldwell, Alfred . . . 42
Callaghan, Andrew J. . . . 25
Camp Augustana . . . 79, 82, 84
Camp Collie . . . 46
Camp Jolly . . . 80
Capone, Al "Scarface" . . . 154
Capron, Wheeler and Whipple . . . 15
Carpenter, Hubbard . . . 42
Carson Pirie Scott and Co. . . . 142
Cedar Point . . . 111
Ceylon Court . . . 25, 37, 42, 54, 64, 85
Chalmers, William . . . 37
Chandler, Frank . . . 42
Chapel on the Hill . . . 82, 84
Chapin, Simeon B . . . 27, 29, 42, 48, 64
Chaplin, Charlie . . . 25
Charles Gossage & Co. . . . 142
Charles Minton Baker House . . . 94
Chicago & Northwestern Railway . . . 18, 20, 99, 113, 144
Chicago Board of Trade . . . 76
Chicago Boys Club . . . 113
Chicago City Railway Company . . . 37
Chicago Club . . . 79, 90
Chicago Community Trust . . . 113
Chicago Daily News . . . 17
Chicago Evening Post . . . 153, 154
Chicago Golf Club . . . 40
Chicago Historical Society . . . 18
Chicago Inner Mission of the Illinois Conference of the Augustana Synod . . 82, 84
Chicago Inter-Ocean . . . 115
Chicago Juvenile Protective Association . . 106
Chicago Park System . . . 42
Chicago Public Library . . . 41
Chicago Railroad . . . 53, 57
Chicago Rawhide . . . 124
Chicago School System . . . 81
Chicago Tribune, The . . . 18, 23, 57, 59, 69
Chicago World's Fair 21, 37, 38, 40, 65, 109, 153
Chicago Yacht Club . . . 46
Chicago's South Parks . . . 42
Chicago's Union Stock Yards . . . 109
Chief Big Foot . . . 11, 29, 88
Chief Black Hawk . . . 88
Chipmunk Club . . . 88
Church, Cyrus . . . 7
Cisco . . . 48, 59, 60, 61, 82
Cisco Beach Camp . . . 82
Cisco Fly . . . 60
City of Lake Geneva . . . 21
Civil War . . . 15, 17, 40, 65, 114, 138
Civil Works Administration . . . 69
Clarke, Mrs. John Carpenter . . . 133
Classic Revival . . . 40
Clear Sky Lodge . . . 41, 42
Cleveland, Horace W.S. . . . 42
Clowry, Colonel R.C. . . . 151
Cobb, Henry Ives . . . 38
Colonial Revival . . . 40
Colton Family . . . 48
Colton, A. D. . . . 76
Colton's Exchange . . . 76
Cook County School system . . . 81
Cooke, John . . . 82
Cooke's Park . . . 82
Cornelian . . . 57
Cornelian Dairy . . . 57
Cotswold . . . 41, 130
Cotsworth, Albert . . . 88
Crane Company . . . 54
Crane Estate . . . 22
Crane, Richard Teller . . . 42, 45, 46, 48, 54, 64
Crow's Nest . . . 88
Cruise of a Schooner . . . 113
Cullen-Harrison Act . . . 27
Curran Jr., O.P. . . . 144
Cygnet . . . 46

## D

Daguerreotypes . . . 65
Daisy . . . 45, 54
Danish Pavilion . . . 153
Davidson, Colonel . . . 46
DeBlase, Steve . . . 57
Deepwood . . . 41
Delafield, Mr. Wallace . . . 52
Delavan . . . 27, 32
DePauw University . . . 114
Depression . . . 21
Detroit Electrical Works . . . 136
Dickinson, Albert . . . 138
Dickinson, Louise . . . 138
Dickinson, Nathan . . . 138, 142
Dickinson, Hannah . . . 142
Dillinger, John . . . 154
Dim . . . 87
Dispatch . . . 22
Distillery . . . 15

Doering, Edmund J. . . . . . . . . . . . . . . .144
Dora . . . . . . . . . . . . . . . . . . . . . . . . . . 45
Doreen . . . . . . . . . . . . . . . . . . . . . . . . 54
Douglas Park. . . . . . . . . . . . . . . . . . . . 40
Drake Hotel. . . . . . . . . . . . . . . . . . . . . 41
Drake, Tracy . . . . . . . . . . . . . . . . . . . . 54
Dreschler, Earl . . . . . . . . . . . . . . . . . .151
Dronley . . . . . . . . . . . . . . . . . . . . . . . . 37
Ducat, General A.C. . . . . . . . . . . . . . . 37
Dummer, Ethel Sturges . . . . . . . . 104, 106
Dummer, Frances . . . . . . . . . . . . . . . 106
Dummer, William Francis "Frank" . . . .104, 106
Dummer's Hill . . . . . . . . . . . . . . . . . . 104
Dunlap, George L. . . . . . . . . . . . . . 37, 53
Dutch Colonial Revival . . . . . . . . . . . . 117
Dwinell, Solomon A. . . . . . . . . . . . . . . . 76

## E

Early Modern . . . . . . . . . . . . . . . . . . . 40
East Delavan Cemetery . . . . . . . . . . . . 11
Eckhart, Bernard A. . . . . . . . . . . . . . .127
Edgewater Beach Apartments . . . . . . . 41
Edgewater Beach Hotel . . . . . . . . . . . . 94
Edgewater Historic District . . . . . . . . . 94
Edgewater Park . . . . . . . . . . . . . . . . . 94
Edgewater Park Tourist Camp, The . . . 94
Edison Electric Company . . . . . . . . . .136
Edison, Thomas . . . . . . . . . . . . . 136, 141
Egan, Wiley M. . . . . . . . . . . . . . . . . . . 37
Eleanor Camp . . . . . . . . . . . . . . . . . . 85
Eleven Gables . . . . . . . . . . . . . . . . . . 94
Elgin Club . . . . . . . . . . . . . . . . . . . . .122
Elgin Park . . . . . . . . . . . . . . . . . . . . . 22
Elizabethan Inn, The . . . . . . . . . . . . . . 94
Elkhorn . . . . . . . . . . . . . . . . . . . . . . . 32
Elmslie, George Grant . . . . . . . . . . . . . 40
Emancipation Proclamation . . . . . . . 15, 58
Emery, Mrs. John . . . . . . . . . . . . . . . .124
Emery, William H. . . . . . . . . . . . . . . . .124
Englewood Baptist Church . . . . . . . . . 92
Englewood Club . . . . . . . . . . . . . . 90, 92
English half-timbered styles . . . . . . . . 41
English Tudor . . . . . . . . . . . . . . . . . .141
Essanay Film Manufacturing Co. . . . . . . 25
Ethel Mary . . . . . . . . . . . . . . . . . . 45, 54
Evanston Girls Industrial School. . . . . . . . . .115

## F

Fair Lawn . . . . . . . . . . . . . . . . . . . . . . 42
Fair Oaks . . . . . . . . . . . . . . . . . 37, 41, 144
Fairbank, Nathaniel K. . . . . . . . . . . 37, 99
Fairfields . . . . . . . . . . . . . . . . 17, 37, 104
Fairlawn . . . . . . . . . . . . . . . . . . . . . . . 64
Family Secrets: Crossing the Color Line . . . . 81
Farming . . . . . . . . . . . . . . . . . . . . . . . 63
Farr Cottage . . . . . . . . . . . . . . . . . . . . 99
Ferris House . . . . . . . . . . . . . . . . . . .122
Ferris, Henry Lakin . . . . . . . . . . . . . . .122
Field & Leiter Department Store . . . . . . 18
Field Museum of Natural History . . . . . 37
Finney, Dr. Theodora Wheeler . . . . . . .143
Finney, William P . . . . . . . . . . . . . . . .143
First Leiter Building . . . . . . . . . . . . . . 40
First National Bank Chicago . . . . .57, 72, 109
First Trust & Savings Bank. . . . . . . . . . 109
Fisher, Ethel . . . . . . . . . . . . . . . . . . . 104
Flat Iron Park. . . . . . . . . . . . . . . . . 32, 99
Floating Booze Bazaar . . . . . . . . . . . . . 54
Flour Mill . . . . . . . . . . . . . . . . . . . . . . . 7
Flowerside Inn . . . . . . . . . . . 29, 41, 42, 64
Folly . . . . . . . . . . . . . . . . . . . . .37, 54, 108
Fontana . . . . . . . . . . . 14, 27, 32, 46, 94, 99
Fontana Community Church . . . . . . . .118
Fontana Park and Public Beach . . . . . . 88, 99
Forest Glen Resort . . . . . . . . . . . . . . . 87
Fort Dearborn . . . . . . . . . . . . . . . . . . . . 8
Fourth of July . . . . . . . . . . . . . . . . . 61, 63
Fox, Charles Eli. . . . . . . . . . . . . . . . . . 41
Freeze, Reka . . . . . . . . . . . . . . . . . . .143
French Country Inn . . . . . . . . . . . . . .154
French, John W. . . . . . . . . . . . . . . . 45, 56
Frost Park . . . . . . . . . . . . . . . . . . . . . 42
Frost, Charles S. . . . . . . . . . . . . . . . . . 38
Frost, Edwin B. . . . . . . . . . . . . . . . . . . 29
Frost, Mrs. Edwin . . . . . . . . . . . . . . . . 108
Fuller, Deacon L.W. . . . . . . . . . . . . . . . . 8
Fuller, Henry Hill . . . . . . . . . . . . . . . . . 52
Furbeck, Warren F. . . . . . . . . . . . . . 37, 88

## G

Gage, Russell . . . . . . . . . . . . . . . . . . . 57
Garbo, Greta . . . . . . . . . . . . . . . . . . . . 97
Garfield Park . . . . . . . . . . . . . . . . . . . 40
Gay, Henry Lord . . . . . . . . . . .88, 107, 108, 141
Gaylynne . . . . . . . . . . . . . . . . . . . . . .107
Geneva . . . . . . . . . . . . . . . . . . . . . 45, 57
Geneva Bay . . . . . . . . . . . . . . . . . . . . 11
Geneva Bay Estates . . . . . . . . . . . . . . 72
Geneva Express, The . . . . . . . . . . . . . 15
Geneva Hotel . . . . . . . . . . . . . . . . . . . 71
Geneva House, The . . . . . . . . . . . . 14, 76
Geneva Inn . . . . . . . . . . . . . . . . . . . . . 8
Geneva Lake . . . . . . . . . . . . . . . . . . . 17
Geneva Lake Conservancy . . . . . . . . .136
Geneva Lake Encampment
    Association of Englewood, IL . . . . . . 90
Geneva Lake Excursion Corporation. . . . . 57
Geneva Lake Herald . . . . . . . . . . . . . . 20
Geneva Lake Historical Society . . . . . . 29
Geneva Lake History Buffs. . . . . . . . . . 29
Geneva Lake Yacht Club . . . . . . . . . . .111
Geneva Lake's Water Safety Patrol . . . . 27
Geneva Manor Subdivision . . . . . . . . . 72
Geneva National . . . . . . . . . . . . . . . .154
Geneva Township . . . . . . . . . . . . . . . 14
George Williams College Camp . . . . .8, 42, 85
Geronimo . . . . . . . . . . . . . . . . . . . . . .127
Gertie . . . . . . . . . . . . . . . . . . . . . . . . . 53
Gertrude . . . . . . . . . . . . . . . . . . . . 46, 54
Gilbert's Restaurant . . . . . . . . . . . 94, 150
Glen Fern . . . . . . . . . . . . . . . 37, 42, 48, 64
Glennon, Edward . . . . . . . . . . . . . . . .151
Glenview Country Club . . . . . . . . . . . . 42
Golden Fleece, The . . . . . . . . . . . . . .115
Golden Idiot, The . . . . . . . . . . . . . . . . 25
Goodsell, Charles M. . . . . . . . . 7, 10, 14, 15
Gossage, Charles . . . . . . . . . . . . . . .142
Graceland Cemetery . . . . . . . . . . . . . . 42
Great Chicago Fire 18, 50, 65, 104, 106, 138, 142
Great Depression . . . . . 27, 69, 71, 72, 106, 154
Great Eastern . . . . . . . . . . . . . . . . . . . 45
Great Lakes Naval Station . . . . . . . . . . 40
Green Gables . . . . . . . . . . . . . . . 25, 26, 37
Green Rabbit . . . . . . . . . . . . . . . . . . . 54

Greer, Ann . . . . . . . . . . . . . . . . . . . . .127
Greer, Frederic "Tombstone" . . . . . . . .127
Grommes & Ullrich . . . . . . . . . . . . . . .133
Grommes, John B. . . . . . . . . . . . . . . .131
Gross & Brooks . . . . . . . . . . . . . . . . . 20
Gross, Daniel . . . . . . . . . . . . . . . . . . . 20
Guido, Frank . . . . . . . . . . . . . . . . . . . 84

## H

H.M. Byllesby and Company . . . . . . . .141
Halley's Comet . . . . . . . . . . . . . . . . . . 23
Harbert, Elizabeth Boynton . . . . . . . . .114
Harkness, Cynthia Kohlsaat . . . . . . . . .118
Harkness, Ken . . . . . . . . . . . . . . . . . .118
Harris, Albert . . . . . . . . . . . . . . . 112, 113
Harris, Norman E. . . . . . . . . . . . . . . . . 37
Harris, Norman Wait . . . . . . . . . . . 23, 112
Harrose Hall . . . . . . . . . . . . . . . . . 42, 64
Harvard . . . . . . . . . . . . . . . . . . . . . 45, 57
Harvard Park . . . . . . . . . . . . . . . . . . . 80
Haskins Electric Company . . . . . . . . . . 23
Hathor . . . . . . . . . . . . . . . . . . . . . 46, 54
Hazeldore . . . . . . . . . . . . . . . . . . . . .127
Healy Estate . . . . . . . . . . . . . . . . . . . . 29
Healy, M.A. . . . . . . . . . . . . . . . . . . . . 29
Heg, James B. . . . . . . . . . . . . . . . . . . 97
Henry Ford . . . . . . . . . . . . . . . . . . . . . 54
Herald, The . . . . . . . . . . . . . . . . . . . . 23
Hermansen Family . . . . . . . . . . . . . . .153
Hermansen, Inar . . . . . . . . . . . . . . . .153
Herrick, Willis S. . . . . . . . . . . . . . . . . . 88
High Gothic . . . . . . . . . . . . . . . . . . . . 40
Hill View . . . . . . . . . . . . . . . . . . . 41, 151
History and Indian Remains of
    Lake Geneva . . . . . . . . . . . . . . . . . 30
History of Arabian Horse Club
    Registry of America, The . . . . . . . .113
History of Walworth County . . . . . . 10, 76
Hogaboom, A.C. . . . . . . . . . . . . . . . . . 21
Hogan, Dr. John E . . . . . . . . . . . . . . . . 22
Hogan, Mary . . . . . . . . . . . . . . . . . . . 22
Hogan, Reverend . . . . . . . . . . . . . . . . 22
Holiday Home . . . . . . . . . . . . . . . . . . 79
Holiday Home Camp . . . . . . . . . . 64, 108
Hollinger, I.V. . . . . . . . . . . . . . . . . . . . 93
Holly Bush . . . . . . . . . . . . . . . . . . 8, 141
Holy Tom . . . . . . . . . . . . . . . . . . . . . . 57
Home Insurance Building . . . . . . . . . . 40
Horticultural Hall . . . . . . . . . . . . 23, 41, 64
Host, Leo J. . . . . . . . . . . . . . . . . . . . . 26
Hotel de Repasz . . . . . . . . . . . . . . . . . 77
Hotel Erb . . . . . . . . . . . . . . . . . . . . . . 97
Hotel Geneva . . . . . . . . . . . . . . . . . 25, 71
Hotel Lakeside . . . . . . . . . . . . . . . . . . 97
Hotel LaSalle . . . . . . . . . . . . . . . . . . . 77
Hotel Lone . . . . . . . . . . . . . . . . . . . . . 79
Hotel Rea . . . . . . . . . . . . . . . . . . . . . . 97
Hotton, J.S. . . . . . . . . . . . . . . . . . . . . 29
House in the Woods . . . . . . . . . . . . 23, 37
House on the Hill . . . . . . . . . 40, 87, 118, 121
Howells, William Dean . . . . . . . . . . . . 81
Hubbard, Rosalie . . . . . . . . . . . . . . . .104
Hugh Garden . . . . . . . . . . . . . . . . . . .133
Hulina, Richard and Bonnie . . . . . . . . .111
Humboldt Park . . . . . . . . . . . . . . . . . . 40
Huml, Jack . . . . . . . . . . . . . . . . . . . . . 84
Hunt and Bohassek . . . . . . . . . . . . . . 40

Hunt, Helm, Ferris and Company . . . . . .122
Hunt, Jarvis . . . . . . . . . . . . . . . . . . . . 38
Huntoon, Colonel J. E. . . . . . . . . . . . . . 76
Hutchinson, Charles L. . . . . . . . . 37, 42, 64

## I

Ice House . . . . . . . . . . . . . . . . . . . 20, 153
Ice King . . . . . . . . . . . . . . . . . . . . . . . 20
Illinois Institute of Technology . . . . . . .130
Illinois Social Science Association . . . . . .115
Illinois Trust and Savings . . . . . . . . . . . 17
Illinois Women's Press Association . . . . .115
Immanuel Woman's Home Association . . 84
Indian Hill Club . . . . . . . . . . . . . . . . . . 42
Inland Scow . . . . . . . . . . . . . . . . . . . . 46
Inwagen, James Van . . . . . . . . . . . . . .141
Iowa's Woman Suffrage Association . . . 114, 115
Iroquois Theater . . . . . . . . . . . . . . . . . 41
Irwin, C. L. . . . . . . . . . . . . . . . . . . . . . 79
Italian Waters . . . . . . . . . . . . . . . . . .107
Ivy Lodge . . . . . . . . . . . . . . . . . . 138, 142

## J

J. Case Company . . . . . . . . . . . . . . . .149
J.P. Smith Ice Company . . . . . . . . . . . . 21
Jenkins, Edward . . . . . . . . . . . . . . . . . 29
Jenkins, Paul B. . . . . . . . . . . . . . 29, 30, 69
Jenney, William LeBaron . . . . . . . . . 40, 42
Jensen, Jens . . . . . . . . . . . . . 42, 133, 136
Jerseyhurst . . . . . . . . . 42, 45, 46, 48, 54, 64
Jesperson, Dr. John . . . . . . . . . . . . . . 84
Jewell Boat Co. . . . . . . . . . . . . . . . . . . 46
Jewell, Thomas . . . . . . . . . . . . . . . . . 46
Jewell, Walter . . . . . . . . . . . . . . . . 46, 57
Johnejack, Emil . . . . . . . . . . . . . . . . . 32
Johnson, Gordon "Butch" . . . . . . . . . . 71
Johnson, Lucretia "Dell" . . . . . . . . . . . 58
Johnson, Wesley . . . . . . . . . . . . . . 45, 57
Johnston Jr., John . . . . . . . . . . . . . . .107

## K

Kahquados, Chief Simon . . . . . . . . . . . 29
Kaiulani . . . . . . . . . . . . . . . . . . . . . . . 46
Kanelos, Elaine . . . . . . . . . . . . . . . . . 33
Kansas City Massacre . . . . . . . . . . . . . 40
Kansas City's Union Station . . . . . . . . . 40
Karpen Chicago Furniture Company . . . .144
Karpen, M. . . . . . . . . . . . . . . . . . . . . .144
Kaye, Arthur . . . . . . . . . . . . . . . . . 22, 141
Kaye's Park Resort . . . . 11, 22, 75, 76, 80, 92, 99
Keeler, David M. . . . . . . . . . . . . . . . . . 15
Keep, Albert . . . . . . . . . . . . . . . . .37, 144
Kemah Farm . . . . . . . . . . . . . . . . . . .113
Kettering, Charles Franklin . . . . . . . . . . 21
King, Albert . . . . . . . . . . . . . . . . . . . . 97
King, Dr. Oscar A. . . . . . . . . . . . . . . . . 97
King, Riley . . . . . . . . . . . . . . . . . . . . . 97
Kinzie, John . . . . . . . . . . . . . . . . . . .8, 29
Kirkland School, The . . . . . . . . . . . . . 106
Knoll, The . . . . . . . . . . . . . . . 143, 144, 146
Knollwood . . . . . . . . . . . . . . . . . . 82, 84
Kohlsaat, Edith . . . . . . . . . . . . . . . . .118
Kohlsaat, Judge Christian C. . . . . . . 87, 118
Kohlsaat, Mrs. Christian . . . . . . . . . . .118
Kunklie Family . . . . . . . . . . . . . . . . . .130

## L

L.E. Myers Construction Co. . . . . . . . . . . .136
Lackner, Francis . . . . . . . . . . . . . . . . . . .151
Ladies Home Journal . . . . . . . . . . . . . . . . 41
Lady of the Lake . . . . . . . . . . 20, 45, 56, 57
Lady of the Lake II . . . . . . . . . . . . . . . . . . 57
Lake Como. . . . . . . . . . . . . . . . . . . 113, 154
Lake Como Beach Association . . . . . . . .154
Lake Como Beach Subdivision . . . . . . . . .154
Lake Como Hotel. . . . . . . . . . . . . . . 153, 154
Lake Geneva Country Club . . . . . . . 124, 141
Lake Geneva Country Clubhouse . . . . . . . 41
Lake Geneva Depot, The. . . . . . . . . . . . . 38
Lake Geneva Fresh Air Association . . . . . . 63
Lake Geneva Garden Club. . . . . . . . . 30, 64
Lake Geneva Garden Show . . . . . . . . . . . 64
Lake Geneva Gardeners and
   Foremens Association. . . . . . . . . . . . .3, 64
Lake Geneva Herald
   . . . . . 17, 21, 22, 23, 60, 61, 63, 65, 76, 99, 107
Lake Geneva Historical
   Pageant Association. . . . . . . . . . . . . . . 29
Lake Geneva Historical Society . . . . . . . .138
Lake Geneva Ice Company . . . . . . . . . . . 21
Lake Geneva Motor Boat Line . . . . . . 46, 57
Lake Geneva News. . . . . . . . . . . . . . . . . 24
Lake Geneva News Tribune . . . . . . . . . . . 69
Lake Geneva Public Library . . . . . . . . . . . 97
Lake Geneva Sanitariums . . . . . . . . . 69, 97
Lake Geneva Schools . . . . . . . . . . . . . . . 58
Lake Geneva Seminary . . . . . . . .15, 94, 138
Lake Geneva Seminary for Young Ladies . . 150
Lake Geneva Steam Line . . . . . . . . . . . . 46
Lake Geneva Steamer Line . . . . . . . . . . . 57
Lake Geneva Women's Club . . . . . . . . . . 29
Lake Geneva Yacht Club . . . . . . . . . . . . .111
Lake House. . . . . . . . . . . . . . . . 14, 15, 76
Lake Michigan . . . . . . . . . . . . . . . . . . . . 22
Lake Shore Drive. . . . . . . . . . . . . . . . . . . 23
Lake Shore Park . . . . . . . . . . . . . . . . . . . 99
Lake Superior . . . . . . . . . . . . . . . . . . 60, 92
Lake View High School . . . . . . . . . . . . . . 81
Lake View Park. . . . . . . . . . . . . . . . . . . . 99
Lakeside Hotel . . . . . . . . . . . . . . . . . . . . 94
Lakewood . . . . . . . . . . . . . . . . . . . . . . .151
L'Arcadie . . . . . . . . . . . . . . . . . . . . . . . .134
LaSalle, Charles . . . . . . . . . . . . . . . . . . .131
Lasalle, O.T. . . . . . . . . . . . . . . . . . . . . . . 48
Leary, Timothy . . . . . . . . . . . . . . . . . . . . 31
Leath, Arthur . . . . . . . . . . . . . . . . . . . . .107
Lee, Charles . . . . . . . . . . . . . . . . . . . . .107
Lee's in the Bay . . . . . . . . . . . . . . . . . . . 85
Lefens Estate. . . . . . . . . . . . . . . . . . . . . 59
Leiter Estate. . . . . . . . . . . . . . . . . . . . . . 72
Leiter Fish Hatchery . . . . . . . . . . . . . . . . 85
Leiter, Joseph . . . . . . . . . . . . . . . . . 37, 63
Leiter, Levi . . . . . . . . 17, 23, 29, 45, 54, 63, 99
Leonard, Josiah Sloan . . . . . . . . . . . . . . . 85
Leonard, Pi . . . . . . . . . . . . . . . . . . . . . . 85
Lewis, Ham & Co. . . . . . . . . . . . . . . . . . 17
Library Park . . . . . . . . . . . . . . . . . . . . . . 99
Liechty, Ernest . . . . . . . . . . . . . . . . . 46, 57
Lincoln Inn . . . . . . . . . . . . . . . . . . . . . . . 79
Lincoln Park Conservatory. . . . . . . . . . . . 40
Lincoln, Mary Todd. . . . . . . . . . . . . . . . . 76
Linden Lodge. . . . . . . 23, 37, 45, 54, 63, 64, 99
Lindquist, C.O. . . . . . . . . . . . . . . . . . . . . 94
Lodge at Geneva Ridge, The . . . . . . . . .154
Lone, John . . . . . . . . . . . . . . . . . . . . . . 79
Long, William . . . . . . . . . . . . . . 25, 48, 79
Loramoor. . . . . . . . . . . . . . . . . . 40, 42, 64
Loreley . . . . . . . . . . . . . . . . . . . . . . . . . 54
Louise . . . . . . . . . . . . . . . . . . . . . . . . . . 54
Luddington Building . . . . . . . . . . . . . . . . 40
Lundahl, Eva Seymour . . . . . . . . . . . . . . 20
Lynne, Gay . . . . . . . . . . . . . . . . . . . . . .107
Lytle, A. E. . . . . . . . . . . . . . . . . . . . . . . . 99
Lytton, Henry C. . . . . . . . . . . . . . . . . . .107

## M

MacDowell, Mary . . . . . . . . . . . . . . . . . 106
Madame Juliani . . . . . . . . . . . . . . . . . . . 94
Madison's Territorial Legislature. . . . . . . . 15
Maher, George W. . . . . . . . . . . . . . . . . . 40
Majestic . . . . . . . . . . . . . . . . . . 22, 45, 57
Manhattan Building . . . . . . . . . . . . . . . . 40
Manning, Warren . . . . . . . . . . . . . . . . . . 42
Manson, George . . . . . . . . . . . . . . . 22, 45
Maple Lawn . . . . . . . . . .17, 42, 46, 54, 104
Maples . . . . . . . . . . . . . . . . . . . . . . . . .115
Marble and Wilson. . . . . . . . . . . . . . . . . 41
Marengo Park . . . . . . . . . . . . . . . . . 79, 93
Marshall and Fox. . . . . . . . . . . . . . . . . . 41
Marshall, Benjamin Howard . . . . . . . . . . 41
Martin Luther King. . . . . . . . . . . . . . . . . 31
Matriark . . . . . . . . . . . . . . . . . . . . . . . . 54
May Fly. . . . . . . . . . . . . . . . . . . . . . . . . 60
McCrea, Reinette Lester . . . . . . . . . . . 108
McGurn, Jack "Machine Gun". . . . . . . . .154
McMullen, R.B. . . . . . . . . . . . . . . . . . . .115
McNamara, Rev. John . . . . . . . . . . . . . . 15
Medieval Revival . . . . . . . . . . . . . . . . . . 40
Metropolitan Block. . . . . . . . . . . . . . . . . 40
Michael Reese Hospital Building . . . . . . .131
Midgley Jr., Thomas . . . . . . . . . . . . . . . . 21
Mid-Summer Fair . . . . . . . . . . . . . . . . . . 63
Milano Café . . . . . . . . . . . . . . . . . . . . . 79
Mill . . . . . . . . . . . . . . . . . . . . . . . .14, 153
Miller House . . . . . . . . . . . . . . . . . . . . . 85
Millionaire Special . . . . . . . . . . . . . .85, 153
Milwaukee Railroad . . . . . . . . . . . . . . . . 57
Minerva. . . . . . . . . . . . . . . . . . . . . . . . . 54
Minier's . . . . . . . . . . . . . . . . . . . . . . . . . 77
Mitchell, John J. . . . . . . . . . . . . 25, 37, 54
Mitchell, Mrs. . . . . . . . . . . . . . . . . . . . . . 64
Mogg, J.J. . . . . . . . . . . . . . . . . . . . . . .117
Mogg, Millard . . . . . . . . . . . . . . . . . . . .117
Mohr, Matthias . . . . . . . . . . . . . . . . 14, 27
Montague & Porter's Park . . . . . . . . . . . 88
Montague, Guerdon . . . . . . . . . . . . . 10, 88
Montgomery Ward Building . . . . . . . . . .131
Moore, Edward . . . . . . . . . . . . . . . . . . .111
Moore, James H. . . . . . . . . . . . . 42, 54, 65
Moore, Judge William H. . . . . . . . . . . . . 42
Moorings . . . . . . . . . . . . . . . . . . . . . . . 37
Moran, George "Bugs". . . . . . . . . . .79, 154
Morton, Sue Dickinson . . . . . . . . . . . . .137
Moser, Millicent . . . . . . . . . . . . . . . . . . .122
Mound . . . . . . . . . . . . . . . . . . . . . . . . . 94
Mound Builders . . . . . . . . . . . . . . . . . . . 29
Movie Theaters. . . . . . . . . . . . . . . . . . . 69
Moving Sidewalk . . . . . . . . . . . . . . . . . . 40
Mudge, Persis Buell . . . . . . . . . . . . . . .138
Muhammad Ali. . . . . . . . . . . . . . . . . . . . 31
Music by the Lake . . . . . . . . . . . . . . . . . 87
Myers, Lewis E. . . . . . . . . . . 42, 54, 134, 136

## N

Napper Boat Company . . . . . . . . . . . 45, 54
Napper, Ted . . . . . . . . . . . . . . . . . . . . . 45
Napper, William Matthew . . . . . . . . . . . . 45
National Child Labor Committee . . . . . . 106
National Education Association . . . . . . . . 81
National Golf Links of America Golf Course. . 40
National Guard. . . . . . . . . . . . . . . . . . . . 32
National Historic Register . . . . . . . . . . . . 40
National Household
   Economics Association . . . . . . . . 114, 115
National Prohibition Act . . . . . . . . . . . . . 26
National Register of Historic Places . . . . . 38
National Security League . . . . . . . . . . .141
Native American . . . . . . . . . . . . . . . . . . 94
Navilio family . . . . . . . . . . . . . . . . . . . .154
Negawni . . . . . . . . . . . . . . . . . . . . . . .141
Nero . . . . . . . . . . . . . . . . . . . . . . . . . . 59
Nettie . . . . . . . . . . . . . . . . . . . . . . . . .146
New Deal . . . . . . . . . . . . . . . . . . . . . . . 69
New Era, The . . . . . . . . . . . . . . . . . . . .115
New York Central Railway System . . . . . .151
Newark Museum . . . . . . . . . . . . . . . . . . 40
Newberry Library . . . . . . . . . . . . . . . . . . 37
Newberry, Lucius . . . . . . . 45, 56, 57, 65, 80
Newberry, Oscar . . . . . . . . . . . . . . . . . . 56
Nieubuurt, Edward J. . . . . . . . . . . . . . .128
Nieubuurt, Minnie . . . . . . . . . . . . . . . . .128
Nightingale Camp . . . . . . . . . . . . . . . . . 80
Nightingale, Florence . . . . . . . . . . . . . . . 81
Nightingale, Professor Augustus F. . . . 80, 81
Nightingale's . . . . . . . . . . . . . . . . . . 60, 92
Normandie. . . . . . . . . . . . . . . . . . . . . . . 54
North Geneva Highlands. . . . . . . . . . . .154
Northport. . . . . . . . . . . . . . . . . . . . . . . . 71
Northwestern Military and
   Naval Academy . . . . . . . . . 24, 41, 46, 141
Northwestern National Bank. . . . . . . . . . 17
Northwestern Railroad . . . . . . . . . . . . . . 53
Northwoodside . . . . . . . . . . . . . . . . . . . 37
Norton, Fanny Rumsey . . . . . . . . . . . . .144
Norton, James Sager . . . . . . . . . . . . . .144
Notter's Lake Como Hotel . . . . . . . . . . .153
Noyes, C.A. . . . . . . . . . . . . . . . . . . . . . 57
Nussbaum, E.T. . . . . . . . . . . . . . . . . . . 71

## O

Oak Hill Cemetery . . . . . .8, 17, 42, 48, 65, 151
Oak Lodge . . . . . . . . . . . . . . . . . . . . . . 45
Oak Park . . . . . . . . . . . . . . . . . . . . . . . 80
Oak Shores. . . . . . . . . . . . . . . . . . . . . .128
Oaks, The . . . . . . . . . . . . . . 30, 37, 45, 46
Oakwood . . . . . . . . . . . . . . . . . . . . . . 150
Oakwood Springs Sanitariums . . . . . . . . 97
Old Settlers Society . . . . . . . . . . . . . . . . 29
Old Tom Pine's. . . . . . . . . . . . . . . . . . .153
Olivett . . . . . . . . . . . . . . . . . . . . . . . 46, 54
Olmsted, Frederick Law . . . . . . . . . . 40, 42
Olmsted, John . . . . . . . . . . . . . . . . . . . 42
O'Malley, Kay Greer . . . . . . . . . . . . . . .127
O'Malley, Michael . . . . . . . . . . . . . . . . .127
Orchard, The . . . . . . . . . . . . . . . . . . . . 104
Orchids. . . . . . . . . . . . . . . . . . . . . . 64, 136
Out of Her Sphere . . . . . . . . . . . . . . . .115

Owl House, The . . . . . . . . . . . . . . . . . . . 76

## P

Paddock, G.L. . . . . . . . . . . . . . . . . . . . .151
Palmer Boat Co. . . . . . . . . . . . . . . . . . . 46
Palmer House . . . . . . . . . . . . . . . . . . . . 18
Palmer Johnson Co. . . . . . . . . . . . . . . . . 46
Palmer, Charles . . . . . . . . . . . . . . . . . . 46
Pappas, Felice . . . . . . . . . . . . . . . . . . . 150
Parkhurst, Mister. . . . . . . . . . . . . . . . . . 93
Passaic . . . . . . . . . . . . . . . . . . . 45, 46, 54
Payne, Christopher. . . . . . . . . . . 10, 14, 153
Percy Baker Farm . . . . . . . . . . . . . 137, 138
Phoenix, Samuel . . . . . . . . . . . . . . . . . . 27
Pier 892 . . . . . . . . . . . . . . . . . . . . . . . . 94
Pinegate . . . . . . . . . . . . . . . . . . . . .40, 121
Pioneer Cemetery . . . . . . . . . . . . . . . . . 48
Pioneer Day . . . . . . . . . . . . . . . . . . . . . 29
Pishcotaqua Park House. . . . . . . . . . 76, 82
Pittsburgh Union Stocks Yards Company . . 109
Point Comfort . . . . . . . . . . . . . . . . . 37, 45
Polaris . . . . . . . . . . . . . . . . . . . . . . . . . 54
Pollard, Bill and Judy . . . . . . . . . . . . . . .145
Pond and Pond. . . . . . . . . . . . . . . . . . . 104
Pond, Allen B. . . . . . . . . . . . . . . . . . . . 106
Pond, Irving K. . . . . . . . . . . . . . . . . . . . 23
Porter & Montague's Park . . . . . . . . . . . 88
Porter, Doric C. . . . . . . . . . . . . . . . . . . . 88
Porter, Henry H. . . . . . . . . . . . . . . . 42, 54
Porter's Park . . . . . . . . . . . . . . . . . . 37, 88
Potawatomi. . . . . . . . . . . . . . . . . . . 11, 141
Potter, E.A. . . . . . . . . . . . . . . . . . . . 46, 54
Powell, Hiram . . . . . . . . . . . . . . . . . . . . .8
Prairie School . . . . . . . . . . . . . . . . . . . .133
Prairie-style . . . . . . . . . . . . . . . . . . . . . 40
President Abraham Lincoln . . . . . . . . 15, 58
President Franklin Roosevelt. . . . . . . . . . 27
President Theodore Roosevelt. . . . . . . . . 46
President Ulysses S. Grant. . . . . . . . . . . 20
President William Howard Taft. . . . . . . . . 46
President Woodrow Wilson . . . . . . . . . . 46
Preston, John . . . . . . . . . . . . . . . . . . . . 22
Princess . . . . . . . . . . . . . . . . . . . . . . . . 54
Pringle, Joe . . . . . . . . . . . . . . . . . . . . .124
Prohibition . . . . . . . . . . . . . . .15, 30, 54, 154
Pullman Company . . . . . . . . . . . . . . . . 40

## Q

Quigley, Captain Edwin . . . . . . . . . . 20, 56
Racine Boat Company . . . . . . . . . . . . . . 54

## R

Railroad . . . . . . . . . . . . . . . . . . . . . 15, 21
Rainbow Point . . . . . . . . . . . . . . . . . . .124
Ralph Williams and his Orchestra . . . . . . . 71
Red Chimney Inn. . . . . . . . . . . . . . . . . .154
Red Cross . . . . . . . . . . . . . . . . . . . . 24, 30
Redwood Cottage . . . . . . . . . . . . . . . . . 94
Reed, Mary . . . . . . . . . . . . . . . . . . . . . . 87
Reed, Miss . . . . . . . . . . . . . . . . . . . . . . 93
Regional News . . . . . . . . . . . . . . . . . . . 71
Rehm, Frank A. . . . . . . . . . . . . . . . . . .131
Rehm, Mrs. Frank A. (Clara) . . . . . . . . . .133
Rehoboth . . . . . . . . . . . . . . . . . . . 42, 104
Reid, George M. . . . . . . . . . . . . . . . . . . 99
Reid's Park . . . . . . . . . . . . . . . . . . . . . . 99
Renaissance Revival . . . . . . . . . . . . . . . 40

Renth, Leston . . . . . 32
Revolutionary War . . . . . 46
Reynolds, Florence . . . . . 145, 146
Richardson, Ida . . . . . 88
Riley, Jim . . . . . 92
Ringer Stadium . . . . . 71
Riots, The . . . . . 31
Ripple, The . . . . . 46, 57
Riviera Ballroom . . . . . 32, 71
Roberts House . . . . . 117
Roberts, Eben E. . . . . . 40, 118, 121
Roberts, Elmer . . . . . 40
Rockefeller, John . . . . . 54
Rockford Camp . . . . . 79, 85
Romanesque . . . . . 38
Romare, Ethel . . . . . 85
Rumsey, Ada . . . . . 18
Rumsey, Amelia "Meme" . . . . . 143
Rumsey, Julian . . . 18, 37, 46, 53, 143, 144, 146
Russell Park . . . . . 87
Russell, Judge . . . . . 32
Russell, Lillian . . . . . 97
Russell, Marcus C. . . . . . 87
Russell, Robert . . . . . 11
Ryerson, Martin A. . . . . . 37, 42, 46, 54

## S

Sanford, Captain Eph . . . . . 57
Schermerhorn . . . . . 40
Schmidt, Dr. Otto. . . . . . 29
Schmidt, Gardner and Martin . . . . . 131
Schmidt, Richard E. . . . . . 131
Sears, Judge Nathaniel C. . . . . . 37, 42, 48
Sears, Mrs. Nathaniel . . . . . 64
Seipp, Catherine . . . . . 46, 151
Seipp, William C.. . . . . . 37
Selfridge, Harry . . . . . 42
Seyfarth, Robert . . . . . 113
Seymour, John . . . . . 20
Shadow Hill . . . . . 18, 37, 143, 144, 146
Shadyside . . . . . 45, 54
Shakyside . . . . . 54
Sharon . . . . . 27
Shaw, George B. . . . . . 151
Shaw, Howard Van Doren . . . . . 41, 130, 134
Shepley, Rutan & Coolidge . . . . . 41
Sheridan Springs . . . . . 21
Sheridan, General Phillip . . . . . 18, 21
Shingle . . . . . 40
Ship, The . . . . . 54
Shore Haven . . . . . 128
Silsbee, Joseph Lyman. . . . . . 40
Simmons, James . . . . . 15, 29
Simonds, Ossian Cole . . . . . 42
Skinner, Martha Rumsey. . . . 143, 144, 145, 146
Skinner, Nathan H. . . . . . 146
Slaney, Catherine . . . . . 81
Smith, George . . . . . 88
Smith, Sydney . . . . . 32
Smithsonian . . . . . 58
Smyth, John M. . . . . . 37
Snug Harbor . . . . . 17, 37, 48, 104, 106
Sorrs B. Barrett House. . . . . . 41
Soutar, Richard. . . . . . 144
Southern California Women's Press . . . . . 115
Spencer & Powers . . . . . 41
Spencer Jr., Robert C. . . . . . 41
Spencer, Mr. . . . . . 127
Spoor, George . . . . . 25
Spring Haven. . . . . . 87
St. Denis Hotel . . . . . 14
St. Moritz. . . . . . 94, 146, 150
St. Paul Railroad . . . . . 57
Stam, Charles . . . . . 85
Stam, Joseph . . . . . 85
Stam, Steven . . . . . 85
Starline . . . . . 122
Starr, Ellen Gates. . . . . . 106
State Bar Association of Wisconsin . . . . . 2
Sterling . . . . . 46
Stevens, Ashton . . . . . 97
Stock Market Crash . . . . . 30, 69
Stockham, Dr. Alice . . . . . 115
Stone Manor . . . . . 37
Story of Telecommunications, The . . . . . 45
Strong, General Henry . . . . . 37
Sturges & Co. . . . . . 17
Sturges, Albert . . . . . 17
Sturges, Buckingham . . . . . 17, 37, 104
Sturges, Buckingham & Co. . . . . . 17
Sturges, George . 17, 20, 37, 46, 48, 99, 104, 106
Sturges, Mary . . . . . 99
Sturges, Mary Delafield . . . . . 106
Sturges, McAllister & Co. . . . . . 17
Sturges, Mrs. George . . . . . 52
Sturges, Shelton . . . . . 17, 99, 104
Sturges, Solomon . . . . . 17, 104
Stuyvesant . . . . . 57
Stuyvesant, Tilford "Til" . . . . . 46, 48, 57
Styberg Jr., E.C. . . . . . 136
Styberg Sr., E.C. . . . . . 136
Suffrage . . . . . 27, 108, 114, 115
Sumachs, The . . . . . 142
Summer Haven . . . . . 144
Sunday Man . . . . . 10
Sunny Hill . . . . . 117
Sunset Hills . . . . . 30
Sunset Ridge . . . . . 37
Surf, The . . . . . 79
Swanson, Gloria . . . . . 25
Swanson, Joseph E. . . . . . 144
Swanson, Ralph E. . . . . . 144
Swift, E.F. . . . . . 23
Syracuse Savings Bank Building . . . . . 40

## T

Tarrant, Edward . . . . . 88
Tarrant, John . . . . . 88
Tarrant, Robert . . . . . 88
Tattle . . . . . 144
Tavern, J.W.O'Brien. . . . . . 30
Temperance . . . . . 10, 14, 15, 26, 57
Thearle, Reverend F.G. . . . . . 92
Thetis. . . . . . 54
Thompson, Agnes . . . . . 109
Thompson, Paduella W. . . . . . 109
Tiffany Pressed Brick Company of Chicago . . 141
Tilford S. . . . . . 46
Time . . . . . 54
Topsy B. . . . . . 45, 54
Town of Geneva . . . . . 15
Tre Brah . . . . . 114
Tribune, The . . . . . 59
Trinke Estates . . . . . 72
Trinke, William F. . . . . . 48, 68, 72
Tucker, Mr. . . . . . 29
Tula . . . . . 45, 54
Turpin, Ben. . . . . . 25
Twist, Lavern . . . . . 84
Tyrawley . . . . . 37

## U

UFO's. . . . . . 30
Ullmann, Ida Emery . . . . . 124
Union Stock Yards Bank . . . . . 17
United States Training Corps for Women . . . 24
Unity Chapel in Spring Green . . . . . 40
University of Chicago . . . . . 37, 38, 42
University of Chicago School of Social Service Administration. . . . . . 106
University of Illinois's Board of Trustees. . . . 81
Utter, George S. . . . . . 20

## V

Valli, Virginia . . . . . 25
Van Blesbroeck, Dr. George . . . . . 30
Van Slyke Creek . . . . . 14
Van Slyke, Catherine . . . . . 14, 48
Van Slyke, James . . . . . 7, 14
Vaughn, Polly . . . . . 104
Vaughan, Howard A. . . . . . 121
Vaughan, Martha . . . . . 121
Vaughan, Stanford S. . . . . . 121
Victorian Gothic . . . . . 38
Vietnam War . . . . . 31
Villa Hortensia . . . . . 23
Villa Immanuel . . . . . 84
Villa Thekla. . . . . . 40
Village of Fontana . . . . . 27
Village of Geneva. . . . . . 15, 21
Volstead Act . . . . . 26, 27
Vralia Camp . . . . . 115

## W

Wacker, Charles . . . . . 42, 64
Wadsworth Hall . . . . . 23, 37
Waldeck . . . . . 151
Walker, George C. . . . . . 37, 45, 54
Walworth . . . . . 27, 46, 57
Walworth Center Cemetery . . . . . 48
Walworth County. . . . . . 32, 68
Walworth County Bar Association. . . . . . 72
Walworth County Fairgrounds . . . . . 32
Walworth County Historical Society . . . . . 29
Walworth County Temperence Movement. . . 15
Walworth II . . . . . 33, 57
Walworth Township . . . . . 27
Walworth, Judge Rueben Hyde . . . . . 27
Warren . . . . . 58
Warren, Greenleaf S. . . . . . 14, 15, 76
Warren, Robert W. . . . . . 14, 48, 76
Warrington Iron Works. . . . . . 46
Warrington, George . . . . . 46, 54
Warwick Park. . . . . . 80, 151
Washburn, Bryant . . . . . 25
Watters, Mister . . . . . 93
Wayne King and his Aragon Ballroom Dance Band. . . . . . 71
Wetherall, Oscar D.. . . . . . 151
Webster House Museum. . . . . . 138
Wells, Harry . . . . . 87
Wesley Woods . . . . . 85
West Parks . . . . . 40
West School . . . . . 108
Western Finals of the National Marble Tournament . . . . . 71
Western Union Telegraph . . . . . 151
Westinghouse . . . . . 141
Weter, Patience. . . . . . 8
Wheeler, Samuel. . . . . . 143, 144
Wheeler, Theodora "Dora" Rumsey 143, 144, 146
Whileaway . . . . . 54
White River. . . . . . 14, 15
Whitecap . . . . . 54
Whiting House . . . . . 76
Wilbur F. . . . . . 57, 59
Williams Bay . . . . . 11, 26, 27, 68, 85, 99
Williams Bay Public Beach and Boat Dock . . . . . 99
Williams' Buck-Horn Hotel. . . . . . 11
Williams, Captain Israel . . . . . 11, 26, 1136
Williams, John . . . . . 151
Willow Landing. . . . . . 143, 144, 146
Willow Park. . . . . . 99
Wilson, Charles L. . . . . . 20
Wilson, John A.. . . . . . 57
Wilson, John P. . . . . . 37
Windmoor . . . . . 133
Wisconsin DNR . . . . . 61, 154
Wisconsin Power and Light Co. . . . . . 136
Wisconsin State Historical Society . . . . . 29
Wisconsin State Senator. . . . . . 72
Wisconsin Territory . . . . . 7
Wisconsin Transportation Company. . 46, 54, 57
Withrow, Judge T. F. . . . . . 45, 54
Women's Civic League of Pasadena. . . . . . 115
Women's Club of Evanston, Illinois . . . 114, 115
Women's Kingdom. . . . . . 115
Women's Suffrage . . . . . 114
Wood, Billy . . . . . 93
World War I . . . . . 68, 72, 141
World's Congress Auxiliary . . . . . 114
World's Unity League . . . . . 114
Wright, Frank Lloyd . . . . . 25, 40, 41
Wright, Mr. B. F. . . . . . 93
Wrigley Estate . . . . . 25
Wrigley Family . . . . . 151
Wrigley Jr., William. . . . . . 25, 26, 107
Wrigley, Phillip . . . . . 25
Wychwood . . . . . 37, 41, 42, 64

## Y

Y.M.C.A.. . . . . . 23, 57, 79
Yerkes Observatory . . . . . 23, 29, 30, 38, 42, 63, 85, 108
Young, Otto. . . . . . 26, 37, 46, 64
Younglands. . . . . . 26, 37, 46, 64

## Z

Zook House . . . . . 130
Zook, R. Harold. . . . . . 41

# REFERENCES

Arnold, C.S. and R.B, druggists, booksellers and jewelers. *Lake Geneva Illustrated*. Lake Geneva, WI: 1889.

Beal, Thomas Prince. *Report of the Secretary of the Class of 1869 of Harvard College, Vol. 8, Dec 31, 1887–Aug 1, 1894*. Boston, MA: Press of Rockwell and Churchill, 1894.

Beckwith, Albert Clayton. *History of Walworth County, Vol. II*. Indianapolis, IN: B.F. Bowan & Company, 1912.

*Biographical Sketch of John Burton*. The Evening Wisconsin Company, Milwaukee, 1898.

Birnbaum, A. and Robin Karson. *Pioneers of American Landscape*. New York, NY: Charles McGraw Hill Publishing, 1976.

Birnbaum, Charles, ed. *Shaping the American Landscape*. Charlottesville, VA: University of Virginia Press, 2009.

Brown, Charles E. and Theodore T. Brown. "Lake Geneva and Lake Como," *The Wisconsin Archeologist*, Vol. 7, No. 3 and Vol. 19, No. 2. Milwaukee, WI: Wisconsin Archeological Society, 1928.

Buckingham, Ebenezer. *Solomon Sturges and His Descendants: A Memoir and a Genealogy*. New York, NY: The Grafton Press, 1907.

Buechler, Steven "M. Elizabeth Boynton Harbert and the Woman Suffrage Movement, 1870–1896," *Signs: Journal of Women in Culture and History*, Vol. 13, No. 1, pp. 78–97. Chicago, IL: The University of Chicago Press, 1987.

Butler Patricia, architectural historian and Sharon Crawford, project historian. *Geneva Lake Area Intensive Survey: An Architectural/Historical Report*. WI: Sponsored by Geneva Lake Land Conservancy, Incorporated and State Historical Society of Wisconsin, 1985.

Chandler, F.R. *Story of Lake Geneva or Summer Homes for City People*. Lake Geneva Villa Association, 1898.

*Citizen's Survey Lake Geneva, Wisconsin, Section X Town Planning and City Beautiful*. 1927.

Cleveland, H.W.S. *Landscape Architecture, as Applied to the Wants of the West*. Amherst, MA: Republished by the Library of American Landscape History, 2000.

Cook, Marlene. "So We Can All be Heard," *Pen Points*. IL, Nov. 2004.

Currey, Josiah Seymour. *Chicago: Its history and its builders: A century of marvelous growth*, Vol. 5. Chicago, IL: S.J. Clarke Publishing Company, 1912.

*Descendents of Riley Button*. Unpublished; date unknown.

Eliot, T.D. "Review," *American Sociological Review*, Vol. 2, No. 2, pp. 275–277. American Sociological Association, 1937.

Flower, Benjamin O. "A Conversation with Elizabeth Morrison Boynton Harbert on The Genesis, Aim, and Scope of the World's Unity League," *The Arena*, Vol. 24, No. 5, pg. 529. Boston, MA: The Arena Publishing Company, 1900.

*Fontana Sesquicentennial Historical Handbook, 1836–1986*. Friends of the Sesquicentennial, 1986.

Fuller, Henry Hill. *Recollections of Lake Geneva*. Unpublished; no date.

Fretz, Reverend Abraham James and N.J. Milton et al. *A Genealogical Record of the Descendants of Jacob Beidler of Lower Milford Township*, Bucks Co., PA. 1903.

Godfrey, Linda "The Como Clubhouse," *The Week*. Delavan, WI: June 13, 1993.

"Wheel of Fame – The Ferris Family Legacy," *The Week*. Delavan, WI: August 1, 1993.

Grossman, James R. and Ann Durkin Keating et al, compilers. *Encyclopedia of Chicago*. Chicago, IL: The University of Chicago Press, 2004.

Hand, E.S. *Auditorium*. Exhibit Publishing Company. Chicago, IL. 1890.

Harvey, Philip R. *The Montague-Douglass Sawmill/Feed Mill*. 2005.

*History of Walworth County, Wisconsin*. Chicago, IL: Western Historical Society in collaboration with Culver, Page, Hoyne Co., 1882.

"Inventory of the Starline, Incorporated, Harvard, Illinois, Records." Date unknown.

Jahus, Virginia. *My Memories of Camp Augustana and Villa Emmanuel*. 2007.

Jenkins, Paul. *The Book of Lake Geneva*. Chicago, IL: Chicago Historical Society and University of Chicago Press, 1922.

— and Charles E. Brown. *History and Indian Remains of Lake Geneva and Lake Como*, Walworth County, Wisconsin. Lake Geneva, WI: Geneva Lake Historical Society, 1930.

*Jens Jensen: Maker of Natural Parks and Gardens*. Baltimore, MD: Johns Hopkins University Press, 1992.

Jensen, Arthur B. *Shawneeawkee Friendly Fontana: A Pictorial History, Second Edition*. Delavan, WI: Advance Printing, 2005.

Krezoski, Gillian M. *From Boom to Bust: John E. Burton and the Northern Wisconsin Iron Mines*. Eau Claire, WI: University of Wisconsin-Eau Claire, 2006.

*Lake Geneva Picturesque and Descriptive*. Artistic Publishing Association.

Larkin, Larry. *Full Speed Ahead: The Story of the Steamboat Era on Lake Geneva*. 1972.

— *Grand and Glorious: Classic Boats of Lake Geneva*. Erin, Ontario: Boston Mills Press, 2002.

Lehman, Nancy Alberth, ed. *Cyrus Church: Early Walworth Settler*. Walworth, WI: Historical Society of Walworth and Big Foot Prairie, Inc, 2006.

Leonard, John William, ed. *Woman's Who's Who of America, 1914–1915*. New York, NY: The American Commonwealth Company, 1914.

Lichtman, Ethel M. *Ethel Sturges Dummer: A Pioneer of Social Activism*. Bloomington, IN: iUniverse, 2009.

Lundahl, Eva Seymour. *Lovely Lake Geneva*. Los Angeles, CA: New Age Publishing Co, 1950.

Marquis, A.N. *The Book of Chicagoans 1905–1936*. Chicago, IL.

McCormick, Mike. "Historical Perspective: Elizabeth Boynton Harbert's mark on the Valley started with the Terre Haute Female College Class of 1862," *TribStar.com*. Terre Haute, IN: TribStar.com, April 15, 2007.

Mulder, Carol June Woodbridge. *Imported Foundation Stock of North American Arabian Horses*, Vol. 3. Los Angeles, CA: Borden Publishing Company, 1995.

Notz, John, Jr. "Prairie on the Lakes: A study of the Prairie School architectural designs on Geneva and Delavan Lakes, Wisconsin." Presented to the Chicago Literary Club, October 7, 1996.

Oslin, George P. *The Story of Telecommunications*. Macon, GA: Mercer University Press, 1999.

*Picturesque Chicago and Guide to the Worl"s Fair*. Lennox Publishing Company, 1893.

*Portrait and Biographical Record of Walworth and Jefferson Counties, Wisconsin*. Chicago, IL: Lake City Publishing Company, 1894.

Probasco, Libby. "Rockford Camp." 2007.

*Prominent Citizens and Industries of Chicago*. Chicago, IL: German Press Club of America, 1901.

Rosen, Robyn L. *Reproductive Health, Reproductive Rights: Reformers and the Politics of Maternal Welfare, 1917–1940*. Columbus, OH: The Ohio State University Press, 2003.

Rumsey, Eliza Voluntine. *Recollections of a Pioneer's Daughter*. Pasadena, CA: The Castle Press, 1936.

Sheldon, Robert D. "A History of the Lake Geneva Club." 1976.

Simmons, James. *The Annals of Lake Geneva, 1835–1897*. Lake Geneva, WI: The Geneva Lake Herald, Lake Geneva, Wisconsin, 1897.

—. *History of Geneva Lake, Wisconsin. Forty Years*, 1835–1875. Lake Geneva, WI: Geneva Lake Herald, 1875.

Sinkevitch, Alice. "The AIA Guide to Chicago," *Chicago Architecture Joint Venture*, 1993 and 2004 ed.

Smeltzer, Carolyn Hope and Martha Kiefer Cucco. *Lake Geneva in Vintage Postcards*. Mount Pleasant, SC: Arcadia Publishing, 2005.

*A Summer Holiday: A brief description of some of the most popular summer resorts in Wisconsin, Michigan and Minnesota, and the routes by which they can be reached*. Chicago, IL: Chicago and Northwestern Railway Company, Rand, McNalley & Co., 1884.

Sweet, Leonard I. "The Female Seminary Movement and Woman's Mission in Antebellum America," *Church History*, Vol. 54, No. 1, pp. 41–55. March, 1985.

Tishler, William, ed. *American Landscape Architecture: Designers and Places*. Washington, D.C.: Preservation Press for the National Trust for Historic Preservation and the American Society of Landscape Architects, 1989.

Urofsky, Melvin I. *Louis D. Brandeis: A Life*. New York, NY: Pantheon Books, 2009.

Volunteers of the Lake Geneva Public Library, compilers. *Lake Geneva Newspaper Obituary Index*. Delavan, WI: Published by the Walworth County Genealogical Society, 2001.

Wade, Louise Carroll. *Chicago's Pride: The Stockyards, Packington, and Environs in the Nineteenth Century*. Urbana-Champaign, IL: University of Illinois Press, 2003.

Willard, Frances E. and Mary A. Livermore, eds. *A Woman of the Century: Fourteen Hundred-Seventy Biographical Sketches Accompanied by Portraits of Leading American Women in All Walks of Life*. Charles Wells Moulton, 1893.

Wittenstrom, Clarence and Edna. "A History of Camp Augustana." 1971.

Workers of the Writers' Program of the Work Projects Administration in the State of Wisconsin. *A Guide to the Badger State*. New York, NY: Duell, Sloan and Pearce, 1941.

## ALSO, THE ARCHIVES OF:

Horticultural Hall, Janesville Gazette, Lake Geneva Cisco, Lake Geneva Herald, Lake Geneva Magazine, Lake Geneva Regional News, Milwaukee Journal, NY Times, Power and MotorYacht, Radcliffe College, The Times (Walworth, Fontana, Williams Bay), The Walworth County, Sunday Wisconsin Holiday News, The Week, The Wisconsin Magazine of History, The Wisconsin State Journal, The University of Chicago

## AND:

All Saints Lutheran Church, Palatine, IL
The Art Institute of Chicago
Chapel on the Hill
 The Clerk of the Circuit Court of Walworth County
Daivd Kiehn, film historian
Doris Reinke Resource Center
Federal Bureau of Investigation
Geneva Lake Museum
Hinsdale Historical Society
The Historical Society of Oak Park and River Forest
Immanuel Womens Home Association
Irving Park Lutheran Church
Lake Geneva Historic Preservation Commission
Lake Geneva Public Library Local Historical Collections
Massachusetts Institute of Technology
Niles Essanay Silent Film Museum and Larry Telles
Norman Saul, Emeritus,
 The University of Kansas, Lawrence, Kansas
The Railroad Commission of the State of Wisconsin
Vaughan Manufacturing
The Walworth County Genealogical Society
The Wisconsin Historical Society
Wisconsin Department of Natural Resources
Woods Hole (MA) Historical Society

COURTESY OF THE FONTANA PUBLIC LIBRARY